# THE SACRAMENTS
# AND THEIR CELEBRATION

# THE SACRAMENTS
## and
# THEIR CELEBRATION

by

**Nicholas Halligan, O.P.**

*Wipf & Stock*
PUBLISHERS
*Eugene, Oregon*

*Nihil Obstat:*
*Very Rev. Philip F. Mulhern, O.P., S.T.M., S.T.D.*
*Censor Deputatus*

*Nihil Obstat:*
*Very Rev. William B. Ryan, O.P., S.T.M., J.C.D.*

*Imprimi Potest:*
*Very Rev. Raymond Daley, O.P., S.T.Lr., J.C.D.*
*Provincial*

*Imprimatur:*
*Rev. Msgr. John F. Donoghue*
*Vicar General*
*Archdiocese of Washington*


Wipf and Stock Publishers
199 W 8th Ave, Suite 3
Eugene, OR 97401

The Sacraments and Their Celebration
By Halligan, Nicholas
Copyright©1986 Alba House, Society of St. Paul
ISBN: 1-59244-931-X
Publication date 10/7/2004
Previously published by Alba House, Society of St. Paul, 1986

# FOREWORD

"Pastors have at their disposal secure norms by which they may correctly direct the exercise of the sacred ministry." Thus the preface to the revised Code of Canon Law, promulgated by John Paul II,[1] who stated: "As a matter of fact, the Code of Canon Law is extremely necessary for the Church. Since the Church is organized as a social and visible structure, it must also have norms: in order that its hierarchical and organic structure be visible; in order that the exercise of the functions divinely entrusted to it, especially that of sacred power and of the administration of the sacraments, may be adequately organized; in order that the mutual relations of the faithful may be regulated according to justice based on charity, with the rights of individuals guaranteed and well-defined; in order, finally, that common initiatives undertaken to live a Christian life ever more perfectly may be sustained, strengthened and fostered by canonical norms."

In the matters of the sacramental ministry, by which the Church's sanctifying office is exercised, the Vatican Council II doctrine and ecclesiology, together with post-conciliar teaching and directives of the Holy See, have been translated into canonical language. This accords with the mission of the Church of Christ where word and sacrament are not separated but intimately united in their distinctiveness. The ministry of the word leads to the ministry of the sacraments, and the sacraments themselves are celebrated in the word. Pastoral ministry in the Church is charged with conveying to all those who respond to the invitation of the grace of Christ the unfathomable and salutary riches of both word and sacrament. The present volume is limited to the consideration of the ministry of the sacraments and their authentic celebration.

The ministry of the sacraments is an "ad-ministration," that is, a ministering *to* the People of God. What the legitimate minister brings to them are the graces of the sacraments and the benefits of the Sacrifice of the Mass, as sacrament and sacrifice have been handed down and understood in the Church and regulated by her authority. It is a worship ministry in which the minister by ordination or deputation offers homage in the name of all. It is an authentic ministry when it is exercised in union with the bishops under the Chief Pastor and thus in accordance with and expressive of their teaching and directive.

The minister who is earnest in fulfilling his ministry with fidelity and pastoral responsibility is responsive to the guidance and direction of the Church in whose name he functions. The burden of this volume is to provide the minister and aspirants to the ministry with authorized norms whereby they may be safely guided in practice in the ministry of the celebration of the sacraments. Each sacrament is treated according to the order of the titles into which the present Code divides the sacrament. Doctrinal and disciplinary materials, previously published by the author, which are still instructive for an understanding of the sacramental ministry are included in this volume.

Although proper theological exploration and canonical interpretation continue to exercise their helpful roles in the understanding of the sacraments and life of worship in the Church, the acceptable celebration of this ministry in the pastoral care of souls is clearly and sufficiently delineated by competent authority in the Church.

The sacramental ministry is considered in the celebration first, of the sacraments of initiation and union: Baptism, Confirmation, Eucharist; second, of the sacraments of reconciliation: Penance, the Anointing of the Sick; third, of the sacraments of community renewal: Holy Orders, Matrimony.

## I. SACRAMENTS OF INITIATION AND UNION

Through the sacraments of Christian initiation men and women, freed from the power of darkness, who have died, been buried, and risen again with Christ, receive the spirit of filial adoption and, with the entire People of God, celebrate the memorial of the Lord's death and resurrection. Through Baptism they are incorporated into Christ, formed into God's people, and obtain forgiveness of all their sins. Raised from their natural human condition to the dignity of adopted children, they become a new creation through water and the Holy Spirit. Hence they are called, and are indeed, the children of God.

Signed with the gift of the Spirit in Confirmation, Christians more perfectly become the image of their Lord. Filled with the Holy Spirit, and thus bearing witness to him before all the world, they forthwith lead the body of Christ to its fullness.

Finally, by sharing in the Eucharist table, they eat the flesh and drink the blood of the Son of Man so that they may have eternal life and show forth the unity of God's people. By offering themselves with Christ, they share in his universal sacrifice: the entire community of the redeemed is offered to God by their priest. They pray for a greater outpouring of the Holy Spirit so that the whole human race may be brought into the unity of God's family.

The three sacraments of Christian initiation closely combine to bring the faithful to the full stature of Christ and to enable them to carry on the mission of the entire people of God in the Church and in the world.[2] They identify the disciple of Christ.

It is through these three sacraments of initiation and unity that a man or woman officially receives identity as a Christian. As sacraments of faith, these three presuppose the gift of faith. It is faith that puts one in contact with the Lord Jesus; it is thus the effective response of each person to the Will of God, who wills that all men be saved. The sacraments incorporate the one receiving them into the Mystical Body of Christ, mature and strengthen him, and give fuller witness to that spiritual contact and incorporation; they are by institution designed to culminate in the most intimate contact and union of all in this life, which takes place in the Eucharist and which is the fulfillment, perfection, and final purpose established for all the other sacraments.

Christian life is a sacramental life. Contact with the Risen Lord Jesus is now made, although not exclusively, through the sacraments which, by positive institution of Christ, guarantee and certify, indicate and signify this contact by a seven-fold benefit conveying to men the everlasting achievement of the Passion, Death, and Resurrection of the God-made-Man.

## II. THE SACRAMENTS OF RECONCILIATION

Man, however, is a free and responsible agent. Even the grace of Christ does not compel him against his will. He may respond to the invitation of Christ in faith and sacrament; he is also capable of refusing, of failing to respond. Similarly, having received any one or all of the sacraments of initiation and unity, he is still a responsible disciple who continues his free acceptance of Christ and deepens this union; yet he is capable withal of neglecting, weakening, and even totally severing this union in love won at so great a price by the crucified and risen Savior. The mystery of personal sin in man is also the mystery of man redeemed by Christ.

Once the bond with Christ is severed by the conscious effort of the Christian, the hope of reconciliation and at the same time of restoration of former status in the Mystical Body is possible only through the gratuitously offered saving grace of the Redeemer, which is embodied in the Sacrament of Penance.

On the other hand, where the union of charity has been impaired by personal sins, even though subsequently forgiven by sacramental absolution, in some way these sins (over and above the abiding presence of fallen nature as it exists in this pilgrim life) more or less leave their consequences upon the individual. When he comes to be in a condition of dangerous debility of health, he is less able to cope with and to control the inner forces to which this condition is susceptible. In this event, through the Sacrament of the Anointing of the Sick he is strengthened, comforted, and enabled to overcome the residue or remnants of former sins, at times even reconciled to Christ in charity through the remission of sins not previously forgiven.

The sacraments of reconciliation — Penance and the Anointing of the Sick — principally regard the sins and the sinfulness of the pilgrim disciple reconciling him in different ways to Christ and to the Church. They purify and prepare the soul for a wholehearted witness of discipleship; they dispose to a more fruitful reception of the graces of the other sacraments.


## III. THE SACRAMENTS OF COMMUNITY RENEWAL

Orders and Matrimony are sacraments of Christian continuation. Sacred or ordained ministers through the handing down of the power of Christ over his Eucharistic and Mystical Body perpetuate and apply in each generation the priesthood of Christ, the fruits of which are for all men for all time. Thus the sanctity of the People of God is maintained and fostered by the sacred and ordained ministry, for those of the faithful who are consecrated by Holy Orders are approved to feed the Church in Christ's name with the Word and the grace of God.[3]

By the sacrament of Matrimony couples mirror the union of Christ and his Church, the community of the People of God with Christ the Head. The community which marriage constitutes, and which by the sacrament is made a holy community, provides children, normally the fruit of mutual love. Thus Christian parents in each generation provide the progeny which the salvific grace of Christ, through the sacramental ministrations of the sacred ministers, constitutes sons of God and joint heirs with Christ of heaven.[4] The union of husband and wife, itself sacramentalized, is conditioned to continue in its own way, within the common priesthood of the People of God, the apostolate of bringing souls to God, which at the same time is the more direct activity of the ordained priesthood.

Thus, these two sacraments, each in a different but related way, exercise spiritual paternity. They are social sacraments instituted by Christ to insure throughout time the continuation of the Christian community or society. They are sacraments of community renewal, of continuation of Christian life in the Church.

# TABLE OF CONTENTS

## CONFIRMATION

## THE MOST HOLY EUCHARIST

## PENANCE

## ANOINTING OF THE SICK

## HOLY ORDERS

# MARRIAGE

# THE SACRAMENTS

# THE SACRAMENTS

The sacraments, instituted by Christ and entrusted to his Church, are, as actions of Christ and the Church, the signs and means whereby the saving grace of Christ is normally bestowed on souls. Each sacrament, by means of its special grace, effects in the soul a particular result, that is, the power of Christ directly touches and moves the soul in a special manner.[1]

All the faithful, therefore, have a right to the sacraments and to their correct celebration.[2] Liturgical actions themselves are not private actions but celebrations of the Church itself.[3] Thus the minister of celebration, who as such functions not in his own name but in that of the Church, is expected to be reverent in his administration of the sacraments so as to reflect the mind of the Church and diligent in the observance of what pertains to their lawful celebration, administration and reception and to the order to be observed in their celebration.[4]

The sacraments require, on the part of recipients, that they be properly disposed and canonically qualified. Ministers, on their part, are to be legitimately qualified and deputed, having the right intention and attention and fulfilling what is requisite for valid and lawful celebration.[5]

## I. MINISTER

### 1. REQUISITE POWER

A sacramental celebration does not depend for its *validity* on the disposition of the minister; its action has its effect from the power of Christ as the due sacramental action is performed (*ex opere operato*). It is not in itself affected by lack of faith, state of grace, or holiness on the part of the minister but only on the fact that the minister is divinely empowered according to the institution of Christ.[6]

## 2. DUE ATTENTION

The minister of a sacrament must have that *attention* without which the administration would not be a truly human action. Attention is the application of the mind to what is being done; it is an act of the intellect (intention is of the will), and is opposed to distraction. Since man cannot always act with full or actual advertence but is sometimes distracted even involuntarily, it is necessary and sufficient to be truly human and responsible that this action proceed in some way from a deliberate will. An *internal attention*, i.e., which is free from all voluntary distraction, is not necessary, since Christ did not intend to require of the minister of his sacraments a condition which at times would be impossible. For a *valid* celebration the minister must have at least *external attention*, i.e., that deliberateness which is responsible for and the cause of the external action of the sacramental rite and which excludes any action physically incompatible with internal attention (if the latter were present or suddenly required). Thus, external attention is the "follow through" resulting from the minister's intention to administer the sacrament, although he is distracted at the time by surrounding circumstances or by thoughts of things other than what he is doing. Lack of external attention implicitly revokes the intention to administer a sacrament and thus invalidates it.

A lawful celebration requires also *internal attention*, which excludes all voluntary distraction. This degree of reverence for the sacredness of the sacramental rite is to be expected from one who is Christ's minister in this action of conferral of grace. A voluntary distraction is usually a slight sin; it may be serious if danger is present of substantial error in the sacramental action, e.g., through carelessness or hastiness in the use of the required material or in the pronunciation of the customary formula. Attention, therefore, answers the question: how much must the individual be aware of what he is doing; intention responds to the query: what must the individual will to do and how must he will it.

## 3. SUFFICIENT INTENTION

The valid celebration of a sacrament demands of the minister a *right intention*. Intention is an act of the will by which a person resolves to do something or to omit something. Being a human or animated instrument of Christ and in order that his action might be therefore intelligent, the minister must will to use his power in conformity with the disposition of the principal agent, Christ. Thus, for a valid sacrament the minister must have a true and serious intention,[7] not only to perform an external rite but also a sacramental rite, i.e., he must have an internal intention.[8] He thereby wills to do through the means of the sacramental sign that which the Church does. His intention determines what this required material and this formula shall signify sacramentally.

In regard to the quality of intention on the part of the minister placing the action, his *intention* is *actual*, (*volitum actualiter*), i.e., his will or intention is being elicited here and now while the sacramental action is in progress, e.g., his intention to administer the Anointing of the Sick at the time he is anointing. Or *virtual*, (*volitum virtualiter*), i.e., his intention was made or elicited at a previous time and never retracted but in some way is now influencing the sacramental action being performed here and now; he is doing what he is now doing precisely because at some time previously he had determined or intended to do it, e.g., having intended to say Mass the priest prepares for and celebrates it but in a distracted manner. Or *habitual* (*volitum habitualiter*), i.e., his intention was made at some previous time and not revoked but here and now it does not exert any positive influence on the action he is performing (it may be said to have negative influence in the sense of not having been retracted and thus remaining as it were in a condition of habit), e.g., a minister baptizing while very intoxicated, insane, or hypnotized. Thus the previously elicited intention, although remaining habitually, because not retracted, is not the reason for and the cause of the action being performed at the moment. (An habitual intention is a disposition to receive but not to act.)

An habitual intention is called: *explicit*, if what was intended was clearly and distinctly apprehended, e.g., a dying unconscious Christian who, when well, expressed by word or sign his desire to receive the last sacraments in danger of death and never later retracted this will is said to have such an intention to receive the sacraments; *implicit*, if what was intended was not clearly and distinctly apprehended but in some way contained in the object explicitly known and willed, e.g., the same dying person who never evidenced this desire when well or ill but yet lived as a Christian or at least never abandoned his religion. Or *interpretative*, i.e., a will or intention which has never been elicited either explicitly or implicitly and does not exist presently, yet it is considered that the individual would have elicited it if he had thought of it or could think of it; as a matter of fact there is no real intention at all but merely a hypothetical one, e.g., an intention of receiving Baptism in an unconscious infidel who has been leading a naturally good life and who knows nothing of Baptism: he would want to be baptized if he knew what it was and meant. The interpretative intention is, in a sense, based upon a presumption of the future, that if the person were to know, he would intended the object. A habitual implicit intention is based upon a presumption of a presently existing (although not active) intention as perceived from some fact or disposition in the past.

An *actual* intention in the administration of a sacrament is always highly desirable and more secure, if not always within the power of the minister. A *virtual* intention suffices for the validity of a sacrament, since it alone (and never an habitual or interpretative intention) positively influences the sacramental action of the minister and causes the union of the required material and the prescribed formula to signify sacramentally. It is of faith[9] that the object of the minister's intention must be *to do what the Church does*. He is performing a sacred rite in the name of Christ and thus must intend what Christ, and therefore the Church of Christ, intends. It suffices that this intention be implicit, i.e., contained in his intention to do what Christ instituted or what the true Church does or what Christians believe in or what is requested of the minister. The latter need not believe in God or in Christ, in the institution of the Church or in the Roman Church, in the sacrament or its efficacy, as long as he intends to do what actually in the Church by Christ's institution is a sacrament.

The intention of the minister must be sufficiently *determined*, i.e., definite and specific regarding the required material and the recipient of the sacrament. Thus (unless the intention is exclusive) it is sufficient to intend, for example, to absolve or to baptize the individual present, although the minister is unaware or even in error that it is a male and not a female, or to consecrate all the hosts before him, although he is unaware of or even in error regarding the exact number. If the intention of the minister is not precise and inclusive in accordance with the nature of the matter or of the recipient of the sacrament, the intention is invalid, e.g., to consecrate some hosts in a ciborium not indicating which ones, or to say "I absolve you" not distinguishing which of two individuals are to be absolved.

The intention must always be *absolute*, as a sacrament may be conferred under a condition only for proportionate cause. In a conflict of *contrary intentions* the one prevails which explicitly or implicitly revokes the other, notwithstanding the chronology of the intentions. Otherwise, if one intention succeeds another, the latter prevails, since it is actually influencing the sacramental action of the minister. If two intentions are simultaneous, the predominant one is that which would have been chosen by the minister if he had known of their repugnance. But if it cannot be so ascertained which prevails, the sacrament is null, for the impossible is intended and one intention destroys the other. In doubt of prevalence or of succession of intention, the sacrament is doubtfully valid.

### 4. FREEDOM FROM SIN AND PENALTY

The *lawfulness* of a sacramental celebration requires the minister to be free from serious sin and from ecclesiastical prohibitions, and that he be properly deputed. The role of minister of Christ in the sacraments demands by consecration and office a holiness which is at least a freedom from grave sin. [10] The minister in serious sin must always at least elicit an act of perfect contrition, if sacramental confession cannot be made. [11]

A minister *certainly sins seriously* who in the state of serious sin fulfills three simultaneously concurring conditions: (1) he is ordained for the sacrament conferred, (2) he confects or celebrates the sacrament (which coincides with its administration in every sacrament except the Eucharist), (3) he does so solemnly (outside of necessity and with the rites and ceremonies prescribed by the Church). Lacking any of the conditions the minister will certainly sin but not always seriously. To celebrate a sacrament without necessary and proper permission or legitimate presumption, outside of necessity, is unlawful and sinful, being a violation of another's right.

### 5. DUTY TO CELEBRATE

The obligation of a minister in the celebration or administration of a sacrament [12] will be qualified by his status, the condition of the petitioner, and the necessity of the request. Ministers of the sacraments are either those entrusted with the care of souls or those not so entrusted. *Ministers with the care of souls* are: local Ordinaries, pastors or their equivalent by law or institution, canonically instituted parochial vicars, military chaplains, hospital or prison or community chaplains, clerical religious superiors.

Their obligations toward that part of Christ's flock entrusted to their care urge in *justice,* from the quasi contract entered into on assuming the office or delegation (clerical religious superiors are probably bound in religion or obedience). *Ministers not having the care of souls* are bound to celebrate or administer the sacraments out of *charity,* lest their neighbor be deprived of a needed spiritual good which has been entrusted to the minister requested.

A *reasonable request* for the celebration or administration of a sacrament is made:   (1) in *common need* or *light necessity,* such as the need to satisfy an obligation to receive the sacrament, e.g., during Paschal time, or to overcome serious sin or to withstand grave temptation which may otherwise be overcome only with difficulty and for which the grace of the sacrament is desired, or out of devotion for spiritual progress;   (2) in *serious need* when only with notable difficulty would the petitioner without the sacrament be able to save his soul, although absolutely he could, e.g., a dying inveterate sinner who has perhaps forgotten how to make an act of contrition or who finds it very difficult;   (3) in *quasi extreme need,* when the petitioner can scarely otherwise save his soul, e.g., an infidel or heretic in danger of death, a dying sinner who cannot elicit an act of perfect contrition;   (4) in *extreme need,* when salvation can be obtained in no other way, e.g., dying unbaptized children or unconscious adult sinners.

The obligation of the minister in each case will be affected by the necessity of the sacrament requested. Thus where the minister is called upon to risk his life, his obligations involve certainly only the absolutely necessary sacraments, viz., Baptism, Penance, and Anointing of the Sick in default of Penance. The minister is also befittingly prepared to celebrate or administer the non-necessary sacraments. A pastor or other minister may also be relieved of his obligation inasmuch as he uses a substitute (unless he is requested by name), or inasmuch as he is impeded or other ministers are readily at hand. For a minister, especially one with the care of souls, to be bound to celebrate or administer a sacrament with the concurrent proximate, very grave, and certain risk of losing his own life there must be a moral certainty of the proportionate need of the recipient *and* a morally certain hope of a successful administration, with no greater evils following upon the fulfillment of this obligation (such as the loss of a pastor depriving many other needy of a shepherd, as in mission countries), e.g., it is improbable that the dying person can be reached before succumbing or before the minister loses his own life.

### 6. REFUSAL TO CELEBRATE

The sacraments must be refused those who are incapable and those who are unworthy of them, since the sacraments require certain conditions and dispositions for their reception as befitting their nature and the action of Christ in them.[13] A sacrament must be denied to one *incapable* to receiving it, since the celebration or administration would be invalid, a simulation, gravely sacrilegious and intrinsically evil, e.g., to baptize an unwilling adult, to absolve an infidel, to ordain a woman.

A sacrament is to be denied to one who, although capable, is *unworthy* to receive it due to sin. The holy things of God should not be given to the indisposed.[14] Fidelity to his office as minister of Christ, charity toward his neighbor lest he cooperate in another's sacrilege, and the avoidance of scandal to the faithful gravely oblige the minister to refuse his administration or celebration. The minister should make himself morally certain of the worthiness of the recipient, which must be positively evidenced in the case of the Baptism of adults, Penance, Orders, and matrimonial impediments; otherwise a presumption of worthiness suffices in the absence of evidence to the contrary.

A sacrament may be *lawfully* celebrated or administered to the unworthy only for a *very grave reason,* all scandal being removed. Such cooperation in another's sin of sacrilege is permitted only for proportionate cause, lest greater evils result from a refusal (but never when a sacrament is asked for out of hatred of the faith or contempt of religion, which would be intrinsically evil). In practice, an excusing reason would be: (1) to avoid violation of the sacramental seal; (2) to avoid grave scandal arising or causing the faithful to be disturbed so that, not knowing the cause of the refusal, they are led to stay away from the sacraments fearing lest they also may be repulsed; (3) to avoid defaming an occult sinner, with consequent general damage to all, or probably even without this damage;[15] (4) to avoid very serious private injury to the minister, such as death or some morally equivalent evil.

Priests with the care of souls have no obligation in *justice* toward non-Catholics, but only to baptized Catholics; non-Catholics are clearly recommended to their care.[15] However, they do have an obligation in *charity* when non-Catholics are in spiritual necessity and can be aided. Non-Catholics should be encouraged to elicit the necessary acts and to retract their errors and then in charity the sacraments may be given to them; in case of doubt they should be further urged but, the doubt remaining, there seems to be no clear obligation binding the minister. The Church normally forbids the administration of the sacraments to baptized non-Catholics outside the danger of death, but allows it in certain circumstances defined in the law.[17] In danger of death unconscious baptized non-Catholics may be absolved and anointed conditionally, if it can be surmised that they are in good faith and implicitly reject their errors, providing scandal is not present.[18] A minister who unlawfully confers the sacraments is liable to ecclesiastical penalties including suspension.[19] He must be very discreet in his refusal of the sacraments, especially publicly, lest those of ill will attempt to prosecute him in civil law for defamation.

### 7. SIMULATION AND PRETENCE OF CELEBRATION

To *simulate* or feign a sacrament is for a minister to change secretly and unlawfully either the required material or the valid formula, or to change or withdraw the necessary intention, so that the sacrament becomes invalid with the recipient and others being led into error. A rite or action (which appears to be sacramental) is falsely placed so that externally it is signified that a sacrament is celebrated, confected or administered, and thus the recipient and others are deceived, e.g., to use grape juice in place of wine at the consecration, to omit an essential word in the formula of absolution or last anointing. Simulation is formal or material as the concealment is intended or permitted. Simulation is *never lawful* under any circumstances, in order to avoid an unworthy reception, to save one's life, or for any reasons whatsoever.[20] It is a grave and sacrilegious lie. Moreover, it is never permitted to give a communicant an unconsecrated host, since it will be at least material idolatry (at least for others), even though he knows it lacks consecration: it is not a simulation of sacramental confection but of administration.

To *dissimulate* or to pretend to celebrate or administer a sacrament is to place a non-sacramental rite or action in circumstance in which others (and *not the recipient*) falsely judge that a sacrament is conferred. The minister intends to hide not the sacrament but the denial or non-conferral of the sacrament. No injury is done to the sacrament, since true or valid material and formula are not employed; there is no lie inasmuch as the bystanders have no right to such knowledge, e.g., in place of absolution to say some prayers and to give a blessing to a penitent who cannot be absolved, or under grave fear to dissimulate refusal of consent in matrimony. The intention is not to deceive others but to hide the truth from them. This deception is lawful for a just cause which is urgent and grave, such as to avoid scandal and infamy.

### 8. REPETITION OF CELEBRATION

To celebrate or confer anew a sacrament already received will depend upon the validity of the previous celebration or conferral and the nature of the sacrament. Sacraments which imprint a character, when it is *certain* that they have been *validly* celebrated or conferred, may *not* without serious sin and sacrilege be readministered in whole or in part to the same subject; likewise, the Anointing of the Sick during the same unchanged danger of death and Matrimony while the same bond exists. Such repetition would be useless and a grave irreverence. Penance may always be repeated, even several times on the same day, as prudence may indicate. The Eucharist of its nature may be repeatedly administered but by ecclesiastical law not more than once on the same day to the same person, except in the cases provided in liturgical prescriptions.

In a *doubt* of the *validity* of a sacramental celebration or conferral, every sacrament *may* be repeated *conditionally*, and certain ones *must* be repeated. However, the doubt must be prudent and reasonable, since an imprudent and rash doubt causes an irreverence to the sacrament; a condition placed in such doubt is considered as not placed, and thus the repetition becomes absolute. All the sacraments may be repeated conditionally lest their fruit be lost to the recipient. Judgment whether a non-necessary sacrament ought to be readministered or celebrated again will be made on the strength of the doubt of its validity, its degree of usefulness to the recipient, and the amount of inconvenience to the minister who is to repeat it. Certain necessary sacraments must be repeated lest grave damage to religion or neighbor result: Baptism, absolution for those dying in mortal sin, Anointing of the Sick for the unconscious moribund, Holy Orders, the consecration of doubtful consecrated hosts.

If there is prudent doubt that a penitent has presented *necessary* material for confession, the form can be repeated but it is not necessary, as there is no obstacle to the reception of Communion. A minister with only slight or negative doubts, such as not recalling having pronounced the words of the formula, must not repeat them, unless the contrary is positively evident or quite probable. In itself it is seriously sinful. In practice, the scrupulous are very often excused from serious sin and often from any sin, since they act either inadvertently or from a perplexed conscience, fearing to offend God if they do not repeat the form in whole or in part. They are obliged to avoid or to eradicate scrupulosity to the best of their ability.

### 9. OBSERVANCE OF PRESCRIBED RITES AND CEREMONIES

*Rite* may be said to refer to the entire legitimate manner of carrying out an act of worship, *ceremonies* to the individual actions and gestures regarding this act, although the term "ceremonies" or even "rubrics" is sometimes used for both. These ceremonies are substantial or *essential* when they regard the legitimate use of required material and prescribed formula in the sacraments, *accidental* when they regard the things instituted by the Church for their more worthy confection and administration, e.g., all those things pertaining to the celebration of Baptism.

The greatest care and reverence must be maintained in celebrating, confecting, administering, receiving the sacraments; the rites, ceremonies, and language of the approved liturgical books must be observed; everyone must follow his own rite as approved by the Church.[21] Thus the obligation to observe the ceremonies is in itself serious and binds the minister in conscience. Ceremonies which are preceptive bind lightly or seriously; those of counsel do not bind under sin, outside of contempt or scandal.

### 10. DUTY TO SAFEGUARD THE SACRAMENTS

#### a. *Attitude*

In the celebration or conferral of the sacraments and the consecration of the Mass it is *never* permitted to follow a merely probable opinion or to pursue a probable course of action and to abandon a safer opinion or course with regard to the *validity* of the sacraments. The validity is to be secured by the safer procedure, even with non-necessary sacraments. A violation is a serious sin against *religion* by irreverence in risking nullity, against *justice* because of the tacit obligation of the pastor by his office (and more probably of any minister) to celebrate or confer the sacrament in a safe manner. Likewise, a recipient may never apply a merely probable opinion in preference to a safer one with respect to validity but only regarding the fruit or grace or effect of the sacrament, since a solid probability of the state of grace suffices for the reception of the sacraments of the living (moral certainty can be gained only by sacramental absolution, and this may involve serious inconvenience, anxieties, scruples). A probable in preference to a safer opinion may be followed when the Church supplies for a defect that may exist, e.g., in defect of jurisdiction in Penance, Confirmation and Matrimony according to the terms of canon 144.

It is permitted in *urgent necessity* to follow a probable opinion or course of actions, since in the supposition a safer one is not obtainable, e.g., to baptize or to anoint in danger of death with doubtful material. In the conferral or reception of a sacrament a solidly safe opinion (i.e., one which safeguards sacramental validity) may be followed, although its contrary may be safer; a safe opinion is a morally certain one and thus more cannot be reasonably demanded, as God obliges to what is certain morally and not metaphysically. A probable opinion may be followed, even regarding validity or in the absence of urgent necessity or suppliance by the Church, in the case of those who otherwise would be in a state of perpetual anxiety of conscience, since the situation then becomes a real and urgent necessity, e.g., a penitent who is in frequent distress over the value of his sorrow, a celebrant who constantly worries about his intention to consecrate, a confessor who scruples over the dispositions of his penitents. When it is a question, not of a valid but of a lawful celebration or administration, a probable practical opinion may be followed, e.g., that a priest conscious of mortal sin and who distributes the Eucharist does not commit a grave sin.

Holy things are to be treated in a holy manner, so that *it is not allowed rashly to expose the sacraments to nullity or unfruitfulness.* On the other hand, *the sacraments are for men,* so that in extreme cases it is permitted to try extreme measures. It is not allowed to confer the sacraments on one who, it is morally certain, lacks either the requisite intention for validity or the good disposition of will required for their fruitful reception. In a case of extreme necessity, when there is no positive prohibition of the Church, the necessary sacraments may be conferred, at least conditionally, if the lack of requisite intention and disposition is not certain and there is at least a minimum probability of the presence of due intention and disposition based on some single act or sign or even on the general quality or character of the former life. In such circumstances the law of charity to succor one's neighbor is more compelling than the law of religion forbidding a minister to risk nullity to a sacrament. As long as there is some *probability* that the sacrament can be valid, nullity to the sacrament is to be risked rather than to expose a soul to the danger of eternal loss. However, there must exist *some probability* of valid reception and not *mere possibility* which is not a reasonable basis for prudent judgment and practice in moral affairs; every sacrament may be *possibly* valid or invalid.

### b. *Validity*

The requisite material of a sacrament is some sensible, concrete material thing to be used (as water poured in Baptism) or sensible action to be employed (as the acts of the penitent expressed in Penance) in the confection or celebration of a sacrament.

The prescribed formula of a sacrament is the words or some other equivalent signs (as a nod expressing consent in Matrimony) which determine or perfect the significance of the required matter in particular, both thus constituting the external sign and producing the sacramental effect. In order to qualify for a sensible sign, the formula must be pronounced vocally (or equivalently, as is possible in Matrimony) and not mentally only.

The required material and prescribed formula in each sacrament must be united by the minister in such a way that they can be truly said to constitute the one sign instituted by Christ. Thus some union of the material and the formula is required for *validity* at least, in order that the words of the formula be verified, with the type of union varying for the different sacraments. Union is either *physical*, if the words of the formula are pronounced at the same instant the matter is applied (to say "I baptize you . . ." and at the very same time to pour the water), or *moral*, if the material and the formula are successively applied (to say "I baptize you . . ." and subsequently to pour the water).

For the *Eucharist* a physical conjunction of both the material and formula being pronounced is always absolutely required. The pronoun "this" (*hoc* and *hic*) in the formulas of consecration is not verified unless the material it designates is physically present to the minister. Normal care should be taken in a Concelebration to pronounce the words with the principal celebrant.

It is common teaching that for the validity of *Baptism, Confirmation, Anointing of the Sick, Holy Orders* a moral conjunction will suffice. The application of the requisite material may be made immediately before or immediately after the formula is pronounced without the words of the formula losing their meaning or verification. Whether any delay (such as less time than it takes to say an *Our Father*) between the application of the material and the pronouncement of the formula invalidates the sacrament is controverted. However, wider latitude in moral union is recognized for *Penance* and *Matrimony*. Since Penance is administered after the manner of a judgment and Matrimony follows the nature of a contract, the penitential judgment may be extended over a notable period of time before being completed, and the matrimonial consent of one party may be supplied later to validate the contract, as long as the consent of the other party perseveres.

The *lawfulness* of sacramental administration requires that the minister observe that union of the two elements prescribed by the Church in her rites. *In the case of the sacraments it is regularly unlawful to use a merely probable opinion at the risk of nullity of the administration.*[22] Thus, in practice, the physical union as prescribed by the rubrics, especially in Baptism, Confirmation, Anointing of the Sick, is to be observed, whatever the theoretical opinion, and even though the sacrament would have to be repeated conditionally.[23] Care should always be taken that the requisite material and the prescribed formula are so united that at least one has begun before the other is finished.

With the exception of Penance and Matrimony (by reason of their character of judgment and of contract) the application of the material and formula of each sacrament must be conjoined by one and the same minister on the same subject of conferral.[24] This is demanded by the signification of the words of the formula. However, many ministers applying the whole material and pronouncing the entire formula at the same time validly confect a sacrament, e.g., many ministers baptizing at the same time the same infant, the formula must be pronounced simultaneously by all. In the Latin Church multiple ministers of a sacrament are usually permitted only in the concelebration of the Eucharist and in the conferral of the episcopal character. If a sacrament is made up of many parts, e.g., in the Eucharist,

Anointing of the Sick, many ministers validly act, each administering a part, as long as each minister places that part of the material corresponding to the formula he pronounces. Thus the signification of the words of the formula is verified if one minister using the prescribed formula anoints the forehead, another the hands. It is gravely unlawful for one minister to consecrate the bread and another the wine at the celebration of the Eucharist except in the case when the principal celebrant of Mass dies immediately after the consecration of the bread.

### c. *Essential elements*

In the administration of the sacraments by fallible ministers it sometimes occurs that the requisite material is not rightly applied or the prescribed formula is altered, due to inadvertence, negligence, error, or deliberate will. In any case the objective change that results will be either substantial or accidental. Judgment of the quality of the change affected will be made not by the criteria of the physical sciences but in accordance with the common usage and estimation of prudent men.

A *substantial* change takes place when in ordinary usage and prudent estimation the material no longer remains of the same species and name as that determined in the sacrament (e.g., to use milk in baptizing), or when the words used in the formula no longer retain the same sense (e.g., to say "I restore you . . ."). A change is *accidental* when the material remains the same in usage and name but altered in some accidental quality (e.g., to use leavened bread or a square host), or when the words of the formula are different but retain the same sense (e.g., to say "I wash you . . ."). However, if the corrupt formula cannot have other than a sacramental sense, it generally remains a valid formula. Thus the separation of individual words or of syllables does not constitute a substantial alteration, unless the interval is long enough to alter the meaning of the sentence (more easily admissible when syllables are separated). In such a case the moral unity of the formula as one complete prayer is destroyed by the interruption and also by such grammatical changes or mistakes as could actually change the meaning of the formula. Substantial alteration may also be risked by faulty articulation or by clipping words through haste. In practice where a complete word is actually interrupted through a pause between syllables, it is advisable to repeat the word, unless the interruption is extremely slight.

A *substantial* change of material and formula always invalidates a sacrament, whereas a *purely accidental* change does not have this effect. It is never permitted and it is always gravely sinful to use a substantially altered material or formula in the sacraments; it is a sin of irreverence to the sacrament, uncharity to the recipient who is thus deprived of a sacramental benefit, injustice on the part of a minister who has by office the care of souls. The use of an accidentally altered element outside of grave (and not always extreme) necessity is slightly or seriously sinful depending upon the degree of voluntary alteration, but clearly seriously sinful when attributable to contempt or to a deliberate will to introduce a new rite of administration. When some grave necessity urges, such an administration may be lawful, e.g., when only non-consecrated water is available in the case of an urgent Baptism.

Since the occasion for using a doubtful formula would very rarely arise, the principles pertinent to the use of doubtful material would apply equally in the case of a doubtful formula. It is never lawful, but rather seriously sinful to use doubtful material when certain material is available, since nullity of the sacrament is risked without sufficient reason; likewise, charity and justice may also be violated. In defect of certainly valid material urgent and grave necessity will permit the use of doubtful material. The administration must be conditional, e.g., "If this is valid material. . ." The conditional administration thus retains due reverence for the sacrament, and the possibility of the sacrament being validly administered provides for the spiritual necessity of the recipient. The necessity will be determined by the nature of each sacrament, e.g., Baptism, Penance and sometimes Anointing of the Sick are necessary for salvation, whereas the Eucharist is not so necessary and the danger of idolatry in the use of doubtful material here can never be tolerated.

The formula prescribed by the Church for each sacrament is absolute, i.e., its truth does not depend upon any condition or circumstance. However, in some cases a *conditional formula* alone will be possible. The condition ought to be — and regularly is presumed to be — with respect to *validity* of the sacrament and not its lawful conferral or reception or fruitfulness. The condition may be of the past, e.g., "if you have not been baptized . . .," or of the present, e.g., "if you are alive . . ." or of the future, e.g., "if you will have restored. . ." Excepting the case of the sacrament of Matrimony, a conditional formula in the sacraments is valid only when the condition is of the past or the present. In such situations, if the condition of the formula is verified, the material and the formula being thereby conjoined, the sacrament is valid; a future condition would impede any physical or moral conjunction of the necessary elements and thus invalidate the administration. Matrimony, following the nature of a contract, can be validly entered into under a future condition. It will take effect at the future verification of the condition, as long as the consent of both parties perseveres.

No sacrament may be administered under a condition without a just cause, because of the danger of nullity and irreverence. As in the case of doubtful material, grave urgency may require a conditional administration where absolute administration is impossible due to a doubt about the material or of the previous administration or of the capacity of the recipient, e.g., with the unconscious. Outside of such necessity as the salvation of the recipient, a just cause will permit but it does not oblige a conditional administration. The justifying cause will vary with different sacraments. To act without sufficient cause would be seriously sinful, but only slightly sinful if the minister is morally certain the condition is verified. The justifying cause may be founded upon *charity*, e.g., if the confessor does not recall imparting absolution to a worthy penitent, or *justice*, e.g., if a sacerdotal ordination is prudently doubted, or *religion*, e.g., if the celebrant prudently doubts having pronounced the words of consecration at Mass. As a general rule, a sacrament may be conferred conditionally when there is danger of it being invalid if administered absolutely, or when a person would be deprived of a great good or his salvation imperiled if the sacrament were denied absolutely.

In every sacramental administration the condition must be expressed *at least mentally*, as the circumstance enters into the very intention of the minister. In practice, it is advisable to express every condition orally in words, in order to assure the placing of the condition. It is controverted whether the intention to administer a sacrament as it should be administered according to the mind of the Church includes implicitly and virtually each necessary condition; or whether this is too generic and indefinite, especially in those instances when the law and the Ritual state very precise conditions, as otherwise there would be no particular point in especially prescribing conditional administration. In any case, the purpose of a condition is not to assure validity but to prevent the serious irreverence of administering a sacrament invalidly when all the requisites for validity are not present.

## II. RECIPIENT

### 1. VALID RECEPTION

1. For the *valid* reception of a sacrament (except Penance) neither faith nor uprightness of life is required, as the sense and practice of the Church shows in not permitting the rebaptism or reordination of heretics rightly baptized or ordained. Baptism, however, is prerequired to all the other sacraments. From the practice of the Church it is certain that no disposition or intention is required of *infants* and the *perpetually insane* to receive validly the sacraments of which they are capable: Baptism, Confirmation and even Orders and the Eucharist.[25] Having no personal sin they need no personal act to be justified, and being unable to cooperate in their own salvation, the intention of Christ and the Church through the will of the minister suffices or supplies for them.

Since no *adult* is justified and saved without his own consent, the *valid* reception of a sacrament requires that he also have an *intention* of receiving it, differing in the various sacraments.[26] It must be a positive act of the will and not a passive attitude, neither willing nor not willing, but here and now the will is said to be not obstructing rather than positively consenting; fear does not invalidate the intention, except in Matrimony by positive law. The intention must be at least *habitual* and may be *implicit*, except for Orders, Matrimony, and the Eucharist (not as Viaticum), when it must be *explicit*. However, in Penance a *virtual* intention is necessary at the time when the required material of the sacrament is placed (at least when the signs of contrition are given); in Matrimony also, since the parties are also ministers. Thus, presupposing an habitual intention, the sacraments are validly received by those who are asleep, drunk, out of their mind or unconscious. (The intentions for the individual sacraments are considered in their appropriate places.) It should be noted that *attention* is not required on the part of the recipient for validity, since a human act proceeds from the intention of the will and not from the attention of the mind, and that the sacraments enjoy the character of gifts, which do not require attention to be truly received.

2. The *lawful* and fruitful reception of the sacraments of the *living*

require also the *state of grace* (known with solid probability), lest the effect of the sacrament be frustrated. A recipient in conscious serious sin commits a further grave sin; the state of grace is first to be regained normally through confession (which is of precept for the Eucharist).[27] To receive the sacraments of the *dead* lawfully adults need to make acts (at least implicit) of faith, hope, and at least attrition, without which acts no adult can be justified. Moreover the recipient must be free of all *censures* prohibiting reception and must observe the prescribed *ceremonies* for each sacrament.

Without sufficient reason it is forbidden to *request* a sacrament for oneself or others from an unworthy minister, i.e., one who it is foreseen will sin in celebrating or conferring it. The request would be a serious or light sin in the measure of the unworthiness of the minister, of offering the occasion for another to sin, of cooperating in it and perhaps risking scandal or the danger of perversion. As long as another minister is not available and scandal is avoided, for any just reason, even reasonable devotion, it is lawful to request a sacrament from a minister who is excommunicated or suspended (but not declared), and thus, a fortiori from one simply unworthy.[28] In doubt of unworthiness it is always lawful to request and to receive a sacrament. The semi-insane and the doubtfully insane are to be given every benefit of sacramental administration befitting due reverence for the sacraments.

# BAPTISM

# BAPTISM

## I. SACRAMENTAL NATURE

Baptism, from the Greek word *Baptizo* meaning to immerse, to bathe, to wash, is a sacrament of the New Law as instituted by Christ in which, by a washing with water, performed by a right-intentioned minister invoking the Holy Trinity a wayfarer on earth is regenerated to divine and supernatural life and aggregated to the Church. Of the three ways in which divine grace may be imparted for justification only Baptism of *water* is truly a sacrament actively justifying by the very fact of its proper conferral. Baptism of *desire* is the sacrament in some way truly sought for and terminating whenever possible in the actual reception of the Baptism of water; it justifies on the strength of the genuine desire. Baptism of *blood* or death suffered for the Christian faith justifies by that very event together with, in the case of adults, at least attrition.

Baptism, the door to life and to the kingdom of God, is the first sacrament of the New Law offered by Christ to all men that they might have eternal life (Jn 3:5). He entrusted this sacrament and the Gospel to his Church when he told his Apostles: "Go, make disciples of all nations, and baptize them in the name of the Father, and of the Son, and of the Holy Spirit" (Mt 28:19). Thus, Baptism is, above all, the sacrament of that faith by which all men who are enlightened by the Spirit's grace respond to the Gospel of Christ. That is why the Church believes it is her most basic and necessary duty to inspire all, catechumens, parents of children still to be baptized, and godparents, to that true and living faith by which they adhere to Christ and enter into or confirm their commitment to the new covenant. To accomplish this, the Church prescribes the pastoral instruction of catechumens, the preparation of the children's parents, the celebration of God's word, and the profession of baptismal faith.

Baptism, moreover is the sacrament by which men and women are incorporated into the Church, built into a house where God lives in the Spirit (Ep 2:22), into a royal priesthood (1 P 2:19) and a holy nation. It is a sacramental bond of unity linking all who have been signed by it.[1] Because of that unchangeable effect (signified in the Latin liturgy by the anointing of the baptized person with chrism in the presence of God's people), the rite of Baptism is held in highest honor by all Christians. It may never lawfully be repeated once it has been validly celebrated, even by our fellow Christians from whom we are separated.

The cleansing with water by the power of the living Word (Ep 5:26), which Baptism is, makes us sharers in God's own life (2 P 1:4) and his adopted children (Rm 8:15; Gal 4:5). As proclaimed in the prayers for the blessing of the water, Baptism is a laver of regeneration (Tt 3:5) as sons of God and of birth on high. The invocation of the Trinity over those who are to be baptized has this effect that those who are signed in this name are consecrated to the Trinity and enter into fellowship with the Father, the Son and the Holy Spirit. They are prepared for this high dignity and led to it by the scriptural readings, the prayer of the community, and the threefold profession of faith.

Far superior to the purifications of the Old Law, Baptism produces all these effects by the power of the mystery of the Lord's passion and resurrection. Those who are baptized are engrafted in the likeness of Christ's death (Rm 6:4-5), buried with him in death (*ibid.*), given life again with him, and with him rise again (Ep 2:6). For Baptism recalls and effects the paschal mystery itself, because by means of it men and women pass from the death of sin into life. Its celebration, therefore, should reflect the joy of the resurrection, especially when it takes place during the Easter Vigil or on a Sunday.[2]

By the sacrament of Baptism, whenever it is properly conferred in the way the Lord determined, and received with the appropriate dispositions of soul, a person becomes truly incorporated into the crucified and glorified Christ and is reborn to a sharing of the divine life, as the Apostle says: "For you were buried together with him in Baptism, and in him also rose again through faith in the working of God who raised him from the dead" (Col 2:12, cf. Rm 6:4).

But Baptism, of itself, is only a beginning, a point of departure, for it is wholly directed toward the acquiring of the fullness of life in Christ. Baptism is thus oriented toward a complete profession of faith, a complete incorporation into the system of salvation such as Christ himself wills it to be, and finally, toward a complete participation in Eucharistic communion.[3]

By his power he is present in the sacraments, so that when a person baptizes it is really Christ himself who baptizes.[4] Thus, by Baptism, we are plunged into the paschal mystery of Christ; we die with him, are buried with him, and rise with him (cf. Rm 6:4; Ep 2:6; Col 3:1; 2 Tm 2:11); we receive the spirit of adoption as children of God "by virtue of which we cry: Abba, Father" (Rm 8:15), and thus become those true adorers whom the Father seeks (cf. Jn 4:23).[5]

Through Baptism we are formed in the likeness of Christ: "For in one Spirit we are all baptized into one body" (1 Cor 12:13). In this sacred rite, a union with Christ's death and resurrection is both symbolized and brought about: "For we were buried with him by means of baptism unto death." And if "we have been united with him in the likeness of his death, we shall be so in the likeness of his resurrection also" (Rm 6:4-5).[6]

Incorporated into the Church through Baptism, the faithful are consecrated by the baptismal character to the exercise of the cult of the Christian religion. Reborn as children of God, they must confess before others the faith which they have received from God through the Church.[7]

In Baptism neophytes receive forgiveness of sins, adoption as children of God, and the character of Christ, by which they are made members of the Church and for the first time become sharers in the priesthood of their Savior.[8]

Thus, Baptism, the gateway to the sacraments, is necessary for salvation in fact or at least in intention. It is validly conferred only by washing with true water together with the required formula of words.[9]

## II. THE CELEBRATION OF BAPTISM

### 1. PREPARATION

#### a. *Ceremony*

In the administration of Baptism the liturgical prescriptions laid down in approved texts are to be observed. In a case of urgent necessity only the valid matter and formula of words are required.[10] Either pouring or immersion may be used, according as the Conference of Bishops may prescribe.[11]

### b. *Participants*

Parents and sponsors of infants[12] to be baptized are to be properly instructed in their respective roles by the pastor personally or through others.[13] Adults[14] intending to receive Baptism are usually admitted through the various stages of the order of initiation, in accordance with the prescribed norms.[15] The one to be baptized should be given a name that is not foreign to a Christian mentality.[16]

### c. *Essential elements*

True and natural water is necessary for Baptism.[17] Water is *true* if it is composed of the requisite elements constituting water; *natural* if it is commonly considered and used as true water, whether naturally or artificially produced, which judgment is arrived at not simply by the results of chemical analysis but by the ordinary estimation and use of prudent men. Such true water is necessary for the sake of the authentic sacramental symbolism. It should be clean, for reasons of health. The baptismal font, or the vessel in which on occasion the water is prepared for the celebration of the sacrament in the sanctuary, should be very clean and attractive. If the climate requires, provision should be made for the water to be heated beforehand.[18]

The following are accepted as *certainly valid material* for the celebration of Baptism: natural water in a liquid state as found in rivers, the sea, wells, springs, fountains, pools, cisterns, baths, swamps, lakes, melted snow or ice or hail, mineral water, sulphur water, dew, condensed vapors, water from sweating walls, water mixed with a small amount of an extraneous element (as in the case of muddy water) as long as the water predominates, putrid water if it still remains true water in common estimation.[19]

Materials are considered *doubtfully valid* when their substances do not certainly imply natural water or their mixture with other elements almost supplants the water. Such doubtful materials are: light tea and coffee, thin soup and broth, light beer, thin ink, water produced from salt or lye or soapsuds, artificial water extracted by distillation from flowers (e.g., rose water) or herbs or flowing from vines or trees or other plants (but all these materials are considered invalid materials by some). In every case of prudent doubt in the concrete situation the resolution should always be in favor of the valid celebration of this so necessary sacrament.

Substances which have never been water or have been so changed as no longer to be or to be considered water are *certainly invalid material*. Such invalid materials are: wine, oil, meat or fat juice, amniotic fluid, fluids from the bodies of animals and men, milk, blood, urine, saliva, tears, sweat, thick soup or gravy, lard, grease, lacquer, shoe polish, foam, phlegm, all things not in a liquid state, water mixed with another substance which predominates and is no longer considered as apt to wash, mud, ink, thick beer or soup or coffee or tea or lye.

Except in the case of necessity, the priest or deacon should use only water that has been blessed for the baptismal rite. If the consecration of the water has taken place at the Easter Vigil, the blessed water should, if possible, be kept and used throughout the Easter season to affirm more clearly the relationship between the sacrament of Baptism and the paschal mystery. Outside the Easter season, it is desirable that the water be blessed for each celebration, in order that the words of blessing may clearly express the mystery of salvation which the Church recalls and proclaims. If the baptistry is supplied with flowing water, the blessing will be given to the water as it flows.[20]

Water which has been corrupted, run out or foul, or otherwise is lacking should not be used. New water should be poured into the previously fully cleaned font and blessed using the formula in the baptismal rite.

In a case of necessity, such as the danger of death, if certainly valid material is lacking or unavailable, doubtfully valid material can and must be used, even with the least probability of its validity (i.e., any material about which there is not certain validity). The use in this instance is conditional: "if this material is valid." The one so baptized is later to be baptized conditionally with certainly valid material.

Either the rite of immersion (dipping), which is more suitable as a symbol of participation in the death and resurrection of Christ, or the rite of infusion (pouring) may lawfully be used in the celebration of Baptism.[21] There must be in the common estimation of men a true washing or ablution, a flowing of water whereby the whole body or the head is washed. A *triple pouring* is made corresponding with the pronouncement of each name of the Trinity, as in the rite. This is probably a serious obligation, even though it pertains only to the lawful conferral of Baptism. The pouring is normally made *on the head*, since the head is the principal part where life integrally resides.

For the validity of a true washing the water should *flow*, even though there be only some drops (merely one or two drops are doubtfully sufficient). Merely to anoint the person to be baptized, e.g., with the thumb moistened with blessed water, is not sufficient.[22] To draw a wet cloth or sponge or wet fingers across the head or forehead is at least doubtfully valid. The water used should flow into the sacrarium or drainage part of the baptismal font and not employed, the water should be poured into a sacrarium or into the ground.

The water that flows must *touch the skin*, otherwise the Baptism is invalid or at least doubtful and thus is to be conferred again conditionally, e.g., if the water touches only the hair, (the hair should be parted to allow the water to flow on the skin, or across the forehead or temples), or only the clothes of the one being baptized. However, Baptism is valid even if the head is covered with sores. (It is invalid if given on the body of the mother of an unborn child to be baptized, highly doubtful when given on the umbilical cord or on one of the two membranes immediately surrounding the fetus in the womb, even though they arise from the fetus. The third membrane which surrounds the fetus exteriorly is from the mother and thus Baptism on it would be invalid.)

The words by which Baptism is conferred in the Latin Church are: "I baptize you in the name of the Father, and of the Son, and of the Holy Spirit."[23] This is the prescribed and *lawful* formula. In judging the *validity* of any other formula which may be used, either intentionally or otherwise, it is absolutely necessary that the following elements be present in the formula: the *minister* or the one baptizing must be expressed, at least implicitly; the *act* of baptizing expressed, in order that the pouring of the water might have significance; the *person baptized* mentioned, since the action is directed to this party; the *unity* of the divine essence, provided for by the words "in the name of"; the *trinity* of Persons, expressed by distinct and also probably by proper names.

The words of the formula are to be pronounced at the same time as the water is poured. Thus, not only moral but also physical simultaneity should be sought, since in practice the safer opinion must be followed.[24]

No one can baptize himself.[25]

## 2. TIME

Although Baptism may be celebrated on any day, to bring out the paschal character of Baptism, it is recommended that the sacrament be celebrated during the Easter Vigil or on Sunday,[26] when the Church commemorates the Lord's resurrection. On Sunday Baptism may be celebrated even during Mass, so that the entire community may be present and the necessary relationship between Baptism and the Eucharist may be clearly seen, but this should not be done too often.[27]

## 3. PLACE

Baptism as a rule is to be celebrated in a church or oratory having a baptismal font, for adults in their own parish church, for infants in the proper parish of their parents.[28] Conferral in a hospital may be permitted by the local ordinary, who for a grave cause may also allow conferral in a private home.[29]

## III. THE MINISTER OF BAPTISM

The ordinary minister is he who in virtue of his *power of Orders* is deputed primarily to confer Baptism. The ordinary ministers of Baptism are bishops, presbyters, and deacons.[30] At every celebration of this sacrament they act in the Church in the name of Christ and by the power of the Holy Spirit. Thus it is incumbent upon them to be diligent in the ministry of the word of God and in the celebration of the sacraments, avoiding any action which the faithful can rightly condemn as favoritism.[31]

Bishops, who are the principal dispensers of the mysteries of God and leaders of the entire liturgical life in the church committed to them, direct the conferral of Baptism, by which a sharing in the kingly priesthood of Christ is granted. For this reason they may wish to confer personally at the Easter Vigil the baptism of adults, at least those who have completed fourteen years of age.[32] The local ordinary may depute others to confer Baptism, but all the faithful should be instructed in the correct manner of baptizing for cases of necessity.[33]

The celebration of Baptism pertains by reason of office to the proper pastor of the one to be baptized. It is a reserved function, since by Baptism one is aggregated to a particular church or parish.[34] No cause is required that a pastor give consent to another priest or deacon to confer Baptism.

## IV. THOSE TO BE BAPTIZED

Every and only a human wayfarer on this earth, who is not yet baptized, is capable of receiving the sacrament of Baptism.[35]

### 1. ADULTS

An *intention* is required of adults, since they are to receive Baptism of their own knowledge and consent (*sciens et volens*).[36] Only in doubt as to the recipient's intention or will to receive the sacrament is Baptism administered conditionally.[37] Thus an adult must have a positive will, which is at least habitual and implicit (as in the desire to become a Christian although ignorant of Baptism) of receiving Baptism, since the present order of divine providence requires that an adult be justified and saved with the accompanying consent of his own free will to this gift of God. The minimum intention may be the basis of the administration of the sacrament only in a case of danger of death, since the safer course must be followed and an explicit intention secured. A general desire to be saved is not sufficiently determined; likewise, goodness and uprightness of life are of themselves inadequate indications of sufficient intention.

There is a *certain obligation* binding the minister to administer conditional Baptism to an adult in danger of death and unable to ask for it, if he has given or if he gives some probable indication of his intention of receiving the sacrament; if he later recovers and doubt remains about the validity of the first Baptism, he is to be baptized again conditionally.[38] Theologians agree that some explicit desire or intention to embrace the Christian religion or the Christian way of life, even with unawareness of Baptism, implicitly contains the desire for Baptism and is a sufficient intention for its reception. It is commonly taught that even conditional Baptism may not be administered to an adult who has given no sign of intention.

An adult shall not be baptized except after due instruction in the faith, and having undergone the catechumenate in accordance with the Rite of the Christian Initiation of Adults;[39] moreover he is to be admonished to repent his sins. The unbaptized who refuses to give up sinful practices cannot be baptized.

But in danger of death, if he cannot be more thoroughly instructed in the principal mysteries of the faith, it suffices for the conferral of Baptism that he in some way manifest his assent to these mysteries and earnestly promise that he will keep the commandments of the Christian religion. Due instruction in the faith and sorrow for sin are thus required in the adult for the lawful reception of the sacrament of Baptism.

The convert to be baptized should have a true and sincere supernatural sorrow, which is at least attrition, for all his actual, especially mortal sins. This will include a motion of hope and an implicit resolve to abandon any bad habits. Out of devotion he may confess his previous sins, but he is not so obliged in an absolute Baptism.

Unless prevented by a grave reason, an adult is to be confirmed immediately after Baptism and to participate in the celebration of the Eucharist, also receiving Communion. [40]

## 2. INFANTS

From the earliest times the Church, to which the mission of preaching the gospel and of baptizing was entrusted, has baptized children as well as adults. For, in the words of Our Lord: "Unless a man is reborn in water and the Holy Spirit, he cannot enter the kingdom of God." The Church has always understood these words to mean that children should not be deprived of Baptism, because they are baptized in the faith of the Church itself, which is proclaimed for them by their parents and godparents, who represent both the local Church and the whole society of saints and believers: "The Church is at once the mother of all and the mother of each." [41]

To fulfill the true meaning of the sacrament, children must later be formed in the faith in which they have been baptized. The foundation of this formation will be the sacrament itself, which they have already received. Christian formation, which is due to children by right, seeks to lead them gradually to learn God's plan in Christ, so that they may ultimately accept for themselves the faith in which they have been baptized. [42] Since the sacraments produce grace where no obstacle exists, it is impossible that there be an obstacle in the case of infants who need no personal disposition for a valid and lawful reception of Baptism.

Infants are to be baptized within the first weeks after birth. This should be arranged by the parents with the pastor either before the birth or as soon as possible afterwards.[43] Pastors and preachers should not fail to admonish the faithful of this serious obligation. Consent for the conferral of Baptism should be given by one or both parents or by whoever lawfully stands in their place.[44]

There should be no delay in baptizing an infant in danger of death, whether of Catholic or non-Catholic parentage, even against parental objection[45] if the child will die before coming to the use of reason.

The children of *lax* or *lapsed* Catholics, i.e., of parents who have fallen into indifferentism, who do not practice the faith without giving it up entirely, who seek the child's Baptism for social reasons, who are invalidly married, etc., may be baptized if the minister judges there is a founded hope of a Catholic upbringing as given by a member of the family, a sponsor, or by the aid of the community of the faithful. The parents should be instructed in their responsibility. If the conditions are not judged sufficient for baptizing, the parents can be invited to inscribe the child for a later Baptism, and pastoral contacts with the parents can be fostered to this purpose. Thus, rather than baptizing all such children presented and hoping for the best, or, on the other hand, tending to refuse Baptism in order not to add to the ranks of the nominal Catholics, the situation might be turned into a pastoral opportunity, perhaps with some deferral of Baptism, to bring the parents to a better appreciation of the meaning and consequences of Baptism both for themselves and for their children.[46]

In the case of a mixed marriage, the hope of Catholic education is present if the Catholic party requests the priest to baptize the child and promises to rear it as a Catholic. If possible, the non-Catholic parent should be advised of the conferral of the Baptism.

The children of a Catholic parent who is dying and merely civilly married to an unbeliever should be baptized, if there is a possible hope that they might in due course be instructed in the true religion and such a promise is given; if no such hope be entertained, administration must be denied, even though Catholic godparents offer them for Baptism.

The *illegitimate* children born of a Catholic with a non-Catholic party may be baptized if the Catholic has control of them and asks for Baptism. Illegitimacy is not sufficient reason to refuse the sacrament, especially when

Catholic education is assured. If it is foreseen that the child after Baptism will be educated outside the faith administration is to be denied.

Abandoned infants or foundlings are to be baptized, unless after a careful investigation there is clear proof of their Baptism.[47] Where it is possible, aborted fetuses, if alive, are to be baptized.[48]

### 3. JURIDIC RITE

The celebration of Baptism not only confers on the recipient personality, rights and obligations in ecclesiastical law but at the same time usually determines the Catholic rite or Ritual Church to which the same person becomes affiliated and must adhere.[49] This is true unless by chance Baptism is conferred by a minister of another rite either unlawfully or even by custom or because of grave necessity when a minister of the candidate's rite was unavailable,[50] in which cases the candidate is enrolled in the Ritual Church in which the Baptism should have been conferred.

If the Ordinary of the parent judges that, for serious reasons, circumstances warrant the Baptism of the child in another rite, he may grant the required permission with the understanding that the child canonically belongs to the rite of the parents.[51] If there is no proper Eastern Rite pastor or hierarch of the parent, the local Latin Ordinary is competent to grant permission.

A child born of Latin Church parents is baptized in the Latin Rite.[52] A child belongs by Baptism to the Latin Church who is born of parents of whom only one is a member of the Latin Church and who agree to have their child baptized in the Latin Church.[53] A child born of parents of whom only one is a member of the Latin Church, but do not agree to have the child baptized in the Latin Church, is to be baptized in the Ritual Church of the father.[54]

Thus, a Latin father and a Melkite mother can agree to have their child baptized in the Latin Rite of the father. If the father is Melkite and the mother Latin, the child may, by agreement, be baptized in the Latin Church. Failing such agreement, the child is to be baptized in the Melkite Church.

A candidate for baptism who has completed his fourteenth year of age can freely choose to belong by Baptism to any Ritual Church, Latin or Eastern.[55]

Unless otherwise legislated, an unbaptized non-Catholic who by Baptism enters into the Catholic Church is free to choose his Ritual Church;

likewise, a baptized non-Catholic who is received into full communion in the Church.

Pastorally, it is important to ascertain the Ritual Church of each parent and to obtain clear expression of any agreement between parents of mixed Latin and non-Latin Rites regarding the Baptism of their child in the Latin Church. It is also important for the pastor or minister of Baptism to respect the obligations and sensitivities of Eastern Rite clergy and faithful.

### 4. RECEPTION INTO FULL COMMUNION

Nothing beyond what is necessary is to be imposed upon one who, born and baptized in a separated ecclesial Community, is received into full communion with the Catholic Church.[56] In this matter the Church's practice is governed by two principles: that Baptism is necessary for salvation and that it can be conferred only once.[57]

There can be no doubt cast upon the validity of Baptism as conferred among separated Eastern Christians. It is enough therefore, to establish the fact that Baptism was administered. Since in the Eastern Churches the sacrament of Confirmation (Chrism) is always lawfully administered by the priest at the same time as Baptism, it often happens that no mention is made of the Confirmation in the canonical testimony of Baptism. This does not give grounds for doubting that the sacrament was conferred.[58] Thus, nothing more is to be required from Eastern Christians coming into the fullness of communion than what a simple profession of Catholic faith requires.[59]

For the admission of one baptized to full communion in the Catholic Church there is required a doctrinal and spiritual preparation in accordance with pastoral needs adapted to each case. The candidate should learn to adhere more and more in his heart to the Church in which he will find the fulness of his Baptism. During the time of this preparation some sharing or communication in worship (*in sacris*) can take place, in accordance with the norms of the Ecumenical Directory. An equalizing of such candidates with catechumens is entirely to be avoided.[60]

The sacrament of Baptism cannot be repeated, and thus it is not permitted to celebrate or confer Baptism again conditionally unless there is present a prudent doubt about the fact or the validity of a Baptism already celebrated or conferred. If, after serious investigation has been made because of such a prudent doubt of fact or validity, it seems necessary to confer

Baptism again conditionally, the minister should opportunely explain the reasons why in this case, it is being celebrated or conferred conditionally.[61] The local Ordinary should see to it in each case what rites should be preserved and what ones omitted in a conditional conferral.[62]

It belongs to the Bishop to admit the candidate. However, the minister who is commissioned to go through with the celebration has the faculty to confirm the candidate in the rite of admission itself, unless the one to be admitted has already validly received Confirmation.[63]

## V. SPONSORS

### 1. OBLIGATION

It is a very ancient custom of the Church that an *adult* is not admitted to Baptism, insofar as possible, without a godparent or sponsor, a member of the Christian community who will assist the adult at least in the final preparation for Baptism and after Baptism will help him or her persevere in the faith and in his or her life as a Christian. In the Baptism of *children* also the godparent should be present to be added spiritually to the immediate family of the one to be baptized and to represent Mother Church. As occasion offers, the godparent will be ready to help the parents bring up their child to profess the faith and to show this by living it. At least in the final rites of the catchumenate and in the actual celebration of Baptism the godparent is present either to testify to the faith of the adult candidate or, together with the parents, to profess the Church's faith, in which the child is being baptized. Each child may have a godfather and a godmother, the word "godparents" (*patrini*) being used in the rite to describe both.[64]

The obligation to have a sponsor or godparent in the celebration of Baptism is considered to be serious and only proportionate and reasonable causes excuse from its observance, e.g., the Baptism would have to be deferred for a long time through lack of a godparent. This obligation rests primarily upon the parents.

When Baptism is repeated *conditionally*, the same godparent, to the extent possible, is used as perhaps in the former Baptism.

The person who asks to be admitted among the catechumens is accompanied by a sponsor, man or woman, who has known and helped the candidate and is witness to his or her morals, faith, and will. It may happen that this sponsor will not have fulfilled the office of godparent during the times of purification, illumination, and "mystagogia." Then another is substituted for him or her in this role.

The sponsor, however, chosen by the catechumen for his or her example, qualities, and friendship, delegated by the Christian community of the place and approved by the priest, accompanies the candidate on the day of election, in the celebration of the sacraments, and at the time of the "mystagogia." It is the task of the sponsor to exhibit in a friendly way to the catechumen the use of the Gospel in his or her (godparent's) own life and in his or her dealings with society, to help the catechumen in doubts and anxieties, to render testimony to the candidate , and to watch over the growth of his or her baptismal life. Already chosen before the "election," the godparent exercises this role publicly from the day of "election" when he or she gives testimony of the catechumen before the community; and the office keeps alive the moment when the neophyte, having received the sacraments, is to be helped to remain faithful to his or her baptismal promises.[65]

### 2. NUMBER

In the celebration of Baptism there should be a sponsor, two at the most (a man and a woman).[66] If there is only one, it is expedient though not necessary that the sponsor be of the same sex as the candidate. Neither father nor mother of the one to be baptized may act as sponsor.[67]

### 3. QUALIFICATIONS

The Church has always opposed the admission to the office of sponsor or godparent of those who are unwilling to perform their obligations in this role or whom she deems unqualified. To guarantee the presence of the required qualifications the common law indicates the conditions that pertain to the assumption of the office. If the proposed sponsor is known to be unfit or unqualified the pastor or minister must refuse permission. This should be done in a prudent and kind manner with an explanation of the laws of the Church in this matter. If the refusal will cause an extremely difficult situation, the pastor or minister could allow the party to assist at the Baptism, thus being constituted a mere witness.

A sponsor is to be appointed by the candidate for Baptism, or by the parents or whoever stands in their place, or failing these, by the pastor or minister. The sponsor should understand the nature of the obligation that is being assumed and should deliberately accept it.[68] The sponsor physically contacts the candidate in accordance with the prescriptions of the baptismal liturgy.[69]

A sponsor may not be less than sixteen years of age, unless a different age has been stipulated by the diocesan bishop or unless the pastor or minister considers that an exception is to be made for a just cause.[70]

A sponsor is to be a Catholic who has been confirmed, has received the sacrament of the Eucharist, and who lives a life of faith which befits the role to be undertaken, and, moreover, does not labor under a canonical penalty, whether imposed or declared.[71]

A baptized person who belongs to a non-Catholic ecclesial community may be admitted only together with a Catholic sponsor, and then simply as a witness to the Baptism.[72]

Because of the close communion between the Catholic Church and the separated Eastern Churches, it is permissible for a *member of one of the separated Eastern Churches* to act as godparent, together with a Catholic godparent, at the Baptism of a Catholic infant or adult, so long as there is provision for the Catholic education of the person being baptized and it is clear that the godparent is a suitable one. A Catholic is not forbidden to stand as godparent in an Orthodox church, if he is so invited. In this case, the duty of providing for the Christian education of the baptized person binds in the first place the godparent who belongs to the Church in which the child is baptized.

However, it is not permissible for a *member of a separated community* (which is not an Orthodox community) to act as godparent in the liturgical and canonical sense at Baptism (or Confirmation). The reason is that a godparent is not merely undertaking his responsibility for the Christian education of the person baptized (or confirmed) as a relation or friend — he is also, as a representative of a community of faith, standing as sponsor for the faith of the candidate. Equally a Catholic cannot fulfill this function for a member of a separated community. However, because of the ties of blood or friendship, a Christian of another communion, since he has faith in Christ, can be admitted with a Catholic godparent as a Christian *witness* of the Baptism. In comparable circumstances a Catholic can do the same for a member of a separated community. In these cases the responsibility for the

Christian education of the candidate belongs of itself to the godparent who is a member of the Church in which the candidate is baptized. Pastors should carefully explain to the faithful the evangelical and ecumenical reasons for this regulation, so that all misunderstanding of it may be prevented.[73]

### 4. PROXY

For a proxy (*procurator*) to act it is necessary that he do so in the name and by the authority of some other determined person and thus his authority must be proved, i.e., certified by qualified witnesses or by a legitimate document, unless the intention of this person is known with certainty by the pastor or minister who baptizes. The latter should know these details in order to investigate whether the designated sponsor has the requisite qualifications. Thus, one not present at a Baptism could not be said to be acting as a godparent merely on the basis that he would act if he knew of the Baptism. A parent or a spouse may act as proxy for a sponsor at Baptism, although they themselves may not be the godparent in the case. Age (except that necessary for the execution of the duty) and sex are immaterial in the choice of proxy. The name of the proxy as well as that of the principal or sponsor must be entered into the baptismal register.

## VI. THE PROOF AND RECORD OF CONFERRED BAPTISM

The baptismal register is the principal record among the parochial books. Every pastor has a serious obligation to note properly the reception of the sacrament of Baptism, as this is the basic document certifying one's membership in the Church and other factors relating to individual juridical status. Pastors ought carefully and without delay to inscribe in the baptismal register the names of those baptized, the minister, parents, sponsors, proxies, witnesses, juridic rite if different, and the place and date of celebration, together with the date and place of birth.[74]

It is important to write clearly and legibly with accurate use of the index, in order to facilitate the issuance of a certificate at some future date.

In recording the Baptism of a child of an unmarried mother the mother's name is to be entered if her maternity is publicly known or if, either in writing or before two witnesses, she freely asks that this be done. Likewise, the name of the father is to be entered, if his paternity is established either by some public document or by his own declaration in the presence of the pastor and two witnesses. In other cases, the name of the baptized person is to be registered, without any indication of the name of the father or of the parents.[75]

With an adopted child, the names of the adopting parents are to be recorded and, at least if this is done in the local civil registration, the names of the natural parents in accordance with §§ 1 and 2, subject however to the prescriptions of the Bishops' Conference.[76]

When Baptism has been administered neither by the pastor nor in his presence, the minister of the Baptism, whoever that was, must inform the pastor of the parish in which the Baptism was administered, so that he may register it in accord with canon 877, 1.[77]

The normal proof of Baptism is through the issuance of a baptismal certificate, which should be of recent date, i.e., issued within the last six months. It must contain all the necessary information as found in the register itself and be signed by the pastor of the place of issuance, or at least his name ought to be written on it and the one issuing the certificate countersigned it, e.g., Reverend Henry Smith, pastor, per Reverend John Jones. The parish seal must be impressed on the certificate. This certificate enjoys the character of a legal public document, but it is full proof, however, of only the fact and date of Baptism and the identity of the minister and sponsors. The pastor, moreover, in making entries into the baptismal record, is merely a public notary and not the judge of what is fitting or expedient. Thus, he is forbidden to make any changes without consulting the local Ordinary; likewise he cannot attest on a baptismal certificate information that differs from the register itself. A baptismal certificate from a non-Catholic sect does not constitute full proof of the reception of valid Baptism.

With children who are *legitimated* by the subsequent valid marriage of their parents, if this fact has been properly noted in the baptismal register, a certificate of Baptism may be issued containing the names of both parents. A true record of *illegitimacy* must be available when the baptized party wishes to enter into marriage, the religious life, or the priesthood. It does not seem that such information is necessary when a baptismal certificate is to be issued only for the purpose of testifying to the fact of Baptism, e.g., for entrance to a Catholic school, or for first Communion. The local Ordinary must decide in all such cases what information, if any, may be withheld or changed.

It sometimes happens that the record of a conferred Baptism for some reason is not extant or that it is not possible to obtain a baptismal certificate or comparable proof. Thus, to prove that Baptism has been conferred, as long as there is no conflict of interest, it suffices to have either the declaration of a single witness who is above suspicion or, if the Baptism was conferred upon an adult, the sworn testimony of the baptized person.[78]

# CONFIRMATION

# CONFIRMATION

## I. SACRAMENTAL NATURE

Confirmation, the Christian's personal Pentecost, is the complement of Baptism, the strengthening and perfecting of the Christian life inaugurated in Baptism and to be consummated in the Eucharist. Those who have been baptized continue the path of Christian initiation through the sacrament of Confirmation in which they receive the Holy Spirit poured out, the same Spirit who was sent upon the Apostles by the Lord on the day of Pentecost. This gift of the Holy Spirit conforms believers more perfectly to Christ and strengthens them so that they may bear witness to Christ for the building up of his body in faith and love. They are so marked with the character or seal of the Lord that the sacrament of Confirmation cannot be repeated.[1]

Through the sacrament of Confirmation those who have been born anew in Baptism receive the inexpressible Gift, the Holy Spirit himself, by which "they are endowed . . . with special strength," and, having been sealed with the character of this same sacrament, are "bound more intimately to the Church" and "are more strictly obliged to spread and defend the faith both by word and by deed as true witnesses of Christ."[2]

As we require the grace of Baptism to form the mind unto faith, so it is of the utmost advantage that the souls of the faithful be strengthened by a different grace, to the end that they be deterred by no danger, or fear of pains, tortures, or death, from the confession of the true faith.[3] Inasmuch as they are reborn as sons of God, the faithful must confess before men the faith which they have received from God through the Church. Then, bound more intimately to the Church by the sacrament of Confirmation, they are endowed by the Holy Spirit with special strength. Hence they are more strictly obliged to spread and defend the faith both by word and deed as true witnesses of Christ.[4] And so, the sacrament by which spiritual strength is conferred on the one born again makes him in some sense a front-line fighter for the faith of Christ.[5] For wherever they live, all Christians are bound to show forth, by the example of their lives and by the witness of their speech, that new man which they put on at Baptism and that power of the Holy Spirit by whom they were strengthened at Confirmation. Thus other men, observing their good works, can glorify the Father and can better appreciate the real meaning of human life and the bond which ties the whole community of mankind together.[6]

It is of faith that Confirmation is a true and distinct sacrament of the New Law,[7] that it confers on the soul an indelible character and thus it may not be repeated.[8] Confirmation is not necessary for salvation by any necessity of means or precept, but it is morally necessary for the Christian. Being a divinely instituted means of perfecting the way of salvation, it may not be neglected. A failure to seek Confirmation when it is opportune is of itself a slight sin, but it can become serious by reason of scandal, contempt, or special spiritual need. Those with the care of souls should see to it that all the baptized come to the fullness of Christian initiation and therefore are carefully prepared for Confirmation.[9]

## II. THE CELEBRATION OF CONFIRMATION

The only valid material for the celebration of Confirmation is sacred chrism (S.C.), that is, pure olive oil mixed with balsam and blessed by a bishop.[10] The chrism is consecrated by a bishop in the Mass which is ordinarily celebrated on Holy Thursday for this purpose.[11] It is never allowed to administer Confirmation without chrism blessed by a bishop, even when administered by a priest, or to receive the chrism from bishops not in communion with the Apostolic See.[12]

Through the anointing with chrism on the forehead, which is done by the imposition of the hand (together with the formula of words), the sacrament is conferred.[13] Validity requires only the imposition of the hand which accompanies the unction. Even though the imposition of hands upon the candidates with the prayer *All powerful God* does not pertain to the valid conferral of the sacrament, it is to be strongly emphasized for the integrity of the rite and the fuller understanding of the sacrament.[14]

The formula in the conferral of Confirmation is: *N., be sealed with the Gift of the Holy Spirit.*[15] Thus the Latin Church adopts the very ancient formula belonging to the Byzantine Rite by which the Gift of the Holy Spirit himself is expressed and the outpouring of the Spirit which took place on the day of Pentecost is recalled.[16]

The sacrament of Confirmation may be celebrated at any time of the year. Ordinarily it is conferred within the Mass in order to express more clearly the fundamental connection of this sacrament with the entirety of Christian initiation.[17]

Although the appropriate place for the celebration of this sacrament is a church, especially because of its normal celebration within the Mass, it may be celebrated in any other worthy place, for a just and reasonable cause in the judgment of the minister, e.g., in danger of death.[18] Within the territory in which they can confer Confirmation, ministers may confirm even in exempt places.[19]

## III. THE MINISTER OF CONFIRMATION

### 1. ORDINARY MINISTER

The original or ordinary minister of Confirmation is the bishop.[20] Normally the sacrament is celebrated by the bishop so that there will be a more evident relationship to the first pouring forth of the Holy Spirit on the day of Pentecost. After they were filled with the Holy Spirit, the Apostles themselves gave the Spirit to the faithful through the laying on of their hands. In this way the reception of the Spirit through the ministry of the bishop shows the close bond which joins the confirmed to the Church as well as the mandate of Christ to be witnesses among men.[21]

Within his own territory the bishop confirms lawfully even one who is not his own subject, unless the latter's own Ordinary has expressly forbidden it. Outside his own territory he needs at least the presumed permission of the local Ordinary, except to confirm his own subjects.[22]

A bishop is bound to confirm his subjects who properly and reasonably request this sacrament or to see to it that the sacrament is provided.[4] Of its nature this is a serious obligation in justice; it admits, however, of lightness of matter. The ample provisions for other ministers in the universal law of the Church greatly assist the bishop in the fulfillment of his obligation to provide the sacrament for the faithful.[24] To neglect or to refuse habitually to administer Confirmation would certainly be a serious sin.

## 2. OTHER MINISTERS

The universal law itself confers the faculty of administering Confirmation upon:[25]

— those equivalent in law to a diocesan bishop, within the confines of their jurisdiction;[26]

— with respect to the person to be confirmed, the priest who by virtue of his office or by mandate of the diocesan bishop baptizes an adult or admits a baptized adult into full communion with the Catholic Church;

— the pastor or indeed any priest with regard to those in danger of death.

One or more specified priests may be given the faculty to confirm by the diocesan bishop, if necessity so requires. Moreover, the priest who by law or by lawful grant confirms may in individual cases invite other priests to join him in administering the sacrament, but for a grave reason.[27]

A priest may confirm the following persons, but only at the stated times:[28]

— adults or children old enough for catechesis, but at the time of their Baptism;

— those validly baptized in non-Catholic Christian Churches, but at the time of their reception into full communion with the Catholic Church;

— those baptized but not confirmed in the Catholic Church who, after having been brought up in or having joined a non-Catholic religion, later seek full reception into the Catholic Church, but at the time of their reception;

— however, a priest may not confirm one who was baptized but not confirmed as a Catholic, who did not join another religion and who, after a period of time (often many years) in which the person was not active in the practice of the faith, now desires to be confirmed and to be actively involved in Church life.

The priest who has the faculty to confirm must use it for those in whose favor it was granted but validly only within the territory assigned to him (except in the case of danger of death), even including those from outside the territory, unless there is a prohibition by their own proper Ordinary.[29]

## IV. THOSE TO BE CONFIRMED

One must be baptized in order validly to receive the sacrament of Confirmation. In addition, if the baptized person has the use of reason, it is required (for lawfulness and fruitfulness) that he be in the state of grace, properly instructed, and able to renew his baptismal promises.[30]

An implicit habitual intention suffices for adults. The sacrament revives when an obstacle of serious sin impeding its effect is removed. Those not in full communion with the Church may not be confirmed until they first become reconciled to the Church.

It is the responsibility of the episcopal conferences to determine more precisely the pastoral means for the preparation of children for Confirmation.[31]

Adults should receive Confirmation immediately after Baptism, unless graver reasons impede. By this connection there are signified the unity of the Paschal mystery, the intimate relationship between the mission of the Son and the pouring forth of the Holy Spirit, and the union of the sacraments by which each divine person with the Father comes to the baptized.[32]

With adults, the same principles should be followed, with suitable adaptations, which are in effect in individual dioceses for the admission of catechumens to Baptism and the Eucharist. In particular, suitable catechesis should precede Confirmation. The relationship of the candidates with the Christian community and with individual members of the faithful should be sufficiently effective to assist them in their formation. This should be directed toward their living the witness of a Christian life and exercising the Christian apostolate, while developing a genuine desire to participate in the Eucharist.[33]

It sometimes happens that the preparation of a baptized adult for Confirmation is part of his preparation for marriage. In such cases, if it is foreseen that the conditions for a fruitful reception of Confirmation will not be satisfied, the local Ordinary will judge whether or not it is better to defer Confirmation until after the marriage.[34]

If one who has the use of reason is confirmed in danger of death, he should be prepared spiritually, so far as possible, depending upon the circumstances of the individual case.[35]

Where it is customary for the candidate of Confirmation to receive a new name, even when Confirmation immediately follows Baptism, this request for a new name should be granted. The new name is recorded in the proper place in the Confirmation register.

A sick person in danger of death should be strengthened by Confirmation before he receives the Eucharist as Viaticum, after the requisite and possible catechesis. In danger of death, however, the sacraments of Confirmation and Anointing of the Sick are not *ordinarily* to be celebrated in the same rite. When circumstances permit, the Rite of Confirmation outside Mass is followed.[36]

In the Latin Church the administration or celebration of Confirmation is generally postponed until about the age of discretion. For pastoral reasons, however, especially to strengthen in the life of the faithful complete obedience to Christ the Lord in loyal testimony to him, episcopal conferences may choose an age which appears more appropriate, so that the sacrament is conferred after appropriate formation at a more mature age.[37]

There should always be the necessary concern that children be confirmed at the proper time, even before the use of reason, when there is danger of death or other serious difficulty. They should not be deprived of the benefit of this sacrament. In the case of a child who has not yet reached the age of reason, Confirmation is conferred in accordance with the same principle and norms as Baptism.[38]

If the candidates for Confirmation are children who have not received the Eucharist and are not admitted to their First Communion at this liturgical celebration or in other special circumstances, Confirmation is celebrated outside of Mass. When this occurs, there should first be a celebration of the word of God.[39]

## V. SPONSORS

Ordinarily there should be a sponsor for each of those to be confirmed. The sponsor brings the candidate to receive the sacrament, presents him to the minister for anointing, and will later help him to fulfill his baptismal promises faithfully under the influence of the Holy Spirit.[40] It is more generally considered that the obligation to have a sponsor or godparent is less serious than at Baptism.

In view of contemporary pastoral circumstances, it is desirable that the godparent at Baptism, if present, also be the sponsor at Confirmation. This expresses more clearly the relationship between Baptism and Confirmation and also makes the duty and function of the sponsor or godparent more effective.[41] Nonetheless, the choice of a special sponsor for Confirmation is not excluded.

Neither the father nor mother can be the sponsor of the candidate.[42] The parents, however, even when the sponsor is present, may present their children for Confirmation. By "present" is meant the simple fact of bringing or accompanying the candidate to the bishop at the end of the Gospel,[43] a natural gesture in the case of young children. But the sponsor functions as such in the actual celebration of the sacrament.

Pastors and ministers should see to it that the sponsor or godparent fulfills the same conditions required for sponsorship in Baptism.[44]

The sponsor must place his right hand on the shoulder of the one to be confirmed at the time of the anointing by the bishop or minister of Confirmation.[45]

## VI. THE PROOF AND RECORD OF CONFERRED CONFIRMATION

The pastor should record the names of the minister, those confirmed, parents and sponsors, the date and place of Confirmation in a special book or Confirmation register, in addition to the notation in the baptismal register which is made according to law.[46]

If the proper pastor of the newly confirmed is not present, the minister should inform him of the Confirmation either personally or through a representative. This is usually done by way of the Confirmation certificate.[47]

In lieu of an authentic Confirmation certificate, proof of Confirmation received follows the same norms as for the proof of Baptism.[48]

# THE MOST HOLY EUCHARIST

# THE MOST HOLY EUCHARIST

## I. SACRAMENTAL AND SACRIFICIAL NATURE

Initiation into Christ and his Church are brought to completion and fulfillment in the Eucharist, the summit and source of the whole Christian life, by means of which the unity of God's people is signified and brought about and the building up of the Body of Christ is perfected. Thus all the sacraments are bound up with and directed to the Eucharist: Baptism and Confirmation as the initiation and strengthening in the Christian life, Penance and the Anointing of the Sick as purifying from sin and its residue whereby the baptized are made worthy participants in the Eucharist, Holy Orders by which an ordained priesthood is provided in every generation to continue the Eucharist, Matrimony by which members for the common priesthood of the true worshippers are handed down.[1]

The Eucharist is at one and the same time a Sacrifice-Sacrament, a Communion-Sacrament, and a Presence-Sacrament. At the Last Supper on the night he was betrayed, our Savior instituted the Eucharistic Sacrifice of his Body and Blood. He did this in order to perpetuate the sacrifice of the Cross throughout the centuries until he should come again, and so to entrust to his beloved spouse, the Church, a memorial of his death and resurrection: a sacrament of love, a sign of unity, a bond of charity, a paschal banquet in which Christ is consumed, the mind filled with grace, and a pledge of future glory given to us. Thus in virtue of Christ's will this sacrament constantly makes actual again the mystery of the sacrifice by which he offered himself to the Father on the altar of the Cross.[2]

The Eucharist is a very great mystery, a mystery which Christ the high Priest instituted and which he commanded to be continually renewed in the Church by his ministers. It is in the Eucharist that the close union of the Mystical Body of Jesus Christ with its Head reaches during this mortal life, as it were, its completion. Thus in the sacrament of the Eucharistic bread the unity of all believers who form one body in Christ is both expressed and brought about. Celebrating the Eucharistic Sacrifice we are, therefore, most closely united to the worshipping Church in heaven. Truly partaking of the body of the Lord in the breaking of the Eucharistic bread, we are taken up into communion with him and with one another.[3]

The Eucharist is the source of perfecting the Church, building up the Church, fashioning it into the true community of the People of God, into a congregation of believers, sealed with the same mark of unity that the first Apostles and disciples of the Lord shared. The Eucharist builds ever anew this community and unity and thus the Church lives by the Eucharist, by the fullness of this sacrament. No Christian community can truly be built up unless it has its basis and center in the celebration of the Eucharist. Renewal in the Eucharist of the covenant between the Lord and man draws the faithful into the compelling love of Christ and sets them afire. From the liturgy, therefore, and especially from the Eucharist, as from a fountain, grace is channeled to us; and the sanctification of man in Christ and the glorification of God, to which all other activities of the Church are directed as toward their goal, are most powerfully achieved. Thus the Lord left behind a pledge of hope and strength for life's journey in that sacrament of faith where natural elements refined by man are changed into his glorified Body and Blood, providing a meal of brotherly solidarity and a foretaste of the heavenly banquet. For all these reasons all Christ's faithful should hold the Eucharist in highest honor.[4]

The word "eucharist" comes from the Greek *eucharistein* signifying "to give thanks," which thanks are due because of the great benefit, the good grace (derived also from the same Greek root), which it confers, containing as it does the Author of grace. In its daily consecration thanksgiving is offered to God for benefits received and for the very institution of the sacrament itself. Many other terms have also been used in Scripture and in Tradition to refer to the divine sacrament and sacrifice.[5]

"This sacrament has a threefold significance: one with regard to the past inasmuch as it is commemorative of Our Lord's Passion, which was a true sacrifice . . ., and in this respect it is called a *sacrifice*. With regard to the present it has another meaning, that of ecclesiastical unity in which men are aggregated through this sacrament; and in this respect it is called *communion* or *synapsis*. With regard to the future it has a third meaning, inasmuch as this sacrament foreshadows the divine fruition, which shall come to pass in heaven; and according to this it is called *viaticum* because it supplies the way of reaching there. . . It is termed a *host* inasmuch as it contains Christ who is 'a host . . . of sweetness.' ''[6]

The Eucharist is thus a sacrament of the New Law as instituted by Christ in which under the consecrated species of bread and wine the Body and Blood of Christ are truly, really, and substantially contained, for the purpose of producing grace after the manner of a spiritual nourishment. This sacrament consists of something permanent from the moment of its consecration, the Real Presence.[7]

It is of faith that the whole and entire Christ is permanently contained under each species and in every part (at least that which is sensible, however small) separated from either species. Thus in every reception of the sacrament the following *effects* or *fruits* may be received: (1) an increase in sanctifying or common or second grace, since the Eucharist is a sacrament of the living; (2) the special grace of this sacrament or sacramental grace, which consists in a spiritual nourishment through union with Christ and his members, thus accomplishing in the spiritual life what material nourishment or food and drink effects in bodily life, namely, sustaining, augmenting, repairing, delighting it; (3) a rich endowment of actual graces and a weakening of concupiscence and the inclination to sin even when habits have been formed; (4) the remission of venial sins and restoration of spiritual strength through the stirring up of charity in this sacrament whereby there is also a preservation from serious sins and all future sins; (5) a remission of the temporal punishment due to sin, not in whole but in part, according to the devotion and fervor of the recipient of the sacrament; (6) a pledge of future glory or consummated union with Christ in the beatific vision; (7) the remission of serious sins or the conferral of first grace, as an accidental effect of the sacrament and under the usual condition.[8]

## II. THE EUCHARISTIC CELEBRATION

Through the ministry of priests the spiritual sacrifice of the faithful is made perfect in union with the sacrifice of Christ, the sole mediator. Through the hands of the priest, who acts in the person of Christ, and in the name of the whole Church the Lord's sacrifice is offered in the Eucharist in an unbloody and sacramental manner until he himself returns. Bishops and priests especially must take care that this sacrament of love stands central in the life of the people of God, so that Christ becomes in truth the life of souls as they repay in worship love for love to him. The clergy should instruct and encourage the faithful to take on an active part in the celebration of Mass, receiving the sacrament with great devotion and frequently, and showing it the reverence of adoration.[9]

## 1. THE MINISTER OF THE MOST HOLY EUCHARIST

### a. *Qualified minister*

The Lord's supper is the assembly or gathering of the people of God, with a priest presiding, to celebrate the memorial of the Lord. When the Church assembles to offer the Sacrifice of the Mass according to the renewed form of celebration, it is made manifest that the Mass is the center of the Church's life. Thus, the celebration of the Eucharist expresses in a particular way the public and social nature of the liturgical actions of the Church, which is the sacrament of unity, namely, the holy people united and ordered under the bishops. The Church is most perfectly displayed in its hierarchic structure in that celebration of the Eucharist at which the bishop presides, surrounded by his priests and ministers, with the active participation of the whole People of God.[10] As dispensers of holy things, especially in the Sacrifice of the Mass priests assume in a unique manner the person of Christ. It is fitting that, by reason of the sign, they participate in the Eucharist and exercise the order proper to them, either by celebrating or concelebrating the Mass, not by limiting themselves to communication like the laity.[11]

It is of faith that only a validly ordained priest can bring into being the sacrament of the Eucharist, acting in the person of Christ. Only a man can be ordained a priest.[12] Any priest may lawfully celebrate the Eucharist, as long as he is not debarred by Church law and observes the canonical norms. He is entitled to offer Mass for anyone, living or dead. A priest, moreover, should be allowed to celebrate the Eucharist, even if he is unknown to the rector of the church, as long as he presents a letter of recommendation not more than a year old, from his diocesan bishop or religious superiors attesting to his worthiness as a priest and requesting that he be admitted to celebrate Mass, or if the rector prudently judges that the priest is worthy and free from penalty.[13]

### b. *Preparation for celebration*

A priest ought not to fail to prepare himself for offering the Eucharistic Sacrifice by devout prayers and after the Sacrifice to give thanks to God for so great a blessing.[14] The remote preparation is the state of grace and a purity of soul which strives to avoid slight sins and the voluntary imperfections which retard the fervor of charity.

Every priest should prepare as well as he can for the liturgical actions he is to perform. He is to keep in mind that the effectiveness of liturgical actions does not consist in the continual search for newer rites or simpler forms, but in an ever deeper insight into the word of God and the mystery which is celebrated. The priest will assure the presence of God and his mystery in the celebration by following the rites of the Church rather than his own preferences. The priest should keep in mind that, by imposing his own personal restoration of sacred rites, he is offending the rights of the faithful and is introducing individualism and idiosyncrasy into celebrations which belong to the whole Church.

The ministry of the priest is the ministry of the Church, and it can be exercised only in obedience, in hierarchical fellowship, and in devotion to the service of God and of his brothers. The hierarchical structure of the liturgy, its sacramental value, and the respect due to the community of the faithful requires that the priest exercise his liturgical service as a faithful minister and steward of the mysteries of God. He should not add any rite which is not contained in the liturgical books.[15]

A priest who is conscious of grave sin may not celebrate Mass without previously having been to sacramental confession, unless there is a grave reason and there is no opportunity to confess. The priest in the latter circumstance is to remember his obligation to make an act of perfect contrition, in which is contained the resolve to go to confession as soon as possible.[16]

### c. *Eucharistic fast*

A priest who is to celebrate the Eucharist is to abstain for at least one hour before communion from all food and drink, with the sole exception of water and medicine. A priest who, on the same day, celebrates Mass twice or three times may consume something before the second or third Mass, even without interval of one hour. Elderly priests and those suffering from some illness may celebrate Mass even if within the preceding hour they have consumed something.[17]

### d. *Frequency of celebration*

In the mystery of the Sacrifice of the Holy Eucharist, which is the chief task which a priest is called upon to perform, the work of our Redemption is constantly renewed. It is, therefore, earnestly recommended that priests celebrate daily. Even if the faithful cannot be present, the Mass is still the act of Christ and the Church, an action in which the priest is always acting for the salvation of the people. Therefore, priests cannot be easily excused from fault who without reasonable cause abstain from daily celebration, since they would seem to depreciate so great a benefit, both for themselves and for the Church at large, and especially if they would cause scandal or wonderment to the faithful.[18]

Unless there is a good and reasonable cause for doing so, a priest may not celebrate the Eucharist without the participation of at least one of the faithful; in which case deacons and lay persons are not permitted to say the prayers, especially the Eucharistic prayers, nor to perform the actions which are proper to the celebrating priest.[19]

A priest may not celebrate more than once a day, apart from those cases allowed to him by the law to celebrate or concelebrate a number of times on the same day. However, if there is a shortage of priests, the local Ordinary may for a good reason allow priests to celebrate twice in one day or even, if there is a pastoral need, three times on Sundays and holydays of obligation.[20] Local Ordinaries may obtain an indult for a greater frequency.

Unless the benefit of the faithful requires or otherwise urges, priests may concelebrate the Eucharist; yet they are fully entitled to offer Mass individually, but not while a celebration is taking place in the same church or oratory.[21]

Concelebration of the Eucharist aptly demonstrates the unity of the Sacrifice and of the priesthood. Moreover, whenever the faithful take an active part, the unity of the People of God is strikingly manifested, particularly if the bishop presides. Concelebration both symbolizes and strengthens the brotherly bond of the priesthood, because by virtue of the sacred ordination and mission which they have in common, all priests are bound together in close brotherhood.

Therefore, unless it conflicts with the needs of the faithful, which must always be consulted with the deepest pastoral concern, and although every priest retains the right to celebrate alone, it is desirable that priests should celebrate the Eucharist in this eminent manner. This applies both to communities of priests and to groups which gather on particular occasions, as also to all similar circumstances. Those who live in community or serve the same church should welcome visiting priests into their concelebration. The competent superiors should therefore facilitate and indeed positively encourage concelebration, whenever pastoral needs or other reasonable motives do not prevent it.

It is the local Ordinary who gives the general guidelines or disciplinary regulations governing concelebration in the diocese, even in churches and semi-public oratories of exempt religious communities. Every Ordinary, including the major superior of non-exempt clerical religious institutes and of societies of clerics living in community without vows, has the right to judge the suitability of, and to give permission for, concelebration in his churches and oratories without the need to consult the local Ordinary. He may also limit the number of concelebrants.

Where there is a large number of priests, the competent superior may permit concelebration several times on the same day, but at different times or in distinct places. No one may concelebrate in a Mass which has already begun.

Without further permission concelebration is permitted at: (1) the chrism Mass and the evening Mass on Holy Thursday; (2) councils, meetings of bishops, and synods; (3) the blessing of an abbot. With permission of the Ordinary: (1) at the conventual Mass and at the principal Mass in churches and oratories when the need of the faithful does not require that all the priests present celebrate individually; (2) at any kind of meeting of priests, either secular or regular: at Masses celebrated on the occasion of a synod or pastoral visitation or whenever priests meet their bishop during a retreat or any other gathering.

In addition to any other faculty to binate or trinate, without further permission it is permissible to celebrate or concelebrate more than once on the same day in the following cases: (1) one who has celebrated or concelebrated the chrism Mass on Holy Thursday may also celebrate or concelebrate the evening Mass; (2) one who has celebrated the Easter Vigil Mass may celebrate or concelebrate the second Mass at Easter; (3) all priests may concelebrate the three Masses at Christmas, provided these are celebrated at the proper times; (4) one who concelebrates with the bishop or his delegate at a synod, at a pastoral visitation, or at a gathering of priests for any reason may celebrate another Mass *for the benefit of the faithful* if the bishop so decides. This holds also for meetings of religious with their own Ordinary; (5) religious who are duty bound to celebrate for the pastoral good of the faithful may also concelebrate on the same day of the conventual or "community" Mass. [22]

### e.  Minister of Holy Communion

The ordinary minister of Communion is a bishop, a priest, or a deacon. The extraordinary minister is an acolyte, or another of the faithful lawfully deputed. [23]

Local Ordinaries have the faculty to permit a suitable person individually chosen as an extraordinary minister for a specific occasion or for a time or, in the case of necessity, in some permanent way, either to give the Eucharist to himself or to other faithful and to take it to the sick who are confined to their homes. This faculty may be used whenever:

a) there is no priest, deacon or acolyte;
b) these are prevented from administering Holy Communion because of another pastoral ministry or because of ill health or advanced age;
c) the number of faithful requesting Holy Communion is such that the celebration of Mass or the distribution of the Eucharist outside of Mass would be unduly prolonged.

Local Ordinaries also have the faculty to permit individual priests exercising their sacred office to appoint a suitable person who in cases of genuine necessity would distribute Holy Communion for a specific occasion. [24]

A priest with the care of souls has an obligation in justice to distribute Communion to his subjects whenever they reasonably request the same, unless he is lawfully impeded by a proportionate cause. He may fulfill his obligation by the ministrations of others. Other priests are bound in charity to minister the Eucharist to the dying, but not in other cases, since necessity is not considered to exist. [25]

The right and duty to bring the Eucharist in the form of Viaticum to the sick belongs to the pastor, parochial vicars, chaplains, and to the community superior, for all who are in the house, in clerical religious institutes or societies of apostolic life. Any priest or minister of Communion must do this in case of necessity or with at least the presumed permission of the above mentioned persons, who are to be later notified.[26]

### 2. PARTICIPATION IN THE MOST HOLY EUCHARIST

#### a. *Qualified recipient*

Any baptized person not forbidden by law can and must be admitted to Holy Communion. They are not to be admitted who are excommunicated or interdicted or who obstinately persist in manifest grave sin.[27] Although the Eucharist as a sacrifice can benefit others inasmuch as it is offered for their salvation, it cannot, received as a sacrament, benefit others, since it is a spiritual food and drink which benefit only the partaker. However, Communion can benefit others as an act of satisfaction made to God for them, as suffrage for them, as Communion quickens charity which renders one more ready to petition God on behalf of others.[28]

The faithful may receive the Eucharist lawfully only from Catholic ministers. They may receive Communion from non-Catholic ministers in whose churches the sacrament of the Eucharist is valid, whenever necessity requires it and genuine spiritual advantage commends it, avoiding all danger of the error of indifferentism, together with the physical or moral impossibility to approach a Catholic minister. Members of Eastern churches not in full communion with the Catholic Church may receive Communion from Catholic ministers if they spontaneously ask for it and are properly disposed. Also members of other churches which the Apostolic See judges to be in the same position as these Eastern churches as far as the Eucharist is concerned. In danger of death or for some other grave and lawfully judged pressing need other Christians not in full communion with the Catholic Church may request the Eucharist from a Catholic minister, if the request is spontaneous, if they cannot approach a minister of their own community, are properly disposed and profess the Catholic faith in respect to the Eucharist.[29] Diocesan regulations should be consulted in all these instances.

One who is conscious of grave sin may not receive the Eucharist without previous sacramental confession unless there is a grave reason together with no opportunity to confess, in which case the communicant should be mindful of the obligation to perfect contrition with the resolve to confess as soon as possible.[30] On the other hand, frequent and even daily reception of the Eucharist should be encouraged among the faithful.[31]

The Eucharist may be given to children only if they possess sufficient knowledge through accurate preparation to understand, in accordance with their capacity, what the mystery of Christ means and are able to receive Communion with faith and devotion. In danger of their death they may be given Communion as long as they can distinguish the Body of Christ from ordinary food and reverently communicate.[32] It is the primary responsibility of parents, and of those taking their place, as well as of the pastor to see to it that children who have reached the use of reason are properly prepared and approach First Communion, but only after First Confession. The pastor may not admit to the Eucharist children who have not reached the age of reason or whom he judges to be insufficiently disposed.[33]

### b. *Eucharistic fast*

One who is to receive the Eucharist is to abstain for at least one hour before Communion from all food and drink, with the sole exception of water and medicine. The elderly and those who are suffering from some infirmity, as well as those who care for them, may receive the Eucharist even if within the previous hour they have consumed something.[34]

The precept to observe the eucharistic fast is a serious obligation founded in the tradition of the Church and based upon due reverence for the Blessed Sacrament. In the context of contemporary legislation very slight violations with regard to the quantity of food or drink or to the time element (unless done out of deliberate irreverence or of contempt) are not serious sins and thus of themselves do not preclude the reception of Communion.

A doubtful and not certain violation of the fast may be resolved in one's own favor, provided that there is no responsibility for the doubt because of a failure to ascertain the hour before deliberately eating and drinking in ignorance of the time.

Anything digestible taken into the stomach from the outside in the manner of eating or drinking, and not as saliva, by respiration or by injection, breaks the eucharistic fast. What is solid food is left to the sound and common judgment of human association or the common estimation of prudent men. Solid food, whether hard or soft, is considered to be that which men are said to eat and with respect to the state in which it is when taken into the mouth, e.g., lozenges, pills, etc. Likewise with drink. It is considered to be that which men are commonly said to drink in the state in which it is taken into the mouth. The drink may be pure or it may be nutritious, i.e., drink into which nutritious materials are mixed, as long as these latter are so dissolved in the fluid material that the whole can be reasonably said to be fluid. Alcoholic drinks are forbidden by the precept of the Eucharistic fast.

Alcoholic drinks are those which are everywhere considered to be and are called alcoholic, e.g., wine, beer, whiskey, gin, rum, liqueurs, etc. A drink is alcoholic whether taken by itself or mixed with something else, no matter how small the quantity of alcohol. Medicine is that which is so considered in the sound and common judgment of men. Common consent generally regards medicine prescribed by a physician as true and proper medicine. In a case of doubt whether a thing is true and proper medicine a sound and present judgment, based on solid and positive probability, may be followed. In fact, where there is a consideration of true and proper medicines, even if they contain alcohol, as long as they qualify as true and proper medicines in the commonly accepted sense of the word, they may be taken by the sick without any limitation of time whatsoever.

### c. *Frequency of reception*

It is strongly recommended that the faithful receive the Eucharist during the Eucharistic celebration, but Communion may be sought, for a just cause, outside of Mass. Communion may be received in any Catholic rite.[35]

One who has already received Communion may receive it a second time on the same day but only within the Mass in which that person participates, except in the case of Viaticum.[36]

In danger of death the Eucharist in the form of Viaticum is to be received, even repeatedly but on separate days, if the danger of death persists.[37]

Those who have made their first Communion are bound by the obligation of receiving Communion at least once a year. Unless for a just reason this precept is fulfilled at another time of the year, it must be fulfilled during the Easter season[38], which in the USA perdures through Trinity Sunday.

## 3. RITES AND CEREMONIES OF EUCHARISTIC CELEBRATION

### a. *Mode of celebration*

The Eucharist may be celebrated in Latin or in any other language but only from legitimately approved texts. Priests and deacons, in celebrating and administering the Eucharist, are to wear the sacred vestments prescribed by the rubrics.[39]

### b. *Rite of celebration*

A priest who is ill or elderly and who is unable to stand may celebrate Mass sitting, while observing the other liturgical norms, but not in public without permission of the local Ordinary. A priest who is blind or suffering from some other infirmity may lawfully use the text of any approved Mass in celebrating the Eucharist, even if there is need of the assistance of another priest, deacon, or properly instructed lay person.[40]

A priest who suffers from alcoholism or from some other illness and who, in the judgment of his own physician, cannot consume even the minimum amount of consecrated wine at Mass, may communicate by intinction in a concelebrated Mass. The local Ordinary can allow a priest, who is in the same condition, and when he also celebrates Mass alone, to communicate himself by intinction, so long as one of the faithful assisting at the Mass consumes what remains of the consecrated wine.[41]

Permission to participate in an inter-ritual Eucharistic concelebration may be granted by the Apostolic Nunciature. Inter-ritual concelebration is a bond of charity and a manifestation of the unity of the Church and of communion among particular churches; only one rite may be employed, that of the host church; concelebrants should be knowledgeable of the rite; provision should be made for the active participation of the faithful; incompatible elements from another rite are not permitted but the concelebrants may retain the vestments and insignia of their own rites, as well as other elements which will not offend the unity of the concelebration or fall under the heading of mixture of rites.[42]

When there is a shortage of priests of a particular rite and a need for a more adequate pastoral care of the faithful of that rite, priests of the Latin Rite may petition an indult of bi-ritualism in order to celebrate also the liturgy of the sacraments in the particular Eastern Rite. Upon the favorable opinion of the Ordinaries of both rites, the Sacred Congregation for the Oriental Churches grants the indult for a limited period. The conditions to be verified in the exercise of the indult are: the care of souls and a determined need; a personal appearance consonant with devotion, with the avoidance of the use of elaborate vestments and either anachronistic or avant-garde rubrics; the conformity of the celebrant not only to the proper ritual of the rite employed but also to local diocesan regulations; the advising of the proper Ordinary or his representative; a Latin priest is not to use the indult to offer an Eastern Rite Mass in a Latin church without the permission of the Ordinary of the rite employed, the same being true of an Eastern Rite priest celebrating a Latin Mass in an Eastern Rite church. A bi-ritual indult may be granted to a permanent deacon for a designated period, but to a transitional deacon only until his ordination to the priesthood, whereupon he must seek a new indult. [43]

### c. Elements Required for Celebration

### 1. Material

The requisite material for the celebration of the Eucharist and the confection of the Sacrament is only wheaten bread, recently made whereby the danger of corruption is avoided, and natural wine from the grape-vine, uncorrupted, and to which a small amount of water is to be added. Unleavened bread alone is to be used in the Latin Rite. [44]

The *bread* must be made from wheat, mixed with natural water, baked by the application of fire heat (including electric cooking) and substantially uncorrupted. The variety of the wheat or the region of its origin does not affect its validity, but bread made from any other grain is invalid material. Bread made with milk, wine, oil, etc., either entirely or in a notable part, is invalid material. Any natural water suffices for validity, e.g., even mineral water or sea water. The addition of a condiment, such as salt or sugar, is unlawful but valid, unless added in a notable quantity. Unbaked dough or dough fried in butter or cooked in water is invalid matter; likewise bread which is corrupted substantially, but not if it has merely begun to corrupt. Therefore, the valid material of this sacrament must be in the common estimation of reasonable men bread made from wheat and not mixed notably with something else so that it is no longer wheat. Those who make altar breads must be satisfied that they have purchased genuine and pure wheat flour.

The bread must be of wheat *flour* and only in case of necessity a white material thrashed or crushed from wheat. It must be free from mixture with any other substance besides wheat flour and water. It is gravely unlawful to consecrate with doubtful material. Altar breads must be fresh or recently baked and must not be allowed to get mouldy, which condition varies with regions, climates, etc. Normally the hosts should be renewed frequently; to use a host more than a month old is generally unlawful, slightly or gravely depending upon the delay in renewal. No more hosts should be consecrated than can be consumed in suitable time. Breads should be clean and unbroken. To use a soiled or broken or disfigured host is slightly or seriously sinful depending upon the extent the host is affected or of the scandal that may arise.[45]

To be valid material *wine* must be made from ripe grapes of the vine and not substantially corrupted; it cannot come from any other fruits or from unripe grapes or from the stems and skins of the grapes after all the juice has been pressed out. In regions where fresh grapes cannot be obtained, it is lawful to use raisin wine, i.e., wine made by adding water to raisins. Wine from which all alcohol has been removed or which on the other hand has more than 20 per cent alcohol or to which foreign ingredients (e.g., water) have been added in equal or greater quantities is invalid material. Wine is likewise invalid which has turned to acid or which is not natural but was manufactured by some chemical process, i.e., by mixing the constituents found in wine so that the product resembles wine. Wine must also be in a potable state, and thus if it is congealed (although most probably valid), it must be melted. The color, strength or origin of wine does not affect its validity.

It is gravely unlawful to use doubtful material and thus it is unlawful to consecrate wine which is just beginning to turn sour or to corrupt. Wine must be naturally fermented and the use of "must" (unfermented grape juice) is gravely unlawful. To be lawful, wine must be pure, free from the lees, diseases, and foreign ingredients. Lawful wine may not contain more than 18 percent alcohol (obtained from the grape); wines which would not ordinarily ferment beyond 12 percent alcohol cannot be fortified beyond this limit. The Holy See has been insistent that sacramental or Mass wine come from sources beyond suspicion, since there are many ways in which wines can be vitiated or adulterated, many methods which are actually used in this country to preserve, age, ameliorate wines. Wines should be purchased regularly only from reputable vendors of Mass wine or only when otherwise guaranteed to be pure and unadulterated.

It is a serious precept which requires that a very small portion of water be mixed with the wine when about to be used in the Holy Sacrifice. This is not necessary by reason of the sacrament but by ecclesiastical precept in order to signify that both water and blood issued from the side of the crucified Savior.[46] It is to be done at the prescribed time and before the offering of the wine. If the minister has forgotten to add the water, he should do so even after the Offertory, but never after Consecration. The quantity to be added is usually three to ten drops. Priests should avoid too great concern over the exact number of drops. Even a single drop, as long as it is sensible, satisfies the precept; even one fifth water (or one fourth if the wine is stronger) is not unlawful, although an excess of one third the amount of wine renders the latter invalid or truly doubtful. If the quantity of water added appears to be more than lawful, the minister should add more wine or take fresh wine and add the correct amount of water.[47]

Communion is to be given under the species of bread alone or, in accordance with liturgical laws, under both species or, in case of necessity, even under the species of wine alone.[48]

Priests must satisfy any obligations deriving from Masses celebrated with invalid matter.

2. Formula of words

The formula of consecration of the bread is: "This is my body which will be given up for you"; of the wine: "This is the cup of my blood, the blood of the new and everlasting Covenant. It will be shed for you and for all so that sins may be forgiven." The words which precede these formulas in no way pertain to the validity of the formula. It is commonly taught today that the essential words of the formula of the Eucharist — and their omission would invalidate the form — are: "This is my body," "This is the cup of my blood" (or "this is my blood"). In practice it is seriously prescribed to pronounce the entire formula; if any of the words from "the blood of the new . . ." on are omitted, the whole formula is to be repeated conditionally.

The dignity of this sacrament wherein the priest speaks in the person of Christ himself requires that the words of consecration be spoken with the greatest care and reverence. At the same time they are to be said in a truly and normally human manner, without scruples, as one speaks important words. The priest should not interrupt the pronouncing of the formula nor repeat it nor bob his head or move his body during its recitation; he would then represent Christ in a ridiculous manner and expose this most sacred action to becoming a distraction to others or even displeasing.

All concelebrants at a concelebrated Mass validly consecrate, even if one accidentally finishes the form sooner than the others, the recitation being considered morally simultaneous.[49] There is a duty to repeat the formula only in a case of a serious and well-founded and not scrupulous doubt. Repetition without a just reason is in itself a serious sin, although a perplexed conscience may excuse. The minister should not be disturbed if he cannot recall having said or said correctly the words required for consecration. If the omission of some essential part is certain or doubtful, the formula should be repeated absolutely or conditionally. If awareness of the omission occurs at the consecration, the formula alone is repeated; if later in the course of the Mass, the repetition begins with the "The day before he suffered. . .", "Before he was given up to death. . .", "On the night he was betrayed. . .", "He always loved . . .", or with the "When supper was ended. . .", "In the same way . . .", in the case of the formula of the wine alone.

The material for the Holy Sacrifice (and at the same time also for the confection of the sacrament) must be physically and morally present to the celebrant or minister who unites the matter with the form. This sacrament requires the maximum of presence and simultaneity of required material with prescribed formula so that the words "*this*" and "*this*" truly signify and are demonstrable. Hosts which are too far removed from the celebrant so as not to be designated by "*this*" but by "*that*," are not validly consecrated because not present.[50]

### 3. Intention

The material to be consecrated must be *definitely* intended by the minister, since by intention the formula determines the significance of the material. Thus the material — and the question in practice offers some difficulty mostly in respect to the hosts — must be *determined* or *properly designated* by the minister's intention. Although an actual intention is preferred, at least a *virtual* intention is required, which intention must be to consecrate the material or at least to do what the Church does.

The bread and wine to be consecrated should be placed on the corporal (or the altar cloth). If there is material to be consecrated or which is consecratable on the altar, but its presence is unknown to the celebrant, *by that very fact* it is not consecrated, since the intention of the minister must in *some sufficient* way designate or include the material that is to be consecrated.

The extent to which the celebrant understands material to be included in his intention, i.e., the meaning which the words "*this*" and "*this*" has for him in order to include all circumstance, can be determined by him once and for all, e.g., at the time of ordination, although it is recommended that this understanding in his own mind be renewed from time to time. On the other hand, his will to consecrate at any particular moment must be actual or at least virtual; unless changed, this will must be considered to be in conformity with his general or prevailing understanding of the terms of the intention. Every priest is urged in the beginning of his priesthood to form a clear intention regarding consecrating the sacred species and to recall it to mind in order to keep it fresh and to avoid anxiety and the danger of doubtful material.

By his intention the minister is considered to will (at least implicitly) to consecrate all that is before him, and thus he consecrates an unknown quantity of hosts in a ciborium or pyx or on the corporal or in his hands, e.g., if at the Communion he should notice that there have been two large hosts stuck together. Small particles remaining in the ciborium or pyx or on the corporal are considered to have been consecrated. Drops of wine adhering to the outside of the chalice are not considered to have been consecrated. Even though the interior surface of the chalice cup is wiped after the wine and water have been poured in for the Sacrifice, drops or a film of wine which sometimes nevertheless adhere to the sides of the cup are to be considered in practice to have been consecrated, since the intention of the minister is to consecrate all consecratable matter in the chalice.

Hosts which are doubtfully consecrated must not be administered to the faithful but rather reserved in the tabernacle and conditionally consecrated at another Mass; if they are few in number, they may be consumed at the same Mass but after the Sacred Blood has been consumed. Hosts which are to be consecrated are to be placed on the corporal (or the altar cloth) at the beginning of Mass, or at least before the Offertory. If for some reason they are brought out shortly after the Offertory, they are to be offered mentally. A serious reason is required if this takes place after the Preface has begun and a very serious reason after the Canon has begun. If one or another person would be deprived for some time of Holy Communion, a small particle from the large Mass host may be given. Under no circumstance may hosts be consecrated after the Mass host has been consecrated.

If consecrated hosts should become mixed with unconsecrated ones, the priest should consecrate the latter at a subsequent Mass and before being distributed to the faithful, either by consecrating the whole amount conditionally, or absolutely only those not consecrated. The same procedure is to be followed if a quantity of unconsecrated wine is added to render the Real Presence doubtful.

Even in a case of extreme necessity it is never allowed to consecrate except *within the Mass*.[51] A consecration which is not accompanied by the principal parts of the Mass is probably invalid. A consecration of one species alone is likewise gravely forbidden. To consecrate one species without the intention to consecrate the other renders the consecration doubtful. If, however, the intention to consecrate the other does exist, the consecration is valid. Thus, in the case of the sudden incapacity of the celebrant, another priest can continue the liturgy of the Mass with the consecration of the other species.

### 4. THE TIME AND PLACE OF EUCHARISTIC CELEBRATION

Mass may be celebrated and Communion distributed on any day and at any hour, except the days and hours excluded by liturgical laws.[52]

The Eucharist is to be celebrated in a sacred place, unless particular necessity requires otherwise, but always in a respectable place, and upon a dedicated or blessed altar, although outside a sacred place a suitable table may be used, using, however, a cloth and a corporal.[53] Diocesan norms should always be consulted.

It is only for the local Ordinary to give express permission, for a just cause, to a priest to celebrate the Eucharist in a place of worship of any church or ecclesial community not in full communion with the Catholic Church, as long as scandal is avoided.[54] .

## III. OFFERINGS GIVEN AT THE CELEBRATION OF THE MASS

### 1. APPLICATION OF THE MASS

The value of the Mass is the intrinsic power which it enjoys to produce its effects or fruits. In itself the Sacrifice of the Mass has an infinite value and efficacy, since Christ, who is of infinite dignity, is both Priest or principal offerer and the sacrificial Victim. Moreover, being substantially the same sacrifice as that of the Cross, it possesses the same infinite value and sufficiency. Thus any one Mass in itself is capable of truly infinite praise and glorification of God, of thanksgiving and propitiation to him, of securing from him the remission of all sins and punishment whatever, as well as beseeching all possible goods and inexhaustible benefits. The Mass, of absolutely infinite value in itself, has a capability which is infinite both intensively and extensively, i.e., as regards the degrees of its effects and as regards the number of its effects and the individuals sharing in them. In other words, it is not possible to assign limits to the efficacy of the Mass either in the number or in the quality of its fruits. It is only in comparison with this essential and proper value and efficacy that the concomitant effectiveness of the impetration, the merit and satisfaction of the Church, of the priest or secondary minister, and of the assisting faithful is to be considered, i.e., inasmuch as the Mass is also man's oblation.

Of the effects which are accomplished by the Mass, the goods and benefits attained or ends and purpose achieved, some of them, viz., the latreutic or the worship of adoration and the Eucharistic or the thanksgiving directly regard God and are infallible and automatic (*ex opere operato*), since due to the holiness and merits of Christ, this Sacrifice is always and unfailingly pleasing and acceptable to God; the others, viz., the impetratory or the entreaties for spiritual and temporal goods, the propitiatory or the reconciliation with God, and the satisfactory or the remission of sins and their temporal punishment, directly regard man and are the fruits and benefits accruing to man from the Mass. These latter especially are called the *fruits of the Mass* and are received in a limited degree and extent. Creatures are not capable of infinite goods. Moreover, the Mass cannot have greater efficacy regarding man than the Sacrifice of the Cross itself, or the sacraments which derive their power from the Cross. Even though the Sacrifice of the Cross is infinite *in itself*, it remains limited *in its application*; otherwise all men would be automatically justified and saved, as likewise one Mass would suffice to save the whole world and eliminate Purgatory. This is the practice of the Church in repeatedly offering Masses to apply both for different persons and also for the same person and for the same benefit. Thus, as with the Sacrifice of the Cross, the Sacrifice of the Mass in the *application* of its effects, in its fruits directed toward man's welfare, depends not only upon the efficacy of the principal cause, Christ, but also upon the dispositions, the willingness or acceptance of those for whom entreaty, propitiation, or satisfaction are offered.[55] These fruits may also increase as a result of the special prayers of the Church, e.g., in a votive or *requiem Mass,* or because of greater external solemnity, e.g., a sung Mass, or due to additional ways of entering into the offering of the Mass, e.g., by offering an alms or stipend for the application of the Mass and also participation in the very Mass offered.

The benefits or fruits received by one from the Mass are threefold:

*General Benefits.* These are by their nature ordained to the good of the whole Church, i.e., of all the faithful, living and departed, who place no obstacle, and even of others that they too might enter into full communion with the Church. As the unbloody repetition of the Sacrifice of the Cross, the Mass is likewise offered up for all; it is essentially an act of public worship. No special application of the celebrant is required beyond a general intention to celebrate according to the mind of the Church. These benefits or fruits are not lessened by the number of individuals sharing in them.

*Special or Ministerial Benefits.* These are applied to some person or purpose by intention of the priest. This is the portion of the fruits or benefits of the Mass which is left to the free application or disposal of the celebrant through the intention he formulates. He alone takes the place of Christ and acts in his person in offering the Sacrifice, and thus he alone applies its fruits. The share of each one in these benefits is probably diminished as they are applied to more persons or purposes.

*Most Special Benefits.* This is the portion of the benefits or fruits which is proper to the priest who offers the Mass and which always accrues to himself; likewise, very special fruits are received by those who in some particular way are united with the priest in offering the Sacrifice, e.g., servers, assistants, attendants at Mass, offerers of the bread and wine, etc. The more intimately one shares in the offering of the Mass, the more fully its benefits are enjoyed. It is improbable that the priest can apply his very special fruits to another, and it is unlawful when the Mass is applied in justice.[56] The number of persons enjoying these benefits does not lessen them.

The application of the Mass, therefore, is the particular determination or disposition which the celebrant makes of the benefits to be enjoyed from the Holy Sacrifice. The beneficiary derives special impetratory, propitiatory, and satisfactory effects, while at the same time adoration and thanksgiving are offered in his name. It is certain teaching that the priest alone has this power by his intention to apply the benefits or fruits of the Mass.[57]

### 2. INTENTION OF THE CELEBRANT

The intention of applying the Mass must be made by the celebrant. It is commonly taught that for validity this intention must be *at least habitual* and *implicit, absolute* or equivalently such. The intention once made must not be retracted, since the application is made in the manner of a donation or transferral of the benefits or fruits, and thus remains valid until revoked. The intention must be made *at least before the consecration*, since the essence of the Sacrifice is in the consecration of both species. An actual and explicit intention is always preferable; in practice a priest should always formulate his intention before beginning Mass (although he may do so some time in advance), so that all the prayers of the Mass might benefit the person or purpose for which the Mass is to be applied. The intention once made must not be retracted before the consecration is completed, if it is to retain its validity and effectiveness.

The intention must be absolute and cannot be conditioned on a future event, since the intention is thereby suspended and the Mass is not offered for that intention. Thus, a Mass cannot be said under the condition that someone will later request a Mass (a stipend cannot be accepted for this), nor for a person under the condition that they will leave the celebrant a legacy, nor for a living person that it will benefit his soul after his death. Equivalently absolute is a condition of the present or past, e.g., if John is not already dead; if I have not already satisfied this stipend, I intend to do so now; if I have, I intend to apply this Mass for such-and-such a person or purpose; if this purpose is not realizable now, I intend this other purpose; etc.

The celebrant's intention must be *sufficiently determined at least implicitly, to a certain person or purpose*. It suffices that he conform his will to the intention explicitly formulated by another, e.g., the intention of the giver, the one noted in the Mass book, the intention of the superior or the sacristan (assuming that it exists), according to the order of stipends received, etc.; the intention is thus objectively and exactly determined and it is not necessary that the person or purpose be known or explicitly determined by the priest. It is permitted to apply a number of Masses to a number of persons or purposes collectively when the priest is unable to remember or does not know the precise order of precedence in the obligations undertaken (whether from the same or from several donors), e.g., ten Masses for the ten obligations undertaken; thus one-tenth share in each Mass is gained by each of the ten and the whole benefit enjoyed upon completion of the ten Masses. It is an invalid intention which is directed to some one on a list without further determination of which one. If the celebrant makes a simple error in application, thinking that the Mass was for a deceased man instead of a woman or a living rather than a deceased person, the application is valid, since normally his intention to fulfill his duty is considered to center on the person for whom applied and not the circumstance.

If the priest has made several different intentions for the same Mass and he has no prevailing or overriding intention for such situations, it is commonly considered that the last intention formulated is the one that is satisfied, being the more actual and the stronger expression of his will. If he has a predominant will in this matter or prevailing intention, then that one is satisfied, e.g., if his prevailing intention is always to say the Mass for which there is the greater obligation, such as a Gregorian series Mass over a manual Mass or a special date obligation over one without attached circumstance. If both intentions made are equal, e.g., two different Gregorian Masses for the same day, it is considered that the second or last made intention is fulfilled. In any doubt, a second Mass can be celebrated on another day for the intention that was not said. If the priest makes no intention or application in the Mass, or one which is invalid, the special or ministerial benefits or fruits probably redound to himself (especially if he has made such a general intention — or to anyone else whom he has intended), or go into the spiritual treasury of the Church. It is recommended that a priest formulate sound prevailing intentions and renew them from time to time.

A second intention in the Mass is the will that the Mass benefit another person or purpose, inasmuch as it does not prejudice the primary intention or application. This is always lawful. It also provides an alternative application of the benefits or fruits in the event that the primary intention for some reason is inapplicable. At the intercessions for the living and of the dead in the Eucharistic Prayer (according to the text selected) as many persons or purposes as desired may be included, as these remembrances are not really applications of the Mass but a form of impetration deriving its special value from association with the Holy Sacrifice. Moreover, the special or ministerial fruits of the Mass may be divided and applied variously, e.g., the impetratory for one, the propitiatory for another, the satisfactory for the departed, etc., even the same fruits being applied to both living and dead. However, this may be done only in those Masses which are not celebrated under any title of obligation in justice, since in the latter case it is considered that the whole benefit of the Mass is willed by the one to whom it is due.

The Mass may be applied to all the *living* without distinction, as long as the Church places no restrictions. Mass may also be applied for all the dead who are in Purgatory. Mass is certainly profitable for the suffering souls in Purgatory, but it is not certain to what extent it profits them or whether a certain soul alone profits. Consequently, it is the practice of the Church to celebrate many Masses for the dead and to pray for all the dead in each Mass.

### 3. OFFERING GIVEN FOR THE MASS

#### a. *Purpose of offerings*

A stipend is a sum of money or some other thing of value which is given to a priest for his maintenance with the understanding that he will offer the Sacrifice of the Mass for a determined purpose. The obligation is one of commutative justice arising from an onerous innominate contract "*do ut facias*" by which the priest is bound in justice to say the Mass or to restore the stipend if he does not or will not celebrate, and the person who has promised a stipend is bound in justice to give it when the Mass has been celebrated. The priest's obligation to satisfy the stipend is certainly serious, regardless of the smallness or largeness of the stipend, since the privation of the special or ministerial fruits is a notable damage.

According to the traditional and approved usage of the Church any priest celebrating or concelebrating is permitted to accept a stipend or offering for applying a Mass according to a definite intention. In this way the faithful contribute to the good of the Church and show their concern for the support of its ministers and works. [58]

The custom of Mass offerings must entirely exclude any semblance of trafficking or commerce. Thus priests are urged to celebrate Mass, even if no offering is forthcoming, for the intention of the faithful, especially of those in need. [59]

### b. *Number of offerings*

Every priest is obliged to offer separate Masses to be applied for the intentions of those for whom an individual offering, no matter how small, has been made and accepted. This obligation binds the priest even if, through no fault of his, the offering received is lost. If a sum of money is offered for the application of Masses but with the number of Masses to be celebrated not indicated, their number is to be reckoned on the basis of the offering established in the place where the donor resides, unless the intention of the donor must lawfully be presumed to have been otherwise. [60]

If the bishops of a province have decreed what offering is to be made for the celebration and application of a Mass it is not lawful for a priest (including members of religious institutes of all kinds) to ask for a larger sum. Where there is no decree the existing custom of the diocese binds (including religious). At the same time, it is permissible to accept, for the application of a Mass, an offering, voluntarily made, which is larger or even smaller than that which is determined by decree or custom. [61]

A priest celebrating many Masses on the same day may apply each Mass for the intention for which an offering was made, but observing the law that, except for Christmas Day, he may retain for himself the offering for only one Mass and giving the others to purposes prescribed by the Ordinary (diocesan or religious). He may take some compensation on the basis of an extrinsic title. A priest, however, concelebrating on the same day a second Mass may not under any title accept an offering for that second Mass. [62]

No one may accept more offerings for Masses to be celebrated by himself than he can satisfy within a year. The time within which Masses are to be celebrated, unless otherwise established, begins from the day the priest who is to celebrate them receives them. [63]

A pastor is bound on each Sunday and holyday which is of obligation in his diocese to apply Mass (without stipend) for the people entrusted to his care.[64]

### c. *Transfer of offerings*

One who transfers Mass stipends to trustworthy priests should do so promptly, transmitting the entire stipend he has received unless it is certainly clear that the excess over and above the established offering in the diocese was given as a personal gift. The donor is responsible for the Masses until such time as he has received notice of the recipient's acceptance of the stipends and their obligation.[65]

All persons, clerical or lay, who in any way are obliged to provide for the celebration of Masses, are to transfer to their Ordinaries (diocesan or religious), in a manner which the latter determine, Mass obligations which have not been satisfied within a year. Certain churches or oratories which possess Mass obligation requests in a larger number than can be celebrated there may send them elsewhere to be celebrated, unless the donors have expressly stipulated otherwise. Those who transfer Masses to others should promptly note in a book both the Masses received and those transferred, indicating their stipends.[66]

Each priest must accurately record the Mass obligations which he has accepted to celebrate and which he has actually satisfied. This insures that in the event of the incapacity or death of the priest the unsatisfied Mass obligations will be more easily perceived and taken care of. The pastor and the rector of a church or other pious place where Mass offerings are usually received are to have a special book in which to list the number, intention, stipend, and fact of celebration of the Masses received. The local Ordinary in churches of the secular clergy and the religious superiors in those of religious institutes and of societies of apostolic life have the duty and right to see that Mass obligations are fulfilled, annually examining the Mass books personally or through others.[67]

### d. *Reduction and condonation of offerings*

*Reduction* is the lessening or reducing of the number of Masses *to be said*, which may be granted for a just cause and is the competency of the

Sacred Congregation for the Clergy. In this case the donors of the stipends suffer no damage, since the deficiency is supplied from the spiritual treasury of the Church. Local Ordinaries have the faculty to reduce, because of diminished revenue and for as long as the situation endures, perpetual legacy Masses to the measure of the stipend legitimately in vogue in the diocese, provided there is no one who is bound and who can be practically compelled to increase the stipend. They likewise have the faculty to reduce obligations or legacies of Masses binding on benefices or other ecclesiastical institutions if the returns from the benefice or institution prove insufficient for the adequate support of the beneficiary and for the discharge of the sacred ministries, if any are attached to the benefice, or for the suitable accomplishment of the purpose proper to the said ecclesiastical institution.[68]

*Condonation* is the forgiveness granted for the *past* omission of Mass obligations, which defect is supplied from the treasury of the Church. The Sacred Congregation for the Clergy may grant a total or partial condonation.[69]

# PENANCE

# PENANCE

## I. SACRAMENTAL NATURE

The Eucharist and Penance are two closely related sacraments. The Eucharist inspires a spirit of penance as a result of the love aroused in its celebration and reception. Penance, for its part, prepares one for a worthier contact and union with the Eucharistic Savior re-presented in his one infinite and eternal Sacrifice.[1] Certainly, if all those who had been regenerated in Baptism had enough gratitude to God to keep forever the justice received in Baptism by his grace and bounty, there would have been no need to institute any other sacrament than Baptism for the remission of sins. But since God is rich in mercy and knows our frail structure, he has also prepared a remedy of life for those who, after Baptism, have given themselves over to the slavery of sin and to the power of the devil. This remedy is the sacrament of Penance, and through it the benefit of Christ's death is applied to those who have fallen after Baptism. However, Penance was not a sacrament before the coming of Christ, and even after his coming it is not a sacrament for anyone who has not been baptized.[2]

At all times all men who were stained by serious sin have needed penance to obtain grace and justice. Properly speaking, penance is a moderated grief for past sins inasmuch as they have offended God, with the intention of removing them. Although a natural virtue of penance is possible, it is of itself of no avail for salvation. Thus a true penitent is one moved by divine grace or a supernatural virtue to detest and to grieve over his sin, inasmuch as it is an injury and an offense to God, and firmly to resolve correction and satisfaction. The benefit or value, as viewed in faith, which is the reparation due to God, is the formal motivation of the penitent. Any person guilty of or even capable of sin is an apt subject of the virtue of penance. Detestation and sorrow are principal in penance; presupposed is the operation of faith, hope, fear, and initial love.[3]

Christian faith teaches that true penance can take away all sins. This means perfect penance or contrition made perfect through charity. For one in a state of serious sin it is necessary for salvation by a necessity both of means and of precept. The virtue of penance operates to justify the sinner solely through the personal penitential act.[4]

The precept of penance does not oblige immediately after the commission of serious sin, although a sinner is obliged to desist immediately from sin and actual affection for it. Being an affirmative precept, it does not always and at every moment oblige but only when a special reason urges. Otherwise one would sin every time he averted to the obligation of penance; an ill person is not taking medicine every time he thinks of it, but only when necessary.

Precisely when the precept of penance obliges is not so clear. Of itself it certainly urges at the moment of death and in probable danger of death (in warfare, a dangerous journey, difficult childbirth, etc.) or of perpetual loss of reason. Outside of such danger, how often in life this obligation of itself binds, or how long one can refrain from eliciting an act of penance before incurring another sin by delaying this act, is not certain. However, a notable delay in repenting is reprobated in Scripture, as it indicates a neglect and contempt of God and a failure in the grave obligation to tend to one's ultimate end.[5]

The precept of penance obliges accidentally or because of the fulfillment of some other duty or obligation: (a) when a sacrament is celebrated or received; (b) when another precept or virtue, e.g., charity, requires a previous act of penance; (c) when an act of penance is necessary to overcome a serious temptation inasmuch as it restores friendship with God; (d) when one wishes to evidence penance externally, which otherwise would be simulation. The violation of the precept of penance obliging only accidentally is not a special sin. Of itself there is no special precept of penance for slight sins, as they may even be left for expiation in the next life; an obligation may arise accidentally, e.g., when they are the only matter in the reception of the sacrament of Penance.

A deliberate will not to do penance or not to repent is a special sin of impenitence; the simple omission of penance is not a special sin unless the obligation binds of itself. Failure in the obligation that binds only accidentally would not be a special sin of impenitence but a transgression of the precept or virtue against which one offends by sinning. Nevertheless, at all times sinners must be warned to sorrow for their sins as soon as they are aware of them, since a protracted enmity with God is an injury to his majesty and most dangerous and destructive for the penitent who must rely on the mercy of God. Confessors inquire about such repentance for the purpose of ascertaining the fulfillment of the positive precept of annual confession and of judging the penitent's state of conscience in order that it might be formed rightly.

Penance or repentance embraces all personal sins. All actual serious sins fully offend God and render the sinner perfectly turned away from God, and thus they are the proper and principal material of penance. Proper but secondary material is all slight sins, since as sins they also in some way offend God. Sins already forgiven are also matter for repentance, since their remission is not infallibly certain to us, their retraction not always perfect, their satisfaction not always full. Mere imperfections are generally not material for penance but rather for the zeal of charity and the motivation of perfection.

The exteriorly manifested acts of the virtue of penance have been raised by Christ to the sacramental level; they have become the material of an effective sign of grace. Faith teaches that, given its institution by Christ, the sacrament of Penance must by a necessity of means be received actually (*in re*) or, when that cannot be done, at least in desire (*in voto*), in order to remove serious sins committed after Baptism. It is certain that after the institution of the sacrament perfect contrition alone is no longer able to destroy sin except through an order or relationship to the sacrament itself which, if not always received actually, is received at least in desire with perfect contrition. An explicit desire is not required, an implicit desire suffices. This is necessarily included in perfect contrition itself, inasmuch as the perfectly contrite will also be prepared to fulfill everything necessary for salvation, even if here and now through inadvertence, forgetfulness, or invincible ignorance the penitent does not think of what these necessary things are. (However sin is remitted, the obligation of receiving absolution remains). The sacrament obliges also by a necessity of precept, operating by the very fact of its celebration with at least imperfect contrition or attrition. [6]

The sacrament of Penance is repeatable. The divine precept of itself obliges seriously at the moment of death and in very probable danger of death or of permanent loss of reason. It cannot be determined with certainty if and when the obligation binds of itself also sometimes in life, or even after every lapse into mortal sin. The sacrament of Penance obliges accidentally, by reason of a natural or positive precept: (a) when the Eucharist is to be received and serious sins have not been confessed or indirectly remitted; (b) when a sacrament must be received or *ex officio* celebrated or administered and an act of perfect contrition cannot be elicited; (c) when a grave temptation or evil habit cannot be overcome without confession. The omission of the sacrament in these cases is not a sin against the divine precept of confessing but a violation of the other obligation which requires confession. The precept does not require immediate confession of sins, lest they be forgotten, but only a confession of those sins of which the penitent is conscious after a diligent examination of conscience. The positive precept of ecclesiastical law (since the IV Lateran Council in 1215) obliges those conscious of serious sin to an annual confession.[7]

The sacrament of Penance has the power to remit through the infusion of sanctifying grace all sins however grievous and however often repeated, and to restore the state of divine friendship. It brings to the well disposed peace and serenity of conscience joined to great consolation of soul. As with the virtue, it takes away the eternal debt or punishment, diminishes the temporal punishment and sometimes (but not always) takes it away fully, revives previous meritorious works, and lessens evil dispositions. It confers a sacramental grace or special supernatural help moving the penitent to an ever-growing hatred of sin and more surely preserving him from sin in the future. Many other benefits are gained from this sacrament by the well-disposed penitent.[8]

The sacrament of Penance is distinctive especially in the fact that it is administered in the manner of a judgment[9] or by a judicial act, whereas the other sacraments consist in a certain consecration: the sinner is the culprit, witness, and accuser; the priest is the judge rendering sentence. Unlike other judgments which tend toward the punishment of the guilty, sacramental judgment is directed to the absolution of the sinner and his reconciliation with God. In this sacrament instituted by Christ all sins committed after Baptism are remitted by the conjunction of the absolution of the priest and the precise placing of certain acts by the penitent. By the same sacrament penitents are reconciled with the Church which they have wounded by sinning.[10]

## II. THE CELEBRATION OF THE SACRAMENT

### 1. INDIVIDUAL ABSOLUTION

The sole means by which any one of the faithful who is conscious of grave sin is reconciled with God and with the Church is by an individual and integral confession with the reception of absolution. Only physical or moral impossibility excuses from this obligation, in which case reconciliation may be achieved by other means also, e.g., an act of perfect contrition.[11]

The *formula* of this sacrament is the words by which the priest as judge passes sentence or absolution on sins; it signifies the use and effect of the power of the keys in the remission of sins. The formula should express the exercise of the judicial power given to the ministers of the Church, to be exercised in the name of God, and the actual effect.[12] For a formula to be *valid* it must contain the essential words: *I absolve you from your sins in the name of the Father, and of the Son, and of the Holy Spirit.*[13] The voluntary omission of an essential word of the formula is a serious sin. Whether voluntary or not, the omission invalidates the sacrament and thus deprives the penitent of sacramental grace. The *lawful* formula is the integral rubrical formula which the Church, in the *Rite of Penance*, prescribes to be employed in absolution. Priests have no right to make up their own formulas.

When the priest wishes to absolve a penitent, he imposes a salutary penance and, after the penance has been accepted, with his hands (or at least his right hand) extended over the head of the penitent, says:

> *May God, the Father of mercies, who through the death and resurrection of his Son reconciled the world to himself and poured forth the Holy Spirit for the remission of sins, grant you through the ministry of the Church pardon and peace. And I absolve you from your sins in the name of the Father, and of the Son,* † *and of the Holy Spirit.*

The penitent responds: *Amen.*

When grave necessity urges in danger of death, the priest may say briefly:

*I absolve you from your sins, in the name of the Father, and of the Son,  †  and of the Holy Spirit.*

The penitent responds: *Amen.*[14]

It is not obligatory to give the introductory blessings before the penitent begins his confession, but this custom should be preserved. The penitent opens his confession by blessing himself in the usual manner. The priest may also give his blessing at the same time. The confessor imparts his absolution while sitting, after the manner of a judge pronouncing sentence; any just cause will excuse from this. The raising of the hand in absolution and the making of the sign of the cross are not required under pain of sin, but the custom and the rubrics are to be observed in this matter.

If sins are confessed to which a censure is attached it suffices for the confessor, observing the norms of law, to intend to absolve a properly disposed penitent also from the censure when pronouncing the formula of absolution. He may, however, before absolving the sins, absolve from a censure with the formula which is to be used when a censure is absolved outside the sacrament of Penance:

*By the power granted me, I absolve you from the bond of excommunication (or suspension or interdict). In the name of the Father, and of the Son, † and of the Holy Spirit.*[15]

If a penitent has incurred an irregularity the priest, according to the norm of law, may dispense from the same, either in confession and after absolution, or outside the sacrament, and with the formula:

*By the power granted me, I dispense you from the irregularity you have incurred. In the name of the Father, and of the Son, † and of the Holy Spirit.*[16]

### 2. GENERAL ABSOLUTION

General absolution, that is, absolution given to a number of penitents, without previous individual confession, may not be imparted by the priest, unless the conditions, which are to be simultaneously verified in the individual cases that follow, are present:[17]

1° when danger of death is imminent and there is not time for the priest or priests to hear the confessions of the individual penitents;[18]

2° when a grave necessity exists; that is, in view of the number of penitents, there is not at hand a supply of confessors who can properly hear the confessions of the individual penitents so that, without any fault of their own, the penitents are forced to be without the grace of the sacrament or of holy Communion for a long time. However, this necessity is not considered to be sufficient when confessors cannot be available simply because of a large gathering of people, such as can occur on some great feastday or pilgrimage.[19]

In the above case (2°) the diocesan bishop judges whether the conditions are present. He can determine cases of such necessity, keeping in mind the criteria agreed upon in the Conference of Bishops.[20]

The conditions of case (2°) implicitly exclude the gathering of a large crowd for the purpose of giving general absolution. Likewise, they are not present if the faithful could find other opportunities for confession and Communion, which are normally offered on a regular basis in their parishes (unless in a remote mission station only infrequently visited by a priest), if not during, then before or after the large gatherings. The granting of general absolution without observing the norms laid down is to be considered a serious abuse, injurious to the welfare of souls and dignity of the sacrament.[21]

Bishops and priests are to arrange pastoral duties so that a sufficient number of priests will be available for confessions for a large gathering. If a serious need arises of giving general absolution apart from cases laid down by the local Ordinary, the priest is obliged, whenever it is possible, to have recourse to the local Ordinary in order to grant the absolution lawfully; if this is not possible, he is to inform the Ordinary as soon as possible of the fact.[22]

For general absolution a penitent must repent of sins committed, have the purpose of keeping from sin, and intend to remove or repair any scandal or loss caused where that may be present. Scandal must be removed in accordance with the personal judgment of one's individual confessor before the penitent receives Communion. This will certainly find some application in the case of divorced Catholics who have remarried outside the Church.

The penitent's sincere intention to bring serious sins to individual confession within a reasonable time is a condition necessary for the validity of general absolution. Thus, the penitent with serious sins forgiven by general absolution should make an auricular confession before receiving absolution in the collective form another time, unless a just cause prevents. Such a penitent may not refuse deliberately or by neglect to satisfy the obligation of individual confession, when it is possible to have a confessor, while waiting for an occasion for collective absolution. [23]

### 3. PLACE AND TIME OF CELEBRATION

The proper place to hear sacramental confession is a church or oratory and, except for a just cause, in confessionals with a fixed grille between penitent and confessor, located in an open place, which the faithful who so wish may freely use.

The reconciliation of penitents may be celebrated at any time on any day, but it is desirable that the faithful know the day and time at which the priest is available for this ministry. They should be encouraged to approach the sacrament at times when Mass is not being celebrated and especially during the scheduled periods. [24]

## III. THE MINISTER OF THE SACRAMENT OF PENANCE

### 1. ORDINARY JURISDICTION

The ministry of the sacrament of penance requires both the power of the priesthood and the power of jurisdiction or governance. Catholic faith teaches that Christ gave to the priest alone the power of binding and loosing, of forgiving and retaining sins. [25] The power of Orders is the efficacious instrument of the conferral of grace. It is a power equally received by all in priestly ordination rendering the recipient capable of sanctifying the people. It bestows the proximate aptitude and disposition to receive jurisdiction over subjects for the purpose of sanctifying them and, in the sacrament of Penance, of absolving their sins. The sacrament of Orders thus causes the penitential judgment to be efficacious.

Jurisdiction is the public power to rule subjects. Ecclesiastical jurisdiction is the public power to rule, to judge, to coerce the baptized with a view to their sanctification and supernatural happiness, which is the end purpose of the Church. This jurisdiction is exercised over all the baptized, as they alone are the subjects of the Church. This includes penitential jurisdiction which is the judicial power to remit or to retain sins in the sacred tribunal of Penance, the faculty of exercising the power of Orders on certain definite persons as legitimately designated subjects, thus making the penitential judgment of the priest to be valid.

It is certain that by divine institution, besides Orders, the priest must possess jurisdiction.[26] A judgment can be made only on one who is subject to the authority of the judge; absolution is a judiciary sentence, and thus the subjects or penitents must be assigned to the priest, even for the valid remission of venial sins. Jurisdiction is received by the commission (*missio*) of a competent superior, which commission to certain subjects may be increased or lessened, suspended or limited as to persons, places, times, cases, sins. Since the other sacraments are not conferred in the manner of a judgment and do not have judicial acts, jurisdiction of itself is not required for them, except for their lawful administration (*licentia*). Thus *a priest may never validly impart absolution unless he possesses penitential jurisdiction in the Church from some valid title*.

*Jurisdiction in the external forum* primarily and directly guides the external social relations of the faithful toward the society of the Church with the accompanying juridical and social effects. It thus determines whether the faithful in view of their conduct are worthy of praise or of blame *before the visible Church*. It is often exercised publicly by the passing of laws, inflicting of penalties, etc.

*Jurisdiction in the internal forum* here guides and directs the internal moral relations of the faithful with God, providing for the private welfare of the faithful in their moral conduct with God. It thus determines whether the faithful in view of their conduct are worthy of praise or blame *before God*. Exercised secretly in this forum of conscience the jurisdiction is private with effects before God alone and carries no judicial effects in the Church unless specially provided for. When this jurisdiction must be exercised in the confessional, i.e., in the sacrament of Penance or in connection with it, it is called *sacramental forum* and is bound by the sacramental seal. When it is not subject to this limitation, it is called *extra-sacramental forum*. Some dispensations may be given in this latter manner. The jurisdiction may be exercised over one who is absent and by letter or messenger (with the exception of sacramental absolution).

Jurisdiction may be *universal* or *particular* depending on whether or not it embraces all persons, places, matters, etc., or is limited in any of these. Exercised with a formal judicial process it is called *judicial*; when exercised without the process it is called *voluntary*, as in the case of dispensations or favors.

Ordinary jurisdiction is that which in virtue of law the incumbent of an ecclesiastical office automatically acquires from that office. It is *proper* when the office is principal and the jurisdiction is exercised in one's name, e.g., a residential bishop; it is *vicarious* when the office is accessory and the jurisdiction, although in a sense proper, is exercised in the name of another, e.g., a vicar general. Ordinary power can be delegated entirely or in part to another, unless the law expressly rules otherwise. Ordinary jurisdiction comes to an end with the loss of office.[27]

Ordinary penitential jurisdiction is enjoyed by bishops who may licitly use it anywhere, unless the diocesan bishop denies it in a particular place. In virtue of their office any local Ordinary, as well as a pastor of a parish, and those who take the place of a pastor, possess the faculty to hear confessions within their jurisdiction.[28]

By virtue of their office superiors of religious institutes or of societies of apostolic life, if clerical and of pontifical right, who by their own law possess executive power of governance, enjoy the faculty to hear the confessions of their subjects and others staying in the religious house day and night, but of their own subjects only if spontaneously requested by them. They may exercise this faculty licitly in any house of the institute or society, unless a major superior denies it concerning his own subjects in a particular case.[29]

## 2. DELEGATED JURISDICTION

Jurisdiction is delegated when it is not attached to an office but is committed to a person. This delegation may be *by law* inasmuch as the law itself grants jurisdiction in certain circumstances, e.g., in danger of death, or *from a competent superior* inasmuch as the special act of the superior expressly grants the jurisdiction whether the person be chosen for his personal qualifications or by reason of the office he holds, e.g., in the case of faculties granted by the Holy See to local Ordinaries.

Only those who are capable of ecclesiastical jurisdiction for the sacrament of Penance may be delegated, and it may be exercised only over those who are subjects of the one delegating.

In the matter of penitential jurisdiction, delegated jurisdiction is of itself personal so that the faculty of *subdelegating* is excluded unless expressly granted. Nor can there be further subdelegation unless this also was expressly granted.[30]

Only the local Ordinary is competent to delegate any and every priest the faculty to hear confessions. Priest members of religious institutes should not use the delegated faculty without at least the presumed permission of their superior. On his part, the superior of a religious institute or of a society of apostolic life, if clerical and of pontifical rite, is competent to delegate any and every priest the faculty to hear confessions of his subjects and of others staying day and night in the house. The faculty to hear confessions may be granted by the local Ordinary or the religious superiors for an indefinite or a definite period of time.[31]

Confessional faculties should not be granted except to priests who have been qualified by an examination or whose suitableness is evident from some other means. The faculty to hear confessions habitually is not to be delegated by the local Ordinary to a priest, even one having a domicile or quasi-domicile in his jurisdiction, without consulting first, as far as possible, that priest's own Ordinary. The faculty to hear confessions habitually is to be granted in writing.[32]

Those who have received the delegated faculty to hear confessions habitually from the Ordinary of the place of incardination or of the place in which they have a domicile can use the same faculty everywhere, unless in a particular case the local Ordinary has refused. If the faculty to hear confessions is revoked by the Ordinary of incardination or domicile, the priest loses this faculty everywhere. If the faculty is revoked by some other Ordinary, the priest loses it only in the territory of the Ordinary who revokes it. An Ordinary who revokes a delegated faculty is to inform the priest's own Ordinary by reason of incardination, or the competent superior in the case of a religious priest.[33]

Those who have received the delegated faculty to hear confessions habitually from a competent religious superior can by the law itself exercise the faculty anywhere in respect to members and others who stay day and night in a house of the religious institute or society, which faculty may be lawfully used, unless some major superior denies it, in a particular case, with regard to his own subjects. If the faculty is revoked by his major superior the priest loses the faculty to hear the confessions of the members of the institute. If the faculty is revoked by another competent superior the priest loses it only with respect to the subjects of that superior's jurisdiction.[34]

The faculty to hear confessions may cease through loss of office, excardination or loss of domicile, as well as by revocation. However, any priest, even one lacking a confessional faculty, validly and licitly absolves from any kind of censures and sins any and every penitent who is in danger of death, even if an approved priest is present. Moreover, in a case of common error, whether of fact or of law, and in positive and probable doubt, whether of law or of fact, of confessional faculty, the Church supplies the faculty for both the external and the internal forum.[35]

### 3. ABUSES OF CONFESSION

The absolution of an accomplice or partner in a sin against the sixth of the Ten Commandments is invalid, except in danger of death.[36] Complicity is present when there is the perpetration with another, male or female, of the same sin of impurity. The crime embraces any sin against the sixth commandment which is on the part of both parties certain, external, and serious by reason of both the internal and the external act.

A priest who in confession, or on the occasion or under the pretext of confession, solicits a penitent to commit a sin against the sixth commandment is to be punished according to law. The crime must be serious both objectively and subjectively. It must be certain that there has been an act of solicitation to impurity which was serious and related to confession. On the other hand, a person who confesses to having falsely denounced to ecclesiastical authority a confessor who is innocent of the crime of solicitation is not to be absolved unless that person has first formally withdrawn the false denunciation and is prepared to repair whatever damage may have been done.[37]

### 4. SEAL OF CONFESSION

The sacramental seal is inviolable and so it is a crime for a confessor in any way to betray a penitent by word or in any fashion at all or for any reason whatsoever. An interpreter, when one is used, is also obliged to observe the sacramental secret, as are all others to whom knowledge of sins from confession shall come in any way.[38] A direct violation of the seal incurs a *latae sententiae* excommunication reserved to the Apostolic See; an indirect violation is to be punished according to the gravity of the offense.[39]

The seal of sacramental confession is the most strict obligation of observing secrecy about those things which have been declared by the penitent in sacramental confession or for the purpose of sacramental absolution, and whose revelation would in some way identify the sin and the sinner. Every and only a sacramental confession, made for the purpose of confessing to a minister of the Church as such and of obtaining absolution, is the root of the obligation of the seal. This is true whether the confession was valid or invalid, merely begun or completed or sacrilegious, whether absolution was deferred or denied. The sacramental seal is inviolable; therefore the confessor shall take scrupulous care lest by word or sign or in any way or for any reason he betray the sinner.[40]

There is no more serious obligation of secrecy than that of the sacramental seal. It allows of no exception whatsoever, no dispensation, no use of extra-legal equity.[41] It does not permit the use of probalilism, i.e., that a confessor adopt a line of action on the ground that in doing so he will probably not violate the seal or give offense to penitents. This is true both when there is a probability of law, i.e., a division among theologians on a given point whether it is or not a matter of the seal or an offense to penitents, or a probability of fact, i.e., a doubt that this or that fact was confessional matter or known only from confession. The confessor cannot use a probable opinion to the detriment of a certain right of another; the penitent has a right to be free from all injury, burden, and grievance on the occasion of his confession of his sins. Thus the confessor is bound to the seal even if he doubts whether something said by the penitent is directed to confession or absolution, because he must judge on the safer side, i.e., on the side of the obligation of the seal. Even under oath the confessor must state that he knows nothing or has heard nothing — which means that he has no *communicable* knowledge.

The sacramental seal is implicit in the institution of Penance by Christ and in the purpose for which he established the sacrament. The obligation arises from the natural law of secrecy and of a quasi contract, from the divine law of reverence for the sacrament which should be made as easy of approach as possible and free from injury to the recipient, and from ecclesiastical law. The obligation binds even after the death of the penitent. Every direct violation of the seal, no matter how slight, is a grievous sin and admits of no lightness of matter. It is a most serious injury to the sacrament, and the faithful are deterred from approaching it when they feel they do not have full security. An indirect violation is a serious sin, but it allows of lightness of matter.

The penitent is not bound by the seal but rather by the obligation of a natural and committed secret concerning the things spoken of or done by the confessor in confession, if their revelation would harm the confessor or bring injury or contempt to the sacrament. It is sometimes necessary for a penitent to speak about a confessor, e.g., when he wishes to have his penance commuted by another confessor, or when he is justified in complaining about a confessor. Confessors on their part should employ great discretion in the confessional, since they cannot defend themselves from the tongues of their penitents.

Outside the confessional even the priest may not lawfully speak to the penitent about a confessional matter without receiving first the free, express, and certain consent of the penitent. The priest should be very slow to request this permission and then only rarely and for serious reasons. In the confession itself the confessor can speak even of the sins confessed in previous confessions, since the past confessions constitute one and the same judgment and tribunal with the present confession. When the penitent of his own initiative speaks of his sins outside of confession, implicitly he is giving the confessor permission to speak of these sins alone and not of previously declared sins. The penitent then can give a more or less ample permission. In any case the confessor is always bound by a natural and committed secret and must avoid scandal and the suspicion of violating the seal. The confessor may not speak of any sins as long as he knows of them only from confessions, even though he is convinced that they are commonly known. He may speak of sins of which he is aware from sources outside of confession but cautiously; he must beware of representing something as certain which previous to the confession he knew only as probable, and refrain from later correcting inaccuracies in view of his confessional knowledge.

Subject to the seal *directly* and *of themselves* are all and only those things which have been revealed for the purpose of sacramental confession and not exclusively for another purpose, e.g., for derision, deception, solicitation to sin of the confessor. In this way are contained under the seal:

1. all sins which are confessed, however slight, and even material sins; sins even though only thought of or proposed but not accomplished or fulfilled; internal or external sins, whether of the past or those to take place in the future; all serious sins whether generically or specifically confessed; all slight sins specifically or numerically confessed; secret sins and also public sins insofar as they have been confessed;

2. the object of sins inasmuch as these are the sins of another, e.g., to confess sinful speech about the sinful pregnancy of a certain girl, to confess hatred of one's father because of his adultery, etc.; the circumstances of sins as such which are thought to be or are necessary or useful in clarifying the case, e.g., certain specific books that have been read, the amount of a theft, the accomplices in a sin whether lawfully or imprudently confessed.

*Of themselves* and *indirectly* under the seal are all those things which of themselves can lead to a knowledge of the sin as declared by the sinner or to an identification of the penitent. Included in this way are: the deferral or denial of absolution; a sacrilegious confession, since the sacramental confession is present in the penitential judgment and not merely in the sacramental absolution; the lack of dispositions of the penitent; the penance imposed, unless it was very light; the confessional advice requested or given.

The confessor is altogether forbidden to use knowledge acquired from confession to the detriment of the penitent, even when all danger of revelation is excluded. Moreover, a person who is in authority can in no way use for the purpose of external governance knowledge about sins which he has received at any time in confession.[42] The situation here is the free use of knowledge which the confessor has gained through confession, as long as there is no danger of direct or indirect revelation. The use of sacramental knowledge is always unlawful when it entails a direct or indirect revelation of confession. Apart from all danger of revelation the confessor is not free to use such knowledge where there may be detriment to the penitent or to penitents in general (even outside the advertence of the latter), or where the faithful generally would be aggrieved or offended, confidence in the sacrament lessened and its frequentation rendered more difficult, or scandal given.

The use of sacramental knowledge can be lawful if there can result no danger of revelation of confessional matter or detriment to the penitent or to others. Thus by knowledge gained from confession the confessor can better his own spiritual life, avoid the occasions of sin, improve his manner of questioning and of instructing penitents and his general celebration or administration of the sacrament, study his problems and consult lawfully with others, pray for his penitent, act more benignly toward them, etc. Preachers may speak of those things which would not have occurred to them if they had not heard confessions, but they must be careful not to speak in a way to render the sacrament disagreeable or to indicate that confessional knowledge is being used, or to mention particular sins in a small community of people.

The confessor must solve his confessional problems with all his diligence by applying good judgment to the knowledge he has acquired, by personal study, prayer, and reflection. Consultation with others on confessional matters must be an extraordinary procedure; it would be looked upon as generally unwise to request the penitent's permission for this. However, even an experienced and sufficiently learned confessor at times needs to seek the advice of another. He should first try to contact a competent consultant who does not know the penitent at all. If there should be any danger of violation of the seal, permission should be first requested of the penitent to seek such counsel. If the request is not granted or if it is judged unwise to make it, the confessor should propose his problem to the consultant as a hypothetical case, revealing only what is necessary in the case and changing the case in other ways so that the penitent cannot be identified and yet the substance of the problem is not changed. In an unusual or complicated case the confessor may request the penitent's consent to handle it outside of confession, e.g., in certain marriage cases or problems of justice.

## 5. QUALITIES OF A CONFESSOR

The priest in the exercise of his office as confessor is to remember that he fulfills the role of judge and equally of healer, and that he is established by God as the minister of divine justice as well as of mercy in order that he may contribute to the honor of God and the salvation of souls. Moreover, in administering the sacrament of Penance the confessor, as minister of the Church, is to adhere faithfully to the doctrine of the magisterium and the norms laid down by competent authority.[43]

The penitential judgment of the confessor, then, is not condemnatory and vindictive but liberative and curative. It belongs to the nature of this sacrament to pass judicial sentence, but its end or purpose is to heal the wounds of sin. As a minister the priest is obliged by religion to procure most carefully the honor of God and the good of the sacrament through its valid and lawful administration. He is bound in justice and charity to secure the good of the penitent by fostering dispositions for a most fruitful reception of the sacrament now and as a safeguard for the future. He is similarly bound to provide for the common good in the exercise of his office by avoiding whatever is injurious to the public good or to individuals through scandal or other evil. Thus, beside sacred orders and the jurisdiction necessary for the sacrament of Penance, the integrity of the confessor's office demands for the spiritual welfare of the souls committed to him certain qualities or characteristics, which can be described as *goodness, knowledge* and *prudence*.

The probity of life expected of the minister of Christ in the confessional is more than the mere state of grace or freedom from serious sin so that a sacrilegious administration might be avoided. In the celebration of Penance he should be free from all unchristian harshness and severity, impatience and hastiness, human respect and sentimental familiarity, vanity and self-adulation. The virtues directive of his office are several and interrelated, but a supernatural zeal and love for souls, sinners especially, must be his most obvious and principal imitation of the Master. The confessor's apostolate of souls is to all sinners without distinction or favoritism, and without reluctance to accept the burdens of the ministry, uniting kindness and gentlemanliness with necessary firmness.

Patience is a virtue which is never out of demand in the life of a confessor — patience with all types of sinners, and constancy and long-suffering when the hearing of confessions becomes monotonous, protracted, or a trial. Humility gives the confessor a practical sympathy with penitents, because he is aware of his own weaknesses and sins and that, but for divine grace, he might be worse than his penitents. Purity is an indispensable safeguard at all times lest the confessional in any way should become a danger to chastity through thought, desire, or action. Meditation on the teachings of the Church and of holy and learned writers concerning the apostolate of penance will, together with constant prayer for assistance and guidance, help to keep alive and to foster the devotion of the priest to this important part of his ministry.

The confessor is gravely bound, outside a case of necessity, to have the knowledge which is required for the proper and competent exercise of his office. He must possess at least the average or ordinary knowledge which is necessary in the circumstances and with regard to the penitents of this day and age; such knowledge must vary also with different confessors as their status and particular ministry varies. Every confessor, however, must know what will secure the substance, validity and lawfulness, integrity and effect of the sacrament both on his and the penitent's part, the common and particular obligations of the states of life of the penitents, the species and changing circumstances of sins, the manner of discernment of serious from slight sins both objectively and subjectively and their numerical distinction, the validity and lawfulness of acts, the principles of justice with the obligations of reparation and restitution, reserved sins and censures, matrimonial impediments dispensable in the confessional, sinful occasions, remedies for sins, fitting and salutary penances and obligations to impose them, the main teachings of ascetical theology and of spiritual direction.

A confessor need not have perfect knowledge whereby he can always and immediately and personally solve all cases. It suffices that he can solve the cases that commonly occur and doubt prudently about the more difficult cases, so as, if necessary, to consult books and those more learned or experienced (in the meantime a penitent may be absolved who is willing to return and to abide by the decisions of the confessor). Otherwise he courts the proximate danger of a bad administration of the sacrament and injury to the penitent. If a case must be solved without delay, e.g., with the dying, the confessor will invoke the Holy Spirit and make the best judgment he can, later checking on his solution. It is worthwhile in practice, especially for neo-confessors, to review their solutions, repair their defects, and thus be fore-armed for the future. A priest sins seriously if he certainly knows he lacks competent knowledge and yet attempts to hear confessions, even out of charity or obedience. The approbation of the bishop or the regular superior does not supply for but rather presupposes requisite knowledge. If a priest *prudently* fears that his lack of knowledge risks nullity of the sacrament, he can absolve only conditionally. However, those who have diligently pursued their seminary studies and have successfully passed the prescribed examinations are presumed to be competent as described (and they ought to exercise their ministry in this conviction), until it becomes otherwise evident and certain.

Alumni of seminaries, both secular and religious, are seriously held to maintain a continual study of the sacred sciences, so that they might exercise the office of confessor with fitness, as is required of other professional men.[44] The natural qualities of good sense and good judgment, most advantageous and necessary in a good confessor, do not substitute for the benefit of theological study and the fruit of the wisdom of others; nor do they provide knowledge of the development of positive legislation in the Church and its interpretation. Experience is no substitute for requisite knowledge, but it is an aid in giving greater insights into human nature, the interior solutions, and a facility in the application of principles and laws. Longstanding experience without study and knowledge has been termed nothing but intimacy with error. A regular review of moral and ascetical theology, canon law, an acquaintance with available ecclesiastical literature, in other words, a continuing education in some forms, is strongly recommended for the retention and development of knowledge already acquired. The confessor, moreover, should expound the common teaching of approved authors in accord with the magisterium of the Church and not his own peculiar viewpoint.[45]

Prudence, the practical wisdom which directs the best means to the end, is exceedingly necessary for the confessor, who must apply principles and precepts, remedies and obligations to the conditions of individual persons and circumstances, avoiding excess and defect, laxity and rigorism. Prudence will direct his ministry in safeguarding the sacrament, leading penitents to the path of Christian living and perfection, and in procuring the common good. Purity of intention, prayer (especially before confessions), docility and earnest industry are means for growing in this prudence.

The confessor must try to adapt his remarks to the concise problem, difficulty, or need of the penitent, i.e., to what the penitent needs and can use, and to refrain from giving a whole course of instructions or long sermons. He ought not to be too hasty in solving difficult cases but give attentive and mature consideration to all the factors, remembering that after all he hears but one side of a situation. He should not guess at an answer nor shirk an evident responsibility to give a definite answer. He should not, unless necessary, send penitents to another confessor or to the pastor, but try to treat the case as satisfactorily as possible. In perplexing cases he should follow a safe and sane norm, doing what, under God, he believes ought to be done in the case, seeking above all to apply solidly probable teaching that is apt to accomplish what the spiritual good of the penitent here and now demands. He should leave the penitent free to go to another confessor; the penitent also must be allowed to abide by a solidly probable opinion that is legitimately applicable in his case. The confessor should never show penitents that he knows them or recognizes them, ask for a name or address, or accept money for Masses in the confessional.

Confidence in other confessors (as well as in parents, teachers, physicians, etc.) must be preserved and not in any way lessened, if this can be avoided. Oftentimes a penitent has misunderstood or misinterpreted the advice or requirements of a previous confessor, or has not explained the case to him in the same way as to the present confessor. Where it is clear or it is suspected that a previous confessor has given wrong advice or made an error, it suffices for the priest to state his lack of understanding of what happened in the previous confession, and that, as the case stands presently before his judgment, his answer is such and such. It is always preferable (and even necessary with an habitual sinner) to find out if the penitent previously received advice and followed it. The penitent should be encouraged to continue or to renew his efforts, if the previous advice still appears advantageous to the penitent; otherwise new counsel is in order.

### 6. OBLIGATIONS OF A CONFESSOR

All to whom the care of souls is committed by reason of office are obliged to provide that the confessions of the faithful entrusted to their care be heard, when they reasonably request confession; they are to be provided with the opportunity of making an individual confession on days and hours arranged for their convenience. Moreover, in a situation of urgent necessity, any and every confessor is bound to hear the confessions of the faithful, and in danger of death any and every priest is so obliged.[46]

Pastors and others to whom in virtue of their office the care of souls has been entrusted are bound by a serious obligation *in justice* to hear, either in person or through another, the confessions of those entrusted to them whenever the latter reasonably request it. This obligation in justice derives from the tacit contract with those from whom they receive sustenance and honor under the condition that they celebrate or administer the sacraments, and with their ecclesiastical superior who appoints them with the understanding that they faithfully discharge their office, of which the celebration of Penance is a part. The gravity of the obligation depends upon the degree of necessity of the penitent.

All confessors are bound *in charity* to hear the confessions of the faithful when reasonably requested. The obligation is in proportion to the spiritual necessity of the penitent.

If the confessor has no doubt about the disposition of a penitent who asks for absolution, it is not to be denied or delayed.[47]

The sacrament of Penance was instituted after the manner of a judgment and thus the absolution or retention of sins is a judicial sentence. By the nature, then, of this sacrament the minister is a *spiritual judge*.

As a judge the minister must know the penitent's case and thus he has an obligation to question about those things concerning the penitent which are necessary to form a prudent judgment, primarily to insure the integrity of the confession and less frequently to discover the penitent's dispositions. It suffices that the confessor make a *prudent* and *probable* judgment regarding the penitent's confession and disposition; complete certitude is not always possible nor required in dealing with internal dispositions. The confessor must employ ordinary diligence; if because of noise, distraction, singing, etc., he does not hear certain sins, he must question the penitent when there is probably serious matter present. He is not bound to recall distinctly at the moment of absolution every sin confessed, but at least generally the state of the penitent. The penitent should not be permitted to gloss over his serious sins, especially in matters of justice and marital relations. The confessor will positively doubt about the penitent's dispositions for absolution if, e.g., he is reluctant or very remiss in confessing all his sins or in admitting guilt, or if he as a recidivist does not evidence genuine sorrow or preparedness to accept remedies and penances, etc.

*To absolve* a certainly well-disposed penitent guilty of serious sin obliges the confessor seriously in justice. For this reason the general rule is to impart absolution. Trustworthy signs of sufficient dispositions are: a spontaneous, sincere, and humble confession and contrition; a confession made despite great difficulties; a positive reversal of former sinful practices;

a sincere resolution to follow the confessor's counsel; great sorrow clearly shown in a habitual sinner; etc.

The confessor must impart absolution even though the penitent holds a different legitimate opinion, as long as he is otherwise properly disposed. The confessor is the judge of the penitent's dispositions and not his moral opinions as long as they are reputable and safe.

*To deny* absolution to those who are judged incapable or unworthy is likewise a serious duty. Otherwise the absolution would be invalid or at least fruitless and a sacrilege, if administered knowingly and willingly. The confessor should do his best to dispose the penitent for absolution. Absolution should be denied, e.g., to those who give no signs of sorrow; to those who are unwilling to reform their lives by abandoning the proximate occasions of sin or removing hatred or enmities or restoring what is possible to rightful possessors, etc. The confessor must be firm in his denial of absolution, especially with priests and those aspiring to Orders or religious profession. He should inform the penitent of the reason in a kind and fatherly manner, urging him to search his soul again and pointing out that the penitent himself is the cause of the confessor's unfortunate inability to impart the divine graces of this sacrament.

*To defer* absolution is a duty of the confessor, if the disposition of the penitent is clearly doubtful and there is no urgent and proportionately serious cause for absolving conditionally. In practice this is rarely advised today, except for a brief time for the obvious good of the penitent, e.g., to step back into the church for further examination and prayer and then to return to confession, or if the confessor prudently judges a delay useful and the rightly-disposed penitent consents. At times it is very difficult in practice to judge the sufficiency of the penitent's dispositions. If both danger of nullity to the sacrament and of notable detriment to the penitent cannot at the same time be avoided, the latter danger should be avoided and the absolution given.

The confessor, in asking questions of the penitent, is to act with prudence and discretion, taking into account the condition and age of the penitent. He is to refrain from asking the name of an accomplice or partner in sin. He is to impose salutary and appropriate penances, in keeping with the kind and number of sins confessed, but considering at the same time the condition of the penitent. The penitent is obliged personally to perform these penances.[48]

The confessor receives his role as *spiritual physician* from the purpose of the sacrament; it pertains to its integrity. Penance not only binds up the wounds and infirmities of sin but also fosters the health and strength of the soul for the future. For this reason the confessor searches the causes and occasions of sins and the dispositions of the penitent and indicates apt remedies. The confessor should make clear what is of obligation and what is of counsel and employ with due caution and adequate understanding those things which can be profitably used from psychology and psychiatry by an expert confessor.

The confessor as *spiritual father* is held in charity more or less, depending on the spiritual state of the penitent and the confessor's possibilities, to propose motives for contrition to those less disposed and thus to prepare them for absolution, e.g., the deformity of sin, the danger of damnation, the shortness and vanity of life, the goodness of God and the gifts of Christ, etc. All penitents, and notably the more needy, should be treated with fatherly love; this love should be signalized by patience, perseverance, and kindness, especially with difficult cases and vexing penitents. Corrections and exhortations must be in the same spirit, avoiding whatever would either terrify or exasperate the penitent. The confessor should not overly spend time with the devout and permit useless conversations. His paternal concern for the penitent should be tempered with caution in the case of women, lest a natural and dangerous affection be aroused on either side.

The confessor as *spiritual doctor* is bound as far as possible to instruct the penitent, in a simple and not prolix but sufficient manner, in those things necessary for a valid and fruitful reception of the sacrament and in the Christian truths and precepts the penitent ought to know, whether the ignorance is culpable or not. By his office the confessor is obliged only to instruct in what is necessary for the administration of the sacrament; by charity he is held to other things.

A confessor is bound in justice to *rectify his error*, culpable or not, affecting the *validity* of the sacrament, even though he agreed to hear the confession only out of charity, if otherwise the penitent would suffer serious damage and it is not known that he will confess again soon. He does not have this obligation if only free matter is confessed or if it is prudently judged that the penitent has already confessed again to another priest. He is also bound to rectify his mistake when he has positively erred with serious culpability in his advice concerning the penitent's obligations in justice. Wrong advice given the penitent concerning his obligations in matters other than justice must be corrected by the confessor as best he can, lest a material sin or violation of a law be permitted without sufficient cause.

### 7. ABSOLUTION FROM PENALTIES

The Church possesses an innate and proper right to constrain with penal sanctions the faithful who commit offenses. The Church in its current discipline has established the following penalties: medicinal penalties or censures, expiatory penalties, and penal remedies and penances.[49]

A censure, as one form of ecclesiastical penalty, is by its nature a medicinal punishment. It is therefore primarily intended to prohibit the offense, to correct the erring ways of the sinner, to withdraw the spirit of contumacy from the offender, and indirectly to repair the public order that has been violated.

A particular censure is laid down either in the general law of the Church or enacted by the authority which is by that same law competent to do so.[50] A penalty which is to be inflicted by a sentence (*ferendae sententiae*) upon the offender does not bind the guilty party until after it has been imposed; but a penalty which is incurred automatically by the very commission of the offense (*latae sententiae*), if the law or precept expressly so states, binds the offender immediately.[51] Censures are of three types: excommunication, suspension, interdict.[52]

No one is subject to the incurrence of a penalty unless the offence committed is an external violation of a law or a precept and is gravely imputable by reason of malice or of culpability. The common law designates those who are not liable to penalty and those in whose cases are factors which affect the impact of the penalty.[53]

The following are the automatic (*latae sententiae*) censures in the common law of the Church:

1. *Reserved to the Apostolic See*:

   a. one who throws away the consecrated species or, for a sacrilegious purpose, takes them away or keeps them: *excommunication*;[54]

    b. one who uses physical force against the Roman Pontiff: *excommunication*;[55]

    c. a bishop who consecrates someone a bishop and the person who receives such a consecration from a bishop without a pontifical mandate: *excommunication*;[56]

    d. a priest who absolves an accomplice or partner in a sin against the sixth commandment: *excommunication*;[57]

    e. a confessor who directly violates the seal of confession: *excommunication*;[58]

2. *Not reserved*:

    a. an apostate from the faith, a heretic or a schismatic: *excommunication*;[59]

    b. one who uses physical force against a bishop: *interdict*; if a cleric, also: *suspension*;[60]

    c. a person who, not being ordained a priest, attempts to celebrate Mass: *interdict*; if a cleric: *suspension*; a person who, though unable to give valid absolution, attempts to do so, or hears a sacramental confession: *interdict*; if a cleric: *suspension*;[61]

    d. a person who makes a false denunciation to an ecclesiastical superior of a confessor of having solicited the penitent to commit a sin against the sixth commandment: *interdict*; if a cleric: also *suspension*;[62]

    e. a cleric who attempts marriage, even if only civilly: *suspension*; a religious in perpetual vows who is not a cleric but who attempts marriage, even if only civilly: *interdict*;[63]

    f. a person who procures a successful abortion: *excommunication*.[64]

Any priest, even though he lacks the faculty to hear confessions, can validly and licitly absolve any penitents who are in danger of death from any censures and sins, even if an approved priest is present. After they have recovered those absolved are obliged to have recourse within a month to a competent superior if there has been an imposed or declared censure or one reserved to the Apostolic See.[65]

An automatic (*latae sententiae*) penalty established by law but not yet declared, and provided it is not reserved to the Apostolic See, can be remitted by the Ordinary for his own subjects or for those actually in his territory or who committed an offense there; moreover, any bishop can do this, but only in the course of sacramental confession.[66]

A penalty which is established by law and had been imposed or declared, and provided it is not reserved to the Apostolic See, can be remitted by the Ordinary who imposed or declared it or by the Ordinary of the place where the offender actually is, after consulting the aforesaid Ordinary, unless because of extraordinary circumstances this is impossible.[67]

Outside the danger of death a confessor can in the internal sacramental forum remit an automatic (*latae sententiae*) censure of excommunication or interdict which has not been declared, if it is difficult for the penitent to remain in a state of serious sin for the time necessary for the competent superior to provide. In this circumstance, in granting the remission, the confessor is to impose upon the penitent, under pain of again incurring the censure, the obligation to have recourse within one month to the competent superior, or to a priest having the requisite faculty, and to abide by his instructions. Meanwhile, the confessor is to impose an appropriate penance and, to the extent demanded, to require reparation of scandal and damage. The recourse, however, may be made even through the confessor, without mention of a name.[68]

## IV. THE PENITENT

### 1. SACRAMENTAL ACTS

"Those who approach the sacrament of Penance obtain pardon from God's mercy for the offense committed against him, and are, at the same time, reconciled with the Church which they have wounded by their sins and which by charity, by example and by prayer labors for their conversion."[69] In order, then, that the faithful may receive the saving remedy of this sacrament they must be so disposed that, repudiating the sins they have committed and having the purpose of amending their lives, they turn back to God.[70] "The parts that the penitents themselves have in the celebration of the sacrament are of the greatest importance. When with proper dispositions they approach this saving remedy instituted by Christ and confess their sins, their own acts become part of the sacrament itself, which is completed when the words of absolution are spoken by the minister in the name of Christ.''[71]

The proper dispositions on the part of the penitent are: contrition, confession, and the resolve of amendment in the acceptance of the penance imposed. Faith teaches that these acts of the penitent so pertain to the sacrament of Penance that without them there cannot be a perfect and integral remission of sins, and also that these acts are the quasi material and parts of this sacrament.[71]

### a. *Contrition*

*Perfect contrition* or contrition in the proper sense is sorrow of soul and detestation for sin committed with the purpose of sinning no more. As an act of penance it justifies with the implicit desire of the sacrament. It arises from a motive of charity, of the love of God above all things (and can remit slight sins even without the sacrament).

*Imperfect contrition* or *attrition* is sorrow for sins committed which springs, not from the perfect motive of charity but from some less exalted but supernatural motive, namely, the baseness of sin or the fear of hell and of the eternal and temporal punishment inflicted by God. These two, to which all other inferior motives are reduced, spring from supernatural faith and actual grace, i.e., they are referred to God. Faith teaches[73] that such attrition, although it cannot of itself lead to justification, disposes the sinner to seek the grace of God in the sacrament of Penance. It is commonly taught that attrition with the actual reception of the sacrament justifies.

For the valid reception of the sacrament any contrition must be *true* and *internal*, that is, not only expressed in words or signs but embraced principally by the heart and soul. It is an act of the will detesting sin committed. It need not be sensibly "felt," as it can be present together with dryness, tedium, etc. Lack of intensity in the act or of an accompanying sensibility does not necessarily affect the penitent's resolution to abandon sin and to fulfill his obligations. The contrition must precede absolution and not be recalled if the latter is to be valid; normally it should exist before confession begins. In some cases the confessor may need to rouse proper dispositions.

Contrition should be *supernatural*, that is, elicited under the movement of actual grace and motivated or referred to God, as noted for perfect and imperfect contrition. The act of penitence should be *formal* and *explicit*, or a positive act by which the will truly and explicitly sorrows for and detests a sin committed as an offense against God. In practice most penitents are not to be greatly disturbed, since in their desire for absolution or in eliciting an act of love there is scarcely lacking a formal act of sorrow. Penitents usually terminate the recounting of their sins with a formula such as ''I am sorry for these and all my past sins.''

The penitent's contrition must be *universal*, extending to all his serious sins not yet directly remitted, even those which are forgotten or unknown. Although it is far better, nevertheless it is not necessary to have sorrow for each serious sin individually and distinctly (although they must be so confessed) but at least implicitly. It is not required to have contrition for all slight sins or even for certain ones. Since they are free material, one can confess and have sorrow for one and not for another. The frequency of slight sins is itself a deformity subject to contrition. True sorrow for slight sins also must be internal, supernatural, and appreciatively supreme, although not always universal. The devout penitent will normally express a sorrow which is universal for all slight sins.

Contrition should be at least *appreciatively supreme*, i.e., the penitent appreciates that no other evil is as great as sin, and he is so displeased over the sin committed that he is generally prepared to forego any good or to risk any harm than to fall into sin again. There is no need for the confessor to compare evils, as the penitent may become disturbed and confused. It suffices for the latter to be prepared to do what he can in the future with God's help. Likewise the contrition need not be intensively supreme or more vehement or more poignantly felt than any other sorrow. Some expressions of sorrow, such as tears, sighs, striking of the breast, etc., are not necessary, but yet not to be frowned on. No particular degree or duration of sorrow is necessary. Perfunctory acts of contrition should be cautioned against and formulas expressing true motives for sorrow taught and promoted.

Contrition is to be elicited with a view to *sacramental* confession and absolution and renewed every time a new serious sin is committed. In practice, whenever a penitent immediately after absolution remembers a serious sin he had forgotten and confesses it, he should make another act of contrition; the same penance or preferably a new one should be imposed.

The contrition necessary for forgiveness, besides sorrow for and detestation of sin committed, must also include a *purpose of amendment*, that is, the resolution (*propositum*) or fixed and firm determination not to sin again. It is explicit and formal, if formulated as a distinct act; implicit and virtual, if included in the act of sorrow (which is the minimum necessary). This resolution is the best indicator of true contrition. It should be *firm*, whereby the penitent here and now seriously and deliberately purposes to sin no more, to amend his life, and to endure with God's help any evil or fear rather than to offend God. The penitent may be aware of his own inconstancy and frailty and judge that he will fall again in the same manner. However, in most cases this does not affect his actual resolution of amendment here and now. With children it is often necessary for the confessor to get them to agree to try to do better in the future. When an adult's disposition is doubtful, e.g., in some cases of birth prevention practice, the confessor will seek an explicit purpose of amendment.

The resolution must be *efficacious*, i.e., the penitent must intend to use the means necessary to avoid sin and its occasions, e.g., prayer and vigilance, to repair as far as he is able any damage done, etc. Such a resolution is efficacious if some means are adopted, but if no means are taken when they easily could be, it is suspect. There can be a doubt of the penitent's resolution if there is a fall immediately after confession. However, relapse into sin is not necessarily a sign of want of true resolution, as habits of sin are not easily nor at once rooted out or frailty quickly overcome.

The will to exclude all serious sins in the future should be *universal*, although the sins need not be thought of individually. It is not required for absolution from slight sins that the purpose of amendment be universal; if only slight sins are confessed, there must be a resolve at least to avoid some definite sin confessed or group of slight sins or the most pernicious of them or those which are fully deliberate or to lessen the number of them, i.e., a will to improve. Confessors should try to arouse penitents who frequently fall into the same sins through negligence, etc., to a more fervent contrition and a firmer resolve to amend.

### b. *Confession*

Sacramental confession is the accusation of one's own sins committed after Baptism, made to an authorized priest for the purpose of obtaining absolution, which confession is necessary by divine precept.[74] *Personal* actual sins, and not merely imperfections, are to be confessed to a spiritual judge who is authorized to judge them for the purpose of absolution. A confession made for some other reason, such as counsel, consolation, or mockery, is not sacramental (and thus not under the seal).

By the ancient custom of the Church confession should be *vocal*. The obligation is grave to confess one's sins orally, unless a just cause in case of necessity requires nods, signs, or writing. Such a just cause is present if the penitent is dumb, or because of illness or some other reason is able to speak only with great difficulty, or he cannot make an integral declaration of sins because of extreme embarrassment, anxiety, or scruples, or if the confessor is hard of hearing and cannot hear the penitent without bystanders also hearing. The deaf and dumb are obliged to confess in signs and nods according to their ability. Those who do not know the language of the confessor should confess by signs and nods as best they can.

A *secret* and *auricular* confession has always been recommended and in use in the Church.[75] Public confession or manifestation of sins is not obligatory. Moreover, a penitent is not bound to choose an interpreter, but such a person when employed is bound by the law of the seal.[76] It can be so arranged that the interpreter does not know the responses of the penitent, e.g., by not facing the penitent who then answers the confessor's questions by nods and by showing a number of fingers.

The penitent should make a confession that is *simple* and *discreet*, being prohibited from narrating what does not pertain to it. He should not list the sins of others nor reveal the name of an accomplice. Sins against the sixth commandment should be told in modest and succinct language, which, however, is sufficiently clear and exact. The penitent should be *humble* in words and gestures and make the confession kneeling, unless just reason excuses. There must be a disposition to accept and to obey the just commands of the confessor as well as to receive humbly his rebukes. The same one who has not been ashamed to commit the sin ought not to be ashamed to confess the sin committed.

Perfect *truthfulness* and *sincerity* ought to be present in every confession so that the penitent manifests his sins as they are in his conscience, as certain or doubtful, mortal or venial, etc., neither denying, lessening, or exaggerating the sins committed. The penitent is bound to reply sincerely to the legitimate questions of the confessor,[77] e.g., about habits of sin, occasions and circumstances of sin, the dispositions of the penitent, etc., without which information the confessor cannot form a prudent judgment as his office requires. If the questions are manifestly indiscreet, the penitent is not bound to reply, and for a just cause he can use a mental restriction in his replies.

To *lie* in confession about a *serious* and necessary matter is a grave pernicious lie and a sacrilege. It perverts the judgment of the confessor; the confession is not integral and the absolution not valid. To *lie* about *non-confessional* matter is not for that reason a sacrilege, as it in no way perverts the penitential judgment. It takes on the sinfulness of the lie in question; as a serious sin it renders the penitent indisposed for absolution.

Confession must be *integral*, that is, complete and entire, so that to one and the same confessor is subjected at the same time the whole necessary matter which has not yet been duly submitted to the keys. *Material* or objective *integrity* embraces absolutely all the serious sins which in reality have been committed since Baptism and not yet confessed. *Formal* or subjective integrity consists in the accusation of all the serious sins which, all things considered, the penitent here and now, according to his capacity and after a careful examination, morally can and must confess according to his conscience, although for a just cause he omits some. All sins must be declared, since the minister is the judge of them all; this sacrament has been instituted in the form of a special judgment in which at the same time all or none of the sins are remitted. Thus integrity is necessary by divine precept for the validity of the sacrament, formal integrity actually and by a necessity of means and precept, material integrity at least *in desire* by a necessity of means, and regularly by precept from which there can be excusing causes. Of itself confession should be materially integral, but formal integrity alone sometimes suffices. It is a serious sin and a sacrilege to omit a sin which one can and must declare here and now in confession.[78]

### c. *Satisfaction*

Satisfaction is the compensation for the temporal punishment due to sins through the good works and the penalties imposed by the confessor and voluntarily accepted by the penitent. Sacramental satisfaction *in desire* is absolutely necessary and essential for the validity of the sacrament.[79] Its actual fulfillment is necessary for sacramental integrity or completeness. By the very fact of being done as it should, it brings about the remission of temporal punishment.

The confessor not only can but he must impose a penance or satisfaction on the penitent.[80] He should impose a salutary and suitable penance based on the kind and number of sins and on the character or condition of the penitent; which penance the penitent must be willing to accept and perform in person. He, as the minister of Christ's power of binding and loosing, should act in accordance with the ways of God who inflicts temporal punishments not only as acts of vindication but as medicinal remedies. To impose other than remedial penalties (except in certain cases) would be against the divine intention and to deprive the penitent of great benefits. He should be guided by justice, prudence, and love and not act arbitrarily. The confessor is excused from imposing a penance when there is physical or moral inability on the part of the penitent, e.g., he is near to death, unconscious, too weak, etc. Even here he often can have the penitent speak the Name of God, kiss a crucifix, strike his breast, or something similar.

It is left to the prudent judgment of the confessor in the confessional to consider what is a grave or a light penance in an individual case. Long drawn out, involved, useless, too difficult or naturally repugnant penances are normally inexpedient. Penances which are commonly considered as grave are: to hear a Mass, to fast or abstain for a day, to recite a third part of the Rosary, to recite the seven penitential psalms, the Way of the Cross, a quarter hour meditation or spiritual reading, at least six times the Our Father and Hail Mary, some notable action on behalf of a neighbor's welfare, etc. A penance which is light in itself may become grave if it is to be repeated several times or because of some added action, e.g., to be said daily for a week, etc. Penances commonly considered to be light are: one of the common litanies, acts of faith and hope and charity, five times the Our Father and Hail Mary, expression of kindness or service to a neighbor, etc.

The lessening of the amount of penance imposed is to be judged not only by the seriousness of the sins confessed but also by the ability of the penitent, since the confessor is not only judge but physician as well, minister of divine mercy as well as justice.

It is certain teaching that the penitent is bound to *accept* the reasonable penance imposed by the confessor. The obligation is serious when the penance given is grave, the material of the confession necessary, and the confessor intends to oblige seriously (which is presumed in such circumstances). The penitent can refuse an unreasonable penance or ask for another from the same or from a different confessor. The confessor should normally acquiesce in the reasonable request of a penitent.

The penitent has a serious obligation to *fulfill* a penance imposed (under the conditions mentioned for acceptance) for serious and necessary material, a light obligation with respect to light or free material (even if the penance given is grave). Culpably to omit the whole or a notable part of a grave penance is itself a serious sin. If the penitent has forgotten his penance, he should ask the confessor what it was; if this is not possible or if the confessor cannot recall it, a new penance can be given on an indication of the penitent's state of soul in the previous confession. Failing this, the penitent can say what he believes the penance was. Unless the confessor makes it otherwise clear, the penance he imposes is to be understood according to the practice in the Church. A penance is satisfied when the same work done out of devotion is performed, e.g., congregational recitation of the rosary. The penitent need have only an habitual intention of satisfying his obligation.

### 2. OBLIGATIONS OF A PENITENT

The faithful are bound to confess, in kind and in number, all serious sins committed after Baptism, of which after careful examination of conscience they are aware, and which have not yet been directly pardoned by the keys of the Church, and which have not been confessed in an individual confession. The faithful are recommended to confess also venial sins.[81] Moreover, all the faithful who have reached the age of discretion are bound faithfully to confess their serious sins at least once a year.[82]

This precept is not satisfied by a sacrilegious confession or by one that is deliberately invalid, since the purpose of the precept — reconciliation with God — is not achieved. Every member of the faithful has the right to confess his sins to the confessor whom he chooses, even though the latter belongs to another rite.[83]

The divine precept obliges only to the confession of *serious* sins not yet directly remitted in the sacrament of Penance.[84] The ecclesiastical determination obliges no more strictly. Even if slight sins are present and no serious sins have been committed in the course of the year, the obligation does not bind, since the purpose of the law — reconciliation with God — is factually realized. The precept, however, is satisfied even by the confession of slight sins. Thus, if one has confessed only venial sins and subsequently within the same year has committed a serious sin, he is not obliged by the precept to confess again that year. This is the understanding and practice of the faithful and a safe norm in practice for the judgment of the confessor.

The precept of annual confession may be variously computed (*tempus utile*), e.g., by the civil year from Jan. 1 to Dec. 31, by the liturgical year from one Advent to the next. The common method is from one Easter to another, or as extended by indult in the U.S.A., from one Trinity Sunday to the next. The faithful usually associate as one the obligation to confess at least once a year and the precept to receive the Eucharist during the Paschal season.

Confession must be *integral*, that is, complete and entire, so that to one and the same confessor is subjected at the same time the whole necessary matter which has not yet been duly submitted to the keys. *Material* or objective *integrity* embraces absolutely all the serious sins which in reality have been committed since Baptism and not yet duly confessed. *Formal* or subjective integrity consists in the accusation of all the serious sins which, all things considered, the penitent here and now, according to his capacity and after a careful examination, morally can and must confess according to his conscience, although for a just cause he omits some. All sins must be declared, since the minister is the judge of them all; this sacrament has been instituted in the form of a special judgment in which at the same time all or none of the sins are remitted. Thus integrity is necessary by divine precept for the validity of the sacrament, formal integrity actually and by a necessity of means and precept, material integrity at least *in desire* by a necessity of means, and regularly by precept from which there can be excusing causes. Of itself confession should be materially integral, but formal integrity alone sometimes suffices.

The *lowest theological species* must be confessed, inasmuch as some sins are more serious than others, and also the *lowest moral species*, inasmuch as sins are distinguished by their formal malices, e.g., justice is differently violated by theft, detraction, homicide. In the event that the penitent does not confess the lowest species, e.g., due to ignorance or forgetfulness, the confessor and penitent must try to determine it as best possible. The next higher species must be confessed. When later recalled, it should be confessed in its lowest species.

The precise and certain *number* of serious sins should be confessed as far as morally possible. If a careful examination does not yield this, the penitent should confess the approximate number. If this is not possible, he should confess the approximate number of times he has committed such a sin or sins each day or week or month or year, or whether in a certain period he has very often, often, or sometimes committed these sins.

*Circumstances* which *change* the nature, i.e., multiply the kinds of species, of sin must be confessed: grave circumstances which are so realized by the sinner, e.g., fornication with a married person. It should be observed that sins are to be confessed in their integrity, not according to the greater knowledge or theological science later acquired by the penitent but according to the knowledge (and thus the voluntariety) possessed at the time they were committed. Of themselves *circumstances* which *aggravate* or increase the malice of sin need not be confessed, e.g., the amount of serious theft, the number of persons, the dignity of the person, etc. (unless it also multiplies the malice). In practice, however, the faithful are accustomed to confess notably aggravating circumstances (and are so to be encouraged) for greater peace of conscience, greater humility and penitence, and to secure richer graces. Exception is made in the case of the scrupulous and ordinarily in matters of chastity.

Although the *external act* does not differ specifically from the internal act, it is the ultimate element of integrity of the sin and completes it in its kind or species. It is likewise forbidden by God and should be declared in confession. The confessor judges differently about the state of the penitent with internal and with external sins, e.g., concerning occasions, the obligation of restitution, etc. This is the understanding of the Church and the practice of the faithful.[85] *Foreseen consequences* must be confessed as being voluntary in cause and thus sinful, e.g., pollution resulting from obscene reading, to miss Sunday Mass due to drunkenness. Evil effects foreseen but retracted or not foreseen at all need not be confessed as not being voluntary and thus sinful (although damage must be repaired).

*Doubtful sins* may regard any of three situations: (1) doubt as to the *existence* of a serious sin, i.e., that it was committed at all. There is no obligation of itself to confess these sins, since a doubtfully committed sin is not sufficient (and thus not necessary) material for absolution; we are bound to confess sins which are on our conscience after a careful examination. They may be confessed, and frequently it is recommended that they be made known, in order to form one's conscience, and especially at the hour of death when the confessor's presence is usually a more secure safeguard than an act of perfect contrition. If a penitent confesses a sin as doubtfully committed, he is not held to confess it as certain if he later recalls it as such. Implicitly the confessor has directly absolved it on the condition that it was committed; (2) doubt as to the *seriousness* of a certainly committed sin. There is no certain obligation to confess these sins, as there is no consciousness of their gravity. In doubt as to full consent or perfect advertence, the favor or presumption is to follow the condition of the penitent: a penitent of tender conscience and unaccustomed to sinning seriously would not be held to confess them, whereas the lax and frequent sinner is to confess them. It is the practice for those who are neither lax nor scupulous to confess a doubtfully serious sin. The uninstructed should declare them, as it is very difficult for the penitent alone to rightly form his conscience; (3) doubt as to the *confession* of a certainly committed serious sin. If the doubt is merely negative, such sins should be confessed, since there is a certain obligation to confess certainly committed serious sins, and this obligation cannot be satisfied by a doubtful fulfillment. If there are positive indications that the sins have already been confessed, e.g., in the case of one who frequently goes to confession and regularly makes a careful examination, the confession need not be made.

No precept can or is intended to oblige to what is *physically* impossible, since no one is obliged to the impossible; therefore, in such a case one is obliged to material integrity. For *moral* inability to excuse from material integrity it must be impossible for the penitent to make a materially integral confession without serious spiritual or temporal damage to himself, the confessor, or to another. Prudent fear of this harm suffices.

The sins thus not directly accused and forgiven must be confessed in the next confession after the cessation of the excusing causes. These causes suspend but do not remove the obligation of material integrity.

The suitable age for the first reception of the Sacrament of Penance is deemed to be that which in the documents of the Church is called the age of reason or of discretion, that is, about the seventh year, more or less. It has been the common and general practice of the Church of putting first Confession before first Communion. Moreover, it is the repeated judgment of the Holy See that this practice is to be retained and observed. The introduction to first Confession may be carried out in various ways for catechetical and pastoral reasons, e.g., by having a communal penitential celebration precede or follow the reception of the Sacrament of Penance.[86]

### 3. FREQUENT AND DEVOUT CONFESSION

"All men who walk this earth commit at least venial and so-called daily sins. All, therefore, need God's mercy to set them free from sin's penal consequences."[87]

"Frequent and reverent recourse to this sacrament [Penance], even when only venial sins are in question, is of great value. Frequent confession is not mere ritual repetition, nor is it merely a psychological exercise. Rather is it a constant effort to bring to perfection the grace of our Baptism, so that, as we carry about in our bodies the death that Jesus Christ died, the life that Jesus Christ lives may be more and more manifested in us. In such confessions, penitents, while indeed confessing venial sins, should be mainly concerned with becoming more deeply conformed to Christ and more submissive to the voice of the Spirit.

"If this saving sacrament is really to be effective in the faithful, it is necessary that it should take root in their entire lives and should inspire them to more zealous service of God and their brothers.

"The celebration of this sacrament is, therefore, always an action by which the Church proclaims her faith, thanks God for the liberty which Christ won for us and offers her life as a spiritual sacrifice in praise of the glory of God, as she hastens to meet Christ."[88]

### 4. NON-CATHOLIC PENITENTS

Those Eastern Christians who, in the absence of sufficient confessors of their own church, spontaneously desire to do so may go to a Catholic confessor. In similar circumstances a Catholic may approach a confessor of an Eastern Church which is separated from the Apostolic Roman See. Thus the Catholic confessor may impart absolution also to the dying separated Eastern Christian who requests it. The dying who are unconscious may also be absolved as in the case of Catholics.

Since the celebration of the sacraments is an action of the celebrating community, carried out within the community, signifying oneness in faith, worship, and life of the community, where this unity of sacramental faith is deficient, as in the case of non-Catholics who are not Eastern Orthodox, the participation of the separated brethren with Catholics, especially in the sacraments of the Eucharist, Penance, and the Anointing of the Sick, is forbidden. The prohibition, then, is because of the usual lack of same faith in these sacraments and not because these persons are unworthy, since in their individual lives by their response to the graces offered them they may be more worthy than some Catholics. Nor can the giving of scandal and the fostering of religious indifferentism be ruled out. However, the Church can for adequate reasons allow access to these sacraments to a separated brother. They may be permitted in danger of death or in urgent need (persecution, in prisons), if the separated brother has no access to a minister of his own communion and spontaneously asks a Catholic priest for the sacraments — so long as he declares a faith in these sacraments in harmony with that of the Church and is rightly disposed. In the case of those separated brethren who have not requested sacramental absolution and are unconscious, the priest may in practice, but without obligation, confer conditional absolution, since it is not morally certain that there exists an adequate intention to receive this sacrament.[89]

# ANOINTING OF THE SICK

# ANOINTING OF THE SICK

## I. SACRAMENTAL NATURE

The sufferings and infirmities of man, especially those which trouble his conscience, affect the Christian as well. But, Christ's disciple is aided and sustained by his faith in the measure that he penetrates the mystery of suffering and courageously bears his sufferings, for which reason also he is beloved of Christ. Sickness and infirmity, not unconnected with man's sinful condition and present despite his diligent care, fill up for the Christian what are lacking on our part of the sufferings of Christ for the salvation of the world. Moreover, the ill and the infirm by their witness are a reminder to others of what is essential and is above; they show that the mortal frailty of man is to be redeemed through the mystery of Christ's own death and resurrection.[1]

Thus, by the sacred anointing of the sick and the prayers of her priests the whole Church commends those who are ill to the suffering and glorified Lord, asking that he may lighten their suffering and save them. She exhorts them, moreover, to contribute to the welfare of the whole People of God by associating themselves freely with the passion and death of Christ.[2] In this sacred Unction, connected with the prayer of faith, there is expressed that faith which is to be aroused in him who administers and above all in him who receives this sacrament. The faith of the sick person and that of the Church will save him — a faith which is mindful of the death and resurrection of Christ whence all sacramental efficacy derives and which looks forward to the future kingdom pledged in the sacraments.[3]

The work of reconciliation with God and with his Church which has taken place in the sacrament of Penance is brought to fulfillment, therefore, in the sacrament of the Anointing of the Sick, which is celebrated in the circumstances of dangerous personal illness or old age. It has always been understood in the Church as the sacrament which completes not only Penance but also the whole Christian life, which ought to be a continual penance. Our benevolent Redeemer has always provided salutary remedies against the weapons of all man's enemies, especially in the sacraments whereby the Christian may during his lifetime keep himself free from spiritual harm. Notably in the circumstance of dangerous and debilitating illness the adversary of our salvation strains more vehemently to bring us to utter spiritual ruin even by tempting us to lose faith in the divine mercy. In a period of such illness (or old age), when strength is weakened against the onslaughts of the devil, the inclinations and anxieties of wounded nature, and the impact of worldly factors, this sacrament, imparting its own special grace, is the strongest defence in the preservation of union with God in grace and charity.[4]

## II. THE CELEBRATION OF THE SACRAMENT

In the Anointing of the Sick the material to be used is olive oil, or, if opportune according to circumstances, another vegetable or plant oil. It must be blessed for this purpose by a bishop or by those whom the law equates with diocesan bishops. The law itself grants this faculty, in case of necessity, to any priest, but only in the celebration of the sacrament itself.[9]

Although it is not certain that the Oil of the Infirm (O.I.) alone renders the celebration of this sacrament valid, in practice and outside of necessity and in the absence of the proper oil, another sacred oil may be employed under a condition ("if this is valid material"), but the sacrament must be later repeated with the properly blessed oil.

The oil is customarily blessed on the Holy Thursday of the same year by the bishop, from whom it must be obtained even by exempt religious.[10] New oils should be obtained promptly by the pastor either personally or through another, even a trustworthy layman, if there is a good cause. Old oil is burned in the sanctuary lamp; oil that is soaked in cotton is to be burned and the ashes placed in the sacrarium, e.g., in the case of a priest who blesses oil for the conferral of this sacrament in the case of true need. The sacred oil should be kept in a decent and appropriate phial sufficiently filled with oil-soaked cotton. It should be kept, when not in use, in an honorable place. The supply of sacred oil should be renewed as often as necessary, if the supply obtained from the bishop of Holy Thursday becomes inadequate.[11]

Although the minimum of a drop of oil is valid material, the thumb of the minister should be dipped into the holy oil for each anointing in order better to secure a sufficient amount for each unction. It must be spread on the forehead and hands (usually in the form of a cross) or, because of the particular condition of the sick person, on another more suitable part of the body (not merely dropped or touched to the sense), the whole formula being pronounced. Both hands are anointed while the second part of the formula is being pronounced.[12] (If a hand is mutilated or cut off, the anointing is made on the nearest portion.)

Thus, in a case of necessity it is sufficient to make a single anointing on the forehead or, because of the particular condition of the sick person, on another more suitable part of the body, the whole formula being pronounced. For a serious reason an instrument may be used.[13]

The communal celebration of the anointing of the sick, for a number of the sick together, who have been appropriately prepared and are rightly disposed, may be held in accordance with the regulations of the diocesan bishop.[14]

The prescribed words or formula of the sacrament of the Anointing of the Sick are: *Through this holy anointing may the Lord in his love and mercy help you with the grace of the Holy Spirit.*

The sick person responds: *Amen.*
*May the Lord who frees you from sin save you and raise you up.*
The sick person responds: *Amen.*

## III. THE MINISTER OF THE ANOINTING OF THE SICK

The proper and only valid minister of the anointing of the sick is a priest. This is a right and an obligation with regard to all priests toward the faithful committed to their pastoral care, viz., the bishop, the pastor and his parochial vicars, priests to whom are committed the institutions for the sick and the elderly, and superiors of clerical religious communities.[16] Any other priest, for a reasonable cause, may administer the sacrament if he has the consent, at least presumed, of the ordinary minister.[17] In prudent doubt of the presence of necessity or of required consent, the priest may always lawfully anoint.

The ordinary minister is seriously bound to celebrate the sacrament of

Unction of the Sick personally or through another.[18] To delay the conferral with exposure of the ill person to dying without it would be a serious sin. However, the minister is not bound to confer the sacrament with special danger to his life, unless it is morally necessary for salvation or more certainly valid than Penance in the case, as in the situation of the unconscious who have not confessed for a long time. He is not so bound in the latter case if the disposition of the candidate (and thus the effect of the conferral) is not certain, or even if certain, a greater evil to common good would result from the death of the priest (e.g., where there is a scarcity of priests, or in mission territories).

The ordinary minister is to prepare the faithful in general and families in particular in such a way that they are led to look forward to this sacred anointing and to receive it promptly and at the opportune time with great faith and devotion. Moreover, those who assist the sick should be taught the role of this sacrament.[19]

When two or more priests are attending a sick person, one may say the prayers and perform the anointing with its formula, while the others may perform the other parts of the rite. All priests may impose hands.[20]

The blessed oil may be carried with him by any priest, so that in a case of necessity he can administer this sacrament.[21]

## IV. THOSE ON WHOM THE ANOINTING OF THE SICK IS CONFERRED

As soon as anyone of the faithful begins to be dangerously ill due to sickness or old age, the appropriate time for him to receive this sacrament has certainly already arrived.[22] Thus this sacrament can be validly conferred only on a person who has been baptized by water, who has or at least has had the use of reason, and who is dangerously ill due to sickness or old age.

Being the completion and consummation of Penance, the Unction of the Sick acts to strengthen the soul against the remnants of sin and the assaults of the devil, all of which the infant (and the perpetually demented) is incapable, not having attained the use of reason. The sacrament therefore requires the existence at some time (although the person may be presently unconscious or demented) of *some use of reason* and thus of a capacity of temptation and inducement to commit at least a slight sin; it strengthens against them. It is not required that sin has been actually committed but only that the person is capable of sinning. Thus the sacrament may be conferred immediately after the Baptism of a dying adult in order to strengthen against temptation, such as the fear of death. It is conferred also on the sick who have lost their senses but who as faithful, sought the Sacred Unction, at least implicitly.[23]

Children in danger of death who have reached their first use of reason should be anointed, even before they have made their first Confession or Holy Communion, in order to be strengthened by this sacrament.[24] As a norm the use of reason is presumed at the age of seven; before that it must be shown to exist, and where it does, it is an abuse to refuse to confer the sacrament. But in doubt as to whether or not a sick person has reached the age of reason, as may happen in the case of children or sub-normal adults, the sacrament may be administered.[25]

The candidate must be *dangerously ill* from *sickness* or *old age*. The danger need not at all be imminent or mortal; a prudent or probable judgment as to its gravity suffices and will eliminate any anxiety on the part of the minister as to its presence. The latter may take into consideration the judgment of others, especially the physician.[26] The sacrament may be given as long as there is true illness which is presently and actually serious and dangerous, thus, for example, excluding the person simply insensible merely from inebriation. Thus a sick person may be anointed before undergoing a surgical operation, as long as a dangerous ailment is the reason for the surgery.[27] Elderly people whose strength has become much weakened, even though no dangerous illness is observed, may be anointed.[28] Since the danger of death must arise from intrinsic causes, no other cause whatever justifies the conferral of this sacrament, e.g., shipwreck, sentence of death, impending air raid or battle, the mere accumulation of years; a pregnancy must present an extraordinary difficulty or danger.

Eastern Christians who are separated in good faith from the Catholic Church, if they ask of their own accord and have the right dispositions, may be granted the sacrament of Unction of the Sick not only in cases of necessity but also in special circumstances when it becomes materially or morally impossible over a long period of time for them to receive the sacraments in their own church, thus depriving them without legitimate reason of the spiritual fruit of the sacraments. Catholics on their part may request the same sacrament from those non-Catholic ministers whose churches possess valid sacraments, as often as necessary or a genuine spiritual benefit recommends such a course of action, and when access to a Catholic priest is physically or morally impossible. The regulations of the diocesan bishop are to be observed.[29]

Separated Christians (who are not of the Eastern Churches) who do not share the same faith in the sacraments, and in the Anointing of the Sick in particular, are forbidden the ministration of this sacrament. However, this may be permitted in danger of death or in urgent need (during persecution, in prison), if the separated brother has no access to a minister of his own communion and spontaneously seeks the sacrament from a Catholic priest — so long as he declares a faith in this sacrament in harmony with that of the Church and is rightly disposed. In other cases the judge of the urgent necessity must be the diocesan bishop. A Catholic in similar circumstances may not request this sacrament except from a minister who has been validly ordained.[30]

As a sacrament of the living, the Unction of the Sick presupposes for its lawful and fruitful reception the state of grace. At the same time, the greater the reverence and devotion, the richer the spiritual fruits that accrue to the soul. If time and the condition of the ill person permits, the sacrament of Penance normally precedes and Viaticum follows the reception of this sacrament, in accordance with the rite of the conferral of the several sacraments.[31]

The sacrament of the Anointing of the Sick may be repeated or given again to a sick person who has already been anointed but later suffers a relapse after a period of convalescence; it may likewise be repeated if, in the course of the same illness, his state becomes more critical.[32] In case of doubt of the existence of the above circumstances, the minister of the sacrament must form a reasonably prudent judgment on whatever evidence he has, giving the sick person the benefit of the doubt, since the sacraments are for men.

Bad Catholics and those who have become unconscious in the very act of sinning (e.g., in a quarrel or a shooting) may be anointed on the basis of a habitual desire to die as a Catholic, unless they have positively manifested the contrary. Those who remain contumaciously impenitent in serious sin (e.g., an invalid marriage) and those who refuse the last sacraments before lapsing into unconsciousness should be denied the sacrament, since they have given no indication of a minimum intention.[33] In any doubt of final impenitence or obstinacy the sacrament is conferred.

If a priest is called to a sick person who has already died, he should offer prayers to God that he might be absolved from his sins and admitted by the divine clemency into the heavenly kingdom. He is not to anoint him. If he doubts whether the person is truly dead, he may confer the sacrament.[34]

## V. VISITATION AND COMMUNION OF THE SICK

All the faithful should share in the solicitude and charity of Christ and his Church toward the sick and suffering by visiting them, comforting them, and offering brotherly help. In particular, pastors and those with the care of the sick should impart the teaching of the faith regarding the role of suffering in the mystery of salvation as it is joined to the suffering of Christ and sanctified and strengthened through constant prayer. It is helpful to pray over them and also to recite with them and others who are present suitable prayers, together with Scripture readings and reflections. The sick should gradually be led to frequent reception of the sacraments of Penance and the Eucharist, and, when opportune, the Anointing of the Sick and Viaticum.[35]

Pastors of souls should be solicitous that the sick who are of adequate age, even though not seriously ill or in imminent danger of death, frequently, if not daily, and especially during Eastertide, receive the Eucharist, which can be administered at any time of the day under the usual safeguards and in accordance with the prescriptions regarding Communion outside of church and without a Mass. The sick who cannot receive the Eucharist under the form of bread may receive under the form of wine, as long as the proper care of the sacred species as prescribed is observed. Those who assist the sick may receive Holy Communion with them.[36]

The liturgy provides a rite for the Communion of one sick person and a shorter rite when many are to be communicated in different rooms.[37]

## VI. VIATICUM

Communion received as Viaticum is considered a special sign of sharing in the mystery, celebrated in the sacrifice of the Mass, of the death of the Lord and his passage to the Father. It is the duty of pastors and those with the special care of the sick to provide them with the strengthening comfort of

Holy Viaticum when they are in proximate danger of death, and especially when they are in full possession of their senses. This may, in accordance with the prescriptions of the rite, be administered within or outside of Mass. The Sacrament of Penance is usually to precede. The Eucharist may be received under the species of wine if it cannot be received under the species of bread. All who participate in the celebration of Mass may receive Communion under both species.[38]

The ordinary ministers of Viaticum are the pastor and his parochial vicars, a priest with the care of the sick in rest homes, the superior of a clerical religious community and, in case of necessity, any priest with at least the presumed permission of the ordinary minister. In the absence of a priest Viaticum may be brought to the sick by a deacon or even by a lay person who has been duly deputed by the bishop to distribute Communion. The deacon follows the rite of the Ritual, the others follow the usual rite for distributing Communion by pronouncing the formula of giving Viaticum.[39]

## VII. CONTINUOUS RITE OF SACRAMENTAL CELEBRATION IN DANGER OF DEATH

The sacramental confession of the sick person in danger of death should be heard, if he is willing and able, before the celebration of Unction and Viaticum. If it is to be made within the celebration itself, it should be done at the beginning of the rite, before the unction. Otherwise, the penitential act is performed within the rite. The confession or penitential act may be concluded with a plenary indulgence in the hour of death.[40]

It should be noted that, unless there is obvious serious sin, the sacrament of Unction may not be refused because the sick person has not gone or will not go to confession. Each case for the reception of this sacrament must be judged on its own merits and any danger of scandal avoided. The benign indulgence of the Church toward her children in face of the presence of danger of death should be kept in mind.

In urgent danger the sick person is given the opportunity, if possible, to confess his sins at least generally. Otherwise, he is quickly anointed with one unction and then Viaticum is given. At the approach of death, if the other sacraments cannot be given, Viaticum (which all the faithful are bound to receive in danger of death) is immediately given so that the dying person might be strengthened with the Body of Christ and fortified with the pledge of the resurrection as he leaves this life.[41]

The sacrament of Confirmation, when conferred on a sick person in danger of death, is usually given separately from the other sacraments. In the legitimate absence of the bishop the law grants the faculty of confirming to pastors and to any priests.[42]

Since in both sacraments, Confirmation in danger of death and the Anointing of the Sick, there is an anointing, they are not usually to be conferred in a continuous rite. If it is necessary, however, Confirmation is immediately conferred before the blessing of the Oil of the Sick, but the imposition of hands that pertains to the rite of Anointing is omitted. The short rite, or in extreme necessity the simple formula with the anointing, may be used.[43]

The rite of commendation of the soul of the dying should be used in order to assist those who are about to leave this life.[44]

# HOLY ORDERS

# HOLY ORDERS

## I. SACRAMENTAL NATURE

By divine institution some among the faithful are, by means of an indelible character by which they are marked, constituted sacred ministers, that is, they are consecrated and deputed to nourish the people of God, each according to his own grade, by fulfilling in the person of Christ the Head the offices of teaching, sanctifying, and ruling.[1] The whole people of God comprises the "universal priesthood" and differs essentially from the "ministerial priesthood" which is rooted in the sacrament of Orders. This latter was constituted in order to enlighten the laity living in the world about the fact that in Jesus Christ we are all a "kingdom of priests" for the Father, which purpose the priest accomplishes through the ministry of the word and of the sacraments, especially the Eucharistic sacrifice, for which he alone is authorized, as well as by a suitable lifestyle.[2] The ministerial priesthood does not draw its origin from the community as though the "call" or "delegation" comes from it. The sacramental priesthood is hierarchical but at the same time — because, having its origin in Christ, it is a gift to be enjoyed as another Christ — it is for the benefit of that community.[3]

The sacrament of Orders is a shared sacrament, fully possessed by the bishops, and in a limited way by the priests or presbyters, and less so by the deacons. Bishops are the principal dispensers of the mysteries of God, the high priests of the flock, from whom the life of Christ in his faithful is in some way derived and dependent. Through those who were appointed bishops by the Apostles, and through their successors down to our own time, the apostolic tradition is manifested and preserved throughout the world. Bishops, exercising the office of pastor and teacher as one who serves, have taken up the service of the community, presiding in place of God over the flock whose shepherds they are, as teachers of doctrine, priests of sacred worship, and officers of good order, in order to continue throughout the ages the work of Christ the eternal Pastor. In the bishops, for whom priests or presbyters are assistants, our Lord Jesus Christ, the supreme High Priest, is present in the midst of those who believe.[4]

Priests or presbyters do not possess the highest degree of the priesthood; they are dependent on the bishops in the exercise of their power. Nevertheless, they are united with the bishops in sacerdotal dignity. By the sacrament of Orders priests are configured to Christ the Priest so that, as ministers of the Head and co-workers of the episcopal order, they can build up and establish his whole body which is the Church. In virtue of this sacrament, as partakers on the level of their ministry of the function of Christ the sole Mediator, priests of the New Testament exercise the most excellent and necessary office of father and teacher among the people of God and for them. Their ministry, which takes its start from the Gospel message, derives its power and force from the sacrifice of Christ. The purpose which priests pursue by their ministry and life is the glory of God the Father as it is to be achieved in Christ, namely, that men knowingly, freely, and gratefully accept what God has achieved perfectly through Christ, and manifest it in their whole lives. By their vocation and ordination priests of the New Testament are truly set apart in a certain sense within the midst of God's people. But this is so, not that they may be separated from this people or from any man but that they may be totally dedicated to the work for which the Lord has raised them up.

Deacons, at the lower level of the hierarchy, are ordained not for the priesthood but for a ministry of service. Strengthened by sacramental grace and in communion with the bishop and his group of priests, they serve the people of God in the ministry of the liturgy, of the word, and of charity.[5]

Order in general is the disposition, arrangement or coordination of many things among themselves in the manner of superior and inferior. It also stands for grade or dignity; thus as regards the clergy it means hierarchical order or sacred hierarchy. The sacrament, called in English "Holy Orders," confers a spiritual power for the purpose of governing the faithful and of providing a ministry of divine worship. The power of Orders or the sacerdotal power regards the Eucharistic Body of Christ (and all the other sacraments and connected things inasmuch as they are ordered to the Eucharist); the power of jurisdiction regards the Mystical Body of Christ or the Church through ruling, governing, and directing the Christian people toward eternal happiness.

It is of faith that Orders is a true sacrament instituted by Christ, and that it imprints an indelible character in the soul distinct from that of Baptism and Confirmation. Thus by divine institution there is an essential distinction between clergy and laity, the ministerial priesthood and the common priesthood. By a necessity of the sacrament itself, Holy Orders presupposes Baptism, and by a necessity of precept, Confirmation.[6]

Because of the indelible character, the sacrament of Orders is not repeatable. Although it may accidentally give first grace, as a sacrament of the living, Orders confers an increase in sanctifying grace, and in an eminent degree, since it is the most worthy sacrament after the Eucharist, to which it is immediately related. Infused at the same time is the sacramental grace proper to it. "The worthy exercise of Orders requires not any kind of goodness but excellent goodness, in order that as they who receive Orders are set above the people in the degree of Order, so may they be above them by the merit of holiness. Hence they are required to have the grace that suffices to make them worthy members of Christ's people, but when they receive Orders they are given a yet greater gift of grace, whereby they are rendered apt for greater things."[7]

## II. THE CELEBRATION AND MINISTER OF ORDINATION

### 1. TIME

Ordination is to be celebrated during Mass, on a Sunday or holy day of obligation, or also, for pastoral reasons, on other days including ordinary weekdays.[8]

### 2. PLACE

Ordination is normally to be celebrated in the cathedral church or, for pastoral reasons, in another church or oratory. A large congregation of faithful and clergy should be invited, who should actively participate according to their proper function.[9]

### 3. MINISTER

Every and only a consecrated bishop is the valid minister of ordination to the diaconate and priesthood.[10] The lawful minister is only the proper bishop of the ordained or a bishop delegated by the proper bishop who issues to him legitimate dimissorial letters.[11] Anyone who is entitled by law to grant dimissorial letters to receive orders may also himself confer these orders, if he is a bishop.[12]

For ordination to the diaconate within the ranks of the secular clergy the proper bishop is the bishop of the diocese in which the candidate has a domicile or the diocese to which he intends to devote himself. For ordination to the priesthood of secular clerics the proper bishop is the bishop of the diocese into which the candidate was incardinated by the diaconate.[13]

The ministries of acolyte and lector are conferred by the Ordinary (the bishop and, in clerical institutes and clerical societies of apostolic life of pontifical right, the major superior).[14] This is the exercise of ordinary jurisdiction and thus may be delegated by the above Ordinary.[15]

*Dimissorial letters can be granted:*

*for the secular clergy:*   by the proper bishop of the ordained; by an apostolic administrator; by a diocesan administrator with the consent of the consultors; an apostolic pro-vicar and pro-prefect with the consent of their councils.

*for the religious clergy:*   by the major superior of a clerical religious institute of pontifical right or of a clerical society of apostolic life of pontifical right for their subjects who, in accord with their constitutions, are perpetually or definitively enrolled in the institute or society. Henceforth, for any other institute or society the law governing secular clergy prevails.[16]

Dimissorial letters, which are not to be granted before all other required testimonials and documents have been obtained, may be sent to any bishop in communion with the Apostolic See, but not to a bishop of a rite other than that of the ordained, except by Apostolic indult.[17] Dimissorial letters are not necessary for the ministries of lector and acolyte.[18]

## III. CANDIDATES FOR ORDINATION

Only a baptized man may validly receive sacred ordination. Of the ministries, lector and acolyte are reserved to men.[19]

For the lawful reception of the sacred orders of diaconate and priesthood the candidate must have satisfied all the prescribed canonical and moral requirements, and be judged useful for the ministry of the Church.[20]

### 1. REQUIREMENTS IN THE CANDIDATES

#### a. *Ministries*[21]

Certain ministries or offices, established by the Church, have been entrusted to the performance of the faithful for the purpose of suitably giving worship to God and for offering service to the People of God according to their needs. Such ministries have entailed duties of a liturgical and charitable nature deemed suitable to varying circumstances. The Latin Church at present retains the ministries or offices of lector and acolyte, since these are especially connected with the ministries of the Word and of the Altar. The institution of other ministries may be requested of the Apostolic See by episcopal conferences.

The Ordinary (the bishop and, in clerical institutes of perfection, the major superior) has the right to accept the petition of candidates or aspirants for the ministries. The ministries are conferred by the aforementioned Ordinary in the proper liturgical rite. A bishop (or major superior) who installs in a ministry a candidate who is not his own proper subject should first receive the permission of the proper Ordinary of that candidate.

For admission to the ministries the candidate should freely make out, in the form of a personal letter, and signed, a petition to the Ordinary (the bishop and, in clerical institutes of perfection and clerical societies of the apostolic life of pontifical right, the major superior) who has the right to accept the petition. The Ordinary should then issue a formal certificate to the candidate as a record of the liturgical institution. A diocesan (and religious) register should be kept in which are inscribed the names of the lectors and acolytes, together with the place, date, and minister of institution.

A suitable age, to be determined by the episcopal conference, is required for installation in the ministries. In the U.S.A. the minimum age is established at eighteen. The bishop may dispense from this in individual cases, e.g., for one who completes high school at a somewhat earlier age. This age should be an assurance of sufficient maturity. In the case of those who may later be candidates for Orders, or of those in pre-theological studies, it will be the occasion for a prior ministry.

Special qualities, to be determined by the episcopal conference, are required, together with a firm will to give faithful service to God and to the Christian people. Thus no one should be installed in either ministry without a period of thorough preparation in all aspects of the respective ministry. In the U.S.A., this period, as well as the program of formation, should be determined by the Ordinary. It should generally be from three to six months long, so that both the specific requirements of the respective ministry and the necessary leadership qualities may be ascertained and developed.

Intervals, determined by the Holy See or the episcopal conference, are to be observed between the conferring of the ministries of lector and acolyte whenever more than one ministry is conferred on the same person. In the U.S.A., a person already installed in one ministry, who later desires institution in the others, should first have already actually exercised the first ministry over a period of at least six months, in order to safeguard the authenticity of the respective ministries.

A person instituted in a ministry for his own diocese (or religious institute) may exercise that ministry in his own diocese in accordance with the diocesan regulations and the rights of the local pastor (or religious superior). For the same person to function in that ministry but in a diocese (or religious institute) not his own, he needs the permission of that diocese in accordance with the regulations of that diocese and the rights of the local pastor (or religious superior). The conferring of ministries does not imply the right to sustenance or salary from the Church.

The *lector* is appointed for a function proper to him, that of reading the Word of God in the liturgical assembly. Accordingly, he is to read the lessons from Sacred Scripture, except for the Gospel, in the Mass and other sacred celebrations. He is to recite the psalm between the readings when there is no psalmist. He is to present the intentions for the prayer of the faithful in the absence of a deacon or cantor. He is to direct the singing and the participation of the faithful. He is to instruct the faithful for the worthy reception of the sacraments. He can also, insofar as necessary, take care of preparing other faithful who by a temporary appointment are to read the Sacred Scripture in liturgical celebrations.

The *acolyte* is appointed in order to aid the deacon and to minister to the priest. It is therefore his duty to attend to the service of the altar and to assist the deacon and the priest in liturgical celebrations, especially in the celebration of Mass. He is also to distribute Holy Communion as an extraordinary minister when the ministers spoken of in canon 910,1 of the Code of Canon Law are not available or are prevented by ill health, age, or another pastoral ministry from performing this function, or when the number of those approaching the Sacred Table is so great that the celebration of Mass would be unduly prolonged.

In the same extraordinary circumstances he can be entrusted with publicly exposing the Blessed Sacrament for adoration by the faithful and afterwards replacing it, but not with blessing the people. He can also, to the extent needed, take care of instructing other faithful who by temporary assignment assist the priest or deacon in liturgical celebrations by carrying the missal, cross, candles, etc., or by performing other such duties.

### b. *Diaconate*[22]

For the nurturing and constant growth of the People of God, Christ the Lord instituted in the Church a variety of ministries which work for the good of the whole body. Thus from the Apostolic age the diaconate has had a clearly outstanding position among these ministries, and it has always been held in great honor by the Church. Deacons have been instituted at a lower level of the hierarchy and upon them hands are imposed unto a ministry of service. Strengthened by sacramental grace, in communion with the bishop and his presbyterium, they serve the People of God in the ministry of the liturgy, of the Word, and of charity. The diaconate, as a hierarchic order, is ennobled with an indelible character and a special grace of its own so that those who are called to it can serve the mysteries of Christ and of the Church in a stable fashion.

One who aspires to the diaconate (transitional or permanent) or the priesthood publicly manifests his will to offer himself to God and the Church so that he may exercise a sacred order. The Church, accepting this offering, selects and calls him to prepare himself to receive a sacred order, and in this way he is properly numbered among candidates for the diaconate or priesthood. Thus it is especially fitting that the ministries of lector and acolyte be entrusted to them and be exercised for a fitting time. For the Church considers it to be very opportune that both by study and by gradual exercise of the ministry of the Word and of the Altar candidates for sacred orders should through intimate contact understand and reflect upon the double aspect of the priestly office. Thus it comes about that the authenticity of the ministry shines out with the greatest effectiveness. In this way the candidates accede to sacred orders fully aware of their vocation, fervent in spirit, serving the Lord, constant in prayer and aware of the needs of the faithful. Dispensation from the reception of the ministries on the part of such candidates is reserved to the Apostolic See.

Entrance into the clerical state and incardination into a diocese are brought about by ordination to the diaconate.

For entrance into the diaconate through the rite of admission the free petition of the candidate, made out in the form of a personal letter, signed, is presented to his Ordinary (the bishop, and in clerical institutes of perfection, the major superior). By the latter's written acceptance of the petition (which may be in the form of a certificate to express the fact of acceptance and to be a record of the liturgical celebration) the selection by the Church is brought about. Professed members of clerical congregations who seek the priesthood are not bound to the rite of admission; thus the certificate of acceptance should be appropriately adapted.

Those can be accepted who give signs of an authentic vocation and, endowed with good moral qualities and free from mental and physical defects, wish to dedicate their lives to the service of the Church for the glory of God and the good of souls.

The liturgical rite of admission to the diaconate is performed by the Ordinary of the candidate (bishop or major superior).

Permission should be sought from the proper Ordinary in the case of a candidate who is not the proper subject of the Ordinary performing the rite. The names of those admitted to candidacy should be inscribed in a diocesan (or religious) register and a formal certificate issued. Upon ordination as deacon notification should be sent to the pastor of the place of Baptism for inscription in the baptismal register.

The intervals established by the Holy See or by the episcopal conference between the conferring, during the course of theological studies, of the ministry of acolyte and the order of deacon are to be observed. In the U.S.A.

the required interval between the conferring of the ministry of acolyte (or, according to circumstances, the conferring of the second ministry) and ordination to the diaconate is six months, in order to provide a lengthy period for the actual and authentic exercise of the ministry in question. Otherwise, a dispensation from the Apostolic See should be sought to proceed without delay to ordination to the diaconate.

Before ordination candidates for the diaconate are to give to their Ordinary (bishop or major superior) a declaration made out and signed in their own hand by which they testify that they are about to receive the sacred order freely and of their own accord. Moreover, before ordination to the diaconate candidates for the priesthood and unmarried deacons are to make a public commitment or special consecration of *celibacy* before God and the Church, for the sake of the kingdom of God, according to the prescribed rule, to which, however, religious in perpetual profession are not bound. Celibacy assumed in this way is a diriment impediment to entering marriage.[23]

The *function* of the deacon, to the extent that he has been authorized by the local Ordinary, is the following:[24]

1) To carry out, with bishop and priest, all the roles in liturgical rites which the ritual books attribute to him;

2) To administer Baptism solemnly and to supply the ceremonies that have been omitted at Baptism in the case of an infant or adult;

3) To have custody of the Eucharist, to distribute it to himself and to others, and to impart Benediction of the Blessed Sacrament to the people with the pyx;

4) To assist at and bless marriages in the name of the Church, with delegation from the bishop or pastor, so long as everything else commanded in the Code of Canon Law is observed (cc. 1108,1; 1111; 1116,2).

5) To administer sacraments, and to preside at funeral and burial rites;

6) To read the Scriptures to the faithful and to teach and preach to the people;

7) To preside over the office of religious worship and prayer services when there is no priest present;

8) To direct Bible services when there is no priest present;

9) To do charitable, administrative, and welfare work in the name of the hierarchy;

10) To legitimately guide outlying communities of Christians in the name of the pastor and the bishop;

11) To foster and aid the lay apostolate.

The deacon is to carry out these offices in complete communion with the bishop and his presbyterium, which means under the authority of the bishop and the priests who preside over the care of souls in that place.

Those who aspire to the *transitional diaconate* must possess the required freedom of choice, careful formation as prescribed by law, and proper instruction concerning the order itself and its obligations. Moreover, they must have, in the prudent judgment of the proper bishop or the competent superior, all things considered, sound faith, right intention, requisite knowledge, good reputation, moral probity, proven virtue, and the other physical and psychological qualities appropriate to the order of the diaconate. [25]

These candidates must have completed their twenty-third year of age, and completed the fifth year of the curriculum of philosophical and theological studies, after which studies, they are, before being promoted to the priesthood, to spend an appropriate time exercising the diaconate and taking part in the pastoral ministry, as determined by the bishop or competent major superior. [26]

Those who aspire to the *permanent diaconate*, besides the qualities prescribed by law, [27] must, if not married, have completed at least twenty-five years of age, but, if already married, have completed at least thirty-five years of age and have their wives' consent. [28]

These candidates are not to be promoted to the permanent diaconate before having completed the time of formation, which should run at least three years and in accordance with the prescriptions of the Apostolic See and the episcopal conference. Unmarried candidates are bound to the public commitment to celibacy; married deacons, who have lost their wives, are incapable of validly entering a new marriage. [29]

### c. Priesthood

Priest or presbyters, in virtue of the ordination they have received and the mission entrusted to them by the bishops, are ordained to serve Christ their Master, Priest, and King, and to share in his ministry. Thus they are given the sacred power of Orders to offer sacrifice, forgive sin, and in the name of Christ publicly to exercise the office of priesthood in the community. The priestly office, joined as it is to that of the bishop, shares the authority by which Christ himself builds up, sanctifies, and rules his Mystical Body. That is why those ordained to the priesthood require, in addition to the basic sacraments which made them Christians, a special sacrament through which, anointed by the Holy Spirit, they are signed with a specific character and are configured to Christ the Priest and are thus able to act in the person of Christ our Head.

Through the Apostles Christ ordained bishops to be successors and sharers in his same consecration and calling. The bishops, in their turn, pass on the functions of their ministry in a lesser degree to priests, who are fellow workers with the bishops in carrying out the apostolic mission entrusted to them by Christ our Lord. The whole object of the ministry and life of priests is, therefore, to give glory to God the Father through Christ our Lord. Whether praying and worshiping, preaching, offering Mass, administering the other sacraments, or doing any other pastoral work, priests are working for the greater glory of God and the divine sanctification of men.[30]

A deacon, therefore, who aspires to share in the ministerial priesthood and freely to undertake its responsibilities and dimensions in contemporary society, must be adequately prepared. Besides the qualities prescribed by law, he must have completed twenty-five years of age and possess sufficient maturity to assume the presbyterate. A dispensation from more than one year of age is reserved to the Apostolic See. Moreover, there must be an interval of at least six months between the diaconate and the priesthood.[31]

Transitional deacons may be refused admission to the priesthood by their proper bishop or competent major superior, but only for a canonical reason, even if it is occult. On the other hand, a deacon who refuses to be promoted to the priesthood may not be forbidden the exercise of his order, unless a canonical impediment so impedes or some other grave reason as judged by the diocesan bishop or competent major superior.[32]

## 2. PREREQUISITES FOR ORDINATION

Candidates for the diaconate must have already received the sacrament of Confirmation as well as received and exercised for an appropriate period the ministries of lector and acolyte. An interval of at least six months must obtain between the conferrals of acolyte and the diaconate.[33]

Before receiving the diaconate a candidate, excepting members in vows in a clerical institute, must have already written and signed in his own hand a petition for admission to the order to his proper bishop or competent major superior, who are to accept it in writing, and have been liturgically inscribed as a candidate by the rite of admission. Also, before promotion to the order of diaconate or to the priesthood a candidate must submit to his proper bishop or competent major superior a declaration written and signed in his own hand testifying that he will spontaneously and freely receive the order and will devote himself permanently to the ecclesiastical ministry, requesting at the same time admission to reception of the order.[34]

An unmarried candidate for the permanent diaconate, and likewise a candidate for the priesthood, is not to be admitted to the diaconate unless he has, in the prescribed rite, publicly before God and the Church undertaken the obligation of celibacy, or unless he has taken perpetual vows in a religious institute.[35]

A retreat of at least five days must be made by a candidate for the diaconate and for the priesthood in a place and in a manner determined by the Ordinary, which fact must be certified to the ordaining bishop.[36]

Admission to sacred orders is subject to the authority of the Church through its competent representatives, who, in calling candidates to assist the bishops in the discharge of their duties as actual pastors of the Christian society, select and accept them according to certain norms required by the nature of the sacrament and the ends and needs of the Church, and also of a particular religious institute in the case of religious candidates. This is the external or public call, the so-called ecclesiastical or canonical vocation to Orders. These norms or requirements at the same time are signs of the presence of a divine interior vocation, which they presuppose or guarantee, make known and complete. Thus the Church cooperates with God who by his special grace interiorly calls the candidate to the service of the Master in Holy Orders. Both a divine interior vocation and the external call of the Church are required of the candidate of Holy Orders.

The right intention essential to vocation is the supernatural motive or desire, free, firm and constant, to procure the glory of God and the salvation of souls; it is a certain supernatural propensity to embrace the clerical life. It is man's response to God's special grace and the primary sign of a divine vocation. The stronger the supernatural motivation of the will, the clearer will be the divine vocation and fitness of the candidate. The intention requisite in the candidate for sacred orders is the determination to go on to the priesthood.

Besides the right intentions necessary in the aspirant for the priesthood, there must also be present those qualities of mind and body which make him fit for that state in life, i.e., the candidate must possess a suitability for a life of dedicated service to God, a fitness for bearing the burdens and tasks of the priesthood. A bishop should not confer sacred orders upon anyone unless he is *morally* certain by reason of *positive* proof that the candidate is canonically fit; otherwise he not only sins most grievously but also runs the risk of sharing in the sins of others. Both the divine vocation and the suitability of the aspirant are not conferred but are rather presupposed by his admission by the bishop to Orders. This admission is not of itself a certain sign of either, as the bishop (or those presenting the candidate to him) may be mistaken. A prudent and founded doubt of fitness in the candidate indicates a lack of requisite qualities and thus he should be rejected. The bishop, of course, ultimately depends wholly or in great part upon the estimation of fitness made by those engaged in the formation of seminarians, whether secular or religious. It is important, then, to use every effort to certify that an exterior appearance of suitability bespeaks an interior reality. It is not enough merely to be aware of nothing bad about the candidate, but there must be a moral certitude of his uprightness of character relative to the sublimity of the degree of orders desired. Suitability includes the whole man with his complexity of faculties and qualities — physical and psychological, intellectual, moral — which fitness should become more evident as the candidate progresses through the period of preparation.

More is required today for the candidate for the priesthood than an absence of bodily defects. He must be completely fit physically and able to handle the tasks and responsibilities of the present-day priesthood (as well as the special burdens of the religious life, in the case of the religious priesthood).

No candidate should seek Orders, or be accepted for or promoted to Orders of whose balanced psychological attitude, sound judgment, and common sense there is not positive proof. Those who give indication of mental illness, nervous disease or psychological disturbance, or traits of vices or mental instability evident in parents or family, should be given special attention, even including expert medical aid and advice. A clear inability or unlikelihood, or a positive doubt of a candidate's fitness or compatibility to carry the burdens of sacred ordination, especially celibacy, with honor to the clerical state is a hindrance to the pursuit of a clerical vocation. It is important to discern the early stage of any psychological abnormality so that the unsuitable may be eliminated or at least detained before advancing further toward orders. A sense of responsibility proportioned to the degree of approach to orders should be characteristic of every candidate.

Intellectual ability and knowledge are indispensable for the priesthood. The specific fundamental knowledge required of candidates for promotion to the diaconate and the priesthood is regulated by law. Moreover, a fuller and wider intellectual formation and performance is required of clerical candidates in the modern age.

"Holiness of life and sound doctrine are, therefore, the two conditions which must be regarded as essential for the promotion of clerics."[37] Holiness is not the goal of the priesthood but the preparation for it. A standard of holiness for the priestly office exceeds even that of the religious state.[38] The seminarian, both secular and religious, should have at least the positive beginnings of the virtues eventually expected in the priesthood. Such suitableness must become more manifest as the candidate aspires to one step after another to the priesthood; seminary training is designed to develop such virtues. The Church in requiring these exterior qualities or evidences of virtue is principally concerned with their interior possession, in which holiness primarily resides. Although all the virtues are present with the state of grace, some especially befit the priest and are be expected to be manifest in the candidate for Orders as signs of vocation: piety or an earnest striving to use the means of perfection, detachment from worldly goods, obedience and docility, zeal and humility, strength and charity, modesty and chastity.

The Church, by her ancient law of *celibacy*, often reaffirmed, in recognition of the supreme becomingness of chastity or modesty and purity in the priest, has consistently striven to maintain the highest standards of chastity in the clergy. The priest is called upon to live not an ordinary life but an heroic life of virtue; consequently the great concern of the Apostolic See also in these days for the proper fitness and preparation in clerical candidates in the matter of chastity. Among the gifts of grace and of nature of which there must be positive proof in order to recognize a divine vocation for the priesthood, chastity must be singled out as the *sine qua non* condition. The chastity must be proven or tried, in that there must be positive evidence of its presence and not merely an absence of deviations; consequently, the seminarian must be a person of proven purity, solidly possessed, profoundly appreciated and zealously cherished. Competent authorities in the external forum, as well as spiritual directors and confessors in the internal forum, should be guided by the mind of the Church in judging with respect to purity the divine vocation and the suitableness of the aspirant.

### 3. IRREGULARITIES AND OTHER IMPEDIMENTS

Impediments to sacred orders are canonical disqualifications which prohibit primarily the reception of sacred orders and secondarily its exercise. They are either perpetual, and thus are termed irregularities, or simple.[39] An irregularity simply renders unlawful the reception or exercise of sacred orders. It can be removed or ceases only by dispensation. An impediment is a temporary disqualification and may cease by dispensation, by lapse of time or by removal of the cause.[40]

The following are the impediments in law and the authority competent to dispense:

*Irregular* as regards the *reception* of sacred orders:[41]

1° one who labors under some form of insanity or other psychic infirmity, because of which, after consultation with experts, he is judged incapable of properly fulfilling the ministry: *Ordinary*

2° one who has committed the offense of apostasy, heresy or schism: *Ordinary*; if public: *Apostolic See*[42]

3° one who has attempted marriage, even civilly, either while himself impeded from entering marriage due to an existing marriage bond, by a sacred order, or by a public perpetual vow of chastity, or with a woman who is validly married or bound by the same vow: *Ordinary*; if public: *Apostolic See*

4° one who has committed voluntary homicide or who has procured an effective abortion, and all who have positively cooperated; whether public or occult: *Apostolic See*

5° one who has gravely and maliciously mutilated himself or another person, or who has attempted suicide: *Ordinary*

6° one who has performed an act of a sacred order which is reserved to those who are in the order of the episcopate or priesthood, while himself lacking the order or having been barred from its exercise by some declared or inflicted canonical penalty: *Ordinary*

*Simply impeded* from *receiving* a sacred order:[43]

1° a man who has a wife, unless he is lawfully destined for the permanent diaconate: *Apostolic See*

2° one who holds an office or exercises administration which is forbidden to clerics[44] of which he must render an account, until he becomes free after having relinquished the office or the position of administration and rendered the account: *Ordinary*

3° a neophyte, unless, in the judgment of the Ordinary, he has been sufficiently tested: *Ordinary*

*Irregular* for the *exercise* of a sacred order already received:[45]

1° one who has unlawfully received a sacred order while bound by an irregularity for the reception of a sacred order: *Ordinary*

2° one who has committed the offence of apostasy, heresy or schism, if the offence is public: *Ordinary*

3° one who has committed the offences which incur the irregularities 3°, 4°, 5°, 6° mentioned above: *Ordinary*; if public: *Apostolic See* but only of 3° if public and of 4° even in occult cases.

*Simply impeded* for the *exercise* of a sacred order:[46]

1° one who has unlawfully received a sacred order while bound by an impediment to the reception of a sacred order: *Ordinary*

2° one who suffers from insanity or some other psychic infirmity, as mentioned in irregularity 1° for receiving a sacred order, until the Ordinary, after consulting an expert, permits the exercise of the same order: *Ordinary*

A dispensation from all irregularities is reserved to the Apostolic See if the fact on which they are based has been brought to the judicial forum. A general dispensation from the irregularities and impediments to receive sacred orders is valid for all the orders.[47]

Ignorance of irregularities and impediments does not exempt from contracting them. These disqualifications are multiplied if they arise from different causes, not however from the repetition of the same cause, except in the case of the irregularity arising from voluntary homicide or the effective procuring of an abortion.[48]

In more urgent occult cases, if the Ordinary (or, in cases of the irregularities 3° and 4° preventing reception of sacred orders mentioned above, the Sacred Penitentiary) cannot be approached and if danger of serious harm or loss of reputation threatens, one who is irregular for the exercise of a sacred order may exercise it, with however the obligation of having recourse as soon as possible to the Ordinary or the Sacred Penitentiary, without mentioning his name, and through the confessor.[49]

All irregularities and impediments are to be mentioned in a petition for dispensation. However, a general dispensation is valid also for those omitted in good faith, with the exception of irregularities contracted by voluntary homicide and effectively procured abortion (even in these two cases the number of offences must be stated for validity), and of others which have been brought to the judicial forum. A general dispensation is not valid for those concealed in bad faith.[50]

#### 4. REQUIRED DOCUMENTS AND EXAMINATION

The documents required and the investigation and certification of the suitable qualitites of the candidates for sacred orders, as prescribed by law, are to be presented to the bishop ordaining his own subjects, who must be satisfied by the evidence before proceeding to the ordination. For a bishop ordaining candidates not his own subjects it suffices for the dimissorial letters of the proper bishop or competent religious superior to certify the necessary information. A bishop, nevertheless, is not to ordain a candidate about whose suitability he has definite reasons to doubt.[51]

## IV. REGISTRATION AND CERTIFICATION OF ORDINATION CONFERRED

The names of those ordained and the ordaining minister, and the place and date of ordination conferred, are to be inscribed in the special register of the curia of the place of ordination, where also all the documents of each ordination conferred are to be kept. Each person ordained is to receive from the ordaining bishop an authentic certificate of the ordination conferred, which, in the case of those not subject to the ordaining bishop, is to be sent to the proper Ordinary for inscription in the special archival register.[52]

The local Ordinary or the competent major superior is to notify the pastor of the place of the ordinand's Baptism, who is to record the ordination in the baptismal register.[53]

# MARRIAGE

# MARRIAGE

## I. SACRAMENTAL NATURE

### 1. MARRIAGE AS AN OFFICE OF NATURE

The Creator of all things established the conjugal partnership as the beginning and basis of human society. The intimate community character of married life and love, established by the Creator and deriving its structure from his laws, is based on the conjugal pact, an irrevocable personal consent. From this act, by which the parties give and receive each other, there arises an institution which by divine ordinance is stable, even in the eyes of society. This bond, which is sacred for the good of the married parties, the children, and society itself, does not depend on the choice of those entering marriage. God, who made marriage, endowed it with its various values and purposes. All these are of the highest importance for the continuance of the human race, for the personal progress and eternal welfare of the members of families, for the dignity, stability, peace, and prosperity of the family itself and of human society as a whole. By their natural character the institutions of marriage and married love are ordained for the procreation and bringing up of children; they reach their peak or crown in these activities. Man and woman, who by the conjugal pact are no longer two but one, help minister to each other in an intimate linking of their persons and activities. They experience the real meaning of their union and achieve it more every day. As a mutual gift of two persons, this intimate union and the good of the children impose total fidelity on the spouses and argue for an unbreakable oneness between them.[1]

The union of man and woman differs radically from every other human association. It constitutes a truly singular reality, the married couple, grounded on the mutual gift of self to one another. Irrevocable indissolubility is the seal on this unity, stamped on the free, mutual commitment of two free persons who now are no longer two but one flesh. Their unity takes on a social and juridical form through marriage and is manifested by a community of life which finds fruitful expression in their bodily self-giving. When spouses marry they express a desire to belong to each other for life, and to this end they contract an objective bond whose laws and requirements, far from involving servitude, are a guarantee, a protection, and a real support.[2]

Matrimony as an office of nature was instituted by God by a positive ordination when, after the creation of Adam, he formed Eve as a companion and helper and blessed their partnership. Implicitly it was instituted by God in the creation of man and woman. God, in creating them to his own image and likeness, showed at the same time that he wished them to be different in sex and apt to generate offspring, that hence through their matrimonial union of mutual love and help the human race might be propagated. Moreover, to fulfill the purpose of creation and to attain the perfection of his nature, the offspring must for many years be nourished and religiously reared, for which nature requires the cooperation of man and woman. And God wished that this stable partnership should be achieved in a way consonant with an intellectual and free nature, i.e., by mutual and free consent.[3]

Thus matrimony is a special design of God and its essentials have been established by him and not by man. It must be accepted as divinely designed and made; it may not be changed or altered to adapt it to man's whims and wishes. Since it is of natural institution, matrimony truly exists among the non-baptized, and natural reason inclines to it. Thus it is in itself lawful, good, and praiseworthy, because of God its author and inasmuch as it is ordained to the purposes he established.[4]

Although matrimony is good and even necessary for the human race, the precept or obligation of contracting it falls upon the race as a whole and not upon each individual, unless accidentally, e.g., to avoid incontinence, to repair an injury, or to fulfill a promise. Each one is free to choose his state of life; no human authority is able *absolutely* to forbid marriage to anyone against his antecedent will and who is capable of carrying out his duties. Moreover, the conjugal act itself is also meritorious when virtuously motivated, e.g., to render the debt in justice, or to beget children out of religious motivation, to foster marital love, and when performed under due conditions the principle of which is that it be done in charity. The shamefulness of concupiscence often accompanying the marital act is not that of fault but of penalty coming from original sin. Even if the intensity of pleasure takes away the reason's use, it does not take away the order of reason, because the marital act is preordered by reason. Even the natural contract is a sacred thing, and thus its principal act is also sacred.[5]

Marriage as an office of nature is essentially a covenant and a bond effected by the mutual exhange of consent; it is more properly the bond which is effected causally by the contractual consent. This conjugal bond is the complex of relations arising from the matrimonial covenant and uniting the spouses in one society, the group of rights and obligations among which the exclusive and perpetual right and obligation of carnal intercourse is proper and exclusive to marriage as distinct from all other unions. The sharing of bed, board, and cohabitation pertains to the integrity and perfection of the conjugal life and not to its essence, as is obvious in a marriage of conscience. The union of the two spirits through mutual love is not precisely the object but rather the condition of a happy married life. Similarly, the union of material goods is a condition for bearing equitably the burdens of marriage; it can be and sometimes is determined by civil agreement. The principal purposes of marriage are usually not to be achieved or well attained unless the integrity of the bond is also had.[6]

The remote material of the contract of marriage is the persons of the contractants, embracing the mutual right to the body of each relative to procreation. The proximate material is the signs or words expressing this reciprocal exchange. The formula is the manner by which the acceptance of each other with mutual rights and obligations is exteriorly manifested.

Marriage by its very nature is destined or ordained for the procreation and education of offspring. This purpose (and thus the right to its fulfillment) is instrinsic to marriage and must be intended, or at least not positively excluded, in contracting the union. If it is lacking, no other purpose of itself suffices for true marital union, although it alone suffices without any other, but not very conveniently. Other purposes also intrinsic to the structure of marriage are: (1) *mutual love*, expressed by the marriage covenant, which bond of love becomes the image and symbol of the covenant which unites God and his people; (2) *mutual help and comfort*. The spouses, endowed by God and nature with different and complementary inclinations and faculties, find mutual help and comfort in marriage, inasmuch as from it springs a happier life together, which is necessary for the education of offspring, and a more tolerable forbearance of the burdens of a common life and of old age. It consists in mutual love and deepest friendship together with other helps and solaces of the spiritual and material orders, e.g., a sharing of goods; (3) *the enjoyment of pleasure and the quieting of concupiscence*. Although this is not essential, it is intrinsic to marriage in this state of fallen nature, as a remedy for weakness. It is an alleviation of concupiscence especially toward a third party and safeguards the achievement of unity of purpose in love. Fallen nature restrains concupiscence within reason only with difficulty; it is less excited to the forbidden if it is granted in marriage lawful things respecting the ordination of marriage. This quieting or healing of concupiscence is the acquisition of the virtue of conjugal chastity.[7]

### 2. MARRIAGE AS A SACRAMENT

"By means of Baptism, man and woman are definitively placed within the new and eternal covenant, in the spousal covenant of Christ with his Church. And it is because of this indestructible insertion that the intimate community of conjugal life and love, founded by the Creator, is elevated and assumed into the spousal charity of Christ, sustained and enriched by his redeeming power. By virtue of the sacramentality of their marriage, spouses are bound to one another in the most profoundly indissoluble manner. Their belonging to each other is the real representation, by means of the sacramental sign, of the very relationship of Christ with the Church."[8]

Matrimony is thus a sacrament of the New Law which confers grace for the sanctification of the lawful union of man and woman and for the religious and holy reception and education of offspring. It is a sign of the union of Christ with his Church, significative and productive of the grace derived from Christ, Head of the Church, whereby the marital union might be supernaturally fruitful of its proportionate likeness to the union of Christ and his Church. Christ while on earth certainly instituted it as a sacrament, elevating the natural bond to the higher state of a sign and cause of grace. He had consecrated and sanctified marriage by his presence in Cana of Galilee and had recalled marriage to its original perfection of unity and indissolubility. It is a teaching of faith that marriage is a sacrament and that a valid matrimonial contract between Christians is by that fact a sacrament. For this reason a matrimonial contract cannot validly exist between baptized persons unless it is also a sacrament by that fact.[9] The distinction between marriage as a natural contract and as a religious act of sacrament can relate only to the *effects* of Christian marriage and not to the marriage itself. Thus, strictly, the baptized cannot celebrate the matrimonial contract as the cause of civil effects and not also as the cause of supernatural effects or as a sacrament.

Elevation implies addition, and matrimony remains after its elevation what it was before, with the power of causing grace added. Thus, whatever properly belongs to a contract, belongs also to the sacrament, e.g., to contract through a proxy. Validly baptized non-Catholics, even if they do not admit or expressly deny that it is a sacrament, when they enter marriage with true consent, by that fact confect and receive a sacrament. Their intention, although erroneous, is sufficient; in the will to celebrate marriage or to contract a valid marriage is included the intention of doing that which in the Church is a sacrament. There is no sacrament and thus no marriage if their positive and prevailing will is not to receive a sacrament, as at least a virtual intention is required in the minister. The marriage of the non-baptized, when *both* spouses become subsequently baptized, automatically becomes a sacrament, even if they are not aware of the fact. The matrimonial contract and consent virtually perdure in the bond itself, which, with the advent of Baptism, becomes a sacred sign.[10] The Church does not require a renewal of consent from such converts; a recommendation to receive the nuptial blessing may be made. If matrimonial consent has been withdrawn expressly, e.g., by a divorce, or if a new marriage is desired, the local Ordinary is to be consulted.

As in the natural contract the material of the sacrament is the outward manifestation of the *conferral* of marital rights; the formula is the external expression of the *acceptance* of these rights.

The ministers of the sacrament of Matrimony are the contracting parties themselves, as in the case of the natural contract. The priest is only the qualified or official witness of the validity and lawfulness of the sacramental contract and thus may be called a minister of the judicial and religious solemnity only.

All can contract marriage who are not prohibited by law. On the other hand, marriage enjoys the favor of law; consequently, when there is a doubt, the validity of a marriage must be upheld until the contrary is proven.[11]

### 3. TYPES OF MARITAL UNION

#### a. *Valid*

A valid or true marriage is a union which fulfills all the conditions requisite for validity, i.e., which is not vitiated by a diriment impediment, by defective consent, or by the failure to observe the required form. A valid marriage produces its juridical effects and makes the parties entering the covenant to be spouses with all the rights and obligations thereof.

*ratified only* (*ratum tantum*).   A valid marriage between baptized persons is called ratified only if it has not been consummated. There must be valid Baptism present in both parties, since there cannot be a sacrament (and consequently its greater obligations) existing on the side of one party and not on the other; marriage does not limp. When a party or the parties who are unbaptized receive Baptism subsequent to having entered into a marriage valid according to the natural law, the marital bond automatically becomes sacramental by reason of the Baptism now present in both parties.

*ratified and consummated* (*ratum et consummatum*).   A valid marriage between the baptized is call ratified and consummated if the parties have performed between themselves *in a human manner* the conjugal act which is in itself apt for the generation of offspring, to which marriage is ordered by its very nature and by which the spouses become one flesh. This act must be one placed after the celebration of the valid marriage. Once the parties cohabit after the marriage celebration, consummation is presumed, until the contrary is proved.

A union entered into according to the laws binding them between two unbaptized parties or between an unbaptized and a baptized party is valid, but it is a natural bond only and not a sacramental bond. Thus, even a marriage between a Catholic and an unbaptized celebrated according to the canonical form is only a natural bond. The marriage of two unbaptized parties is governed only by the natural law and just civil laws. When one party alone is baptized (even though a non-Catholic), the marriage is by that fact ruled by ecclesiastical law, unless exempt in some respect, e.g., those baptized as non-Catholics are exempted from the Catholic canonical form of marriage.

### b. *Invalid* (*invalidum*)

An invalid or null and void marriage is a union lacking some condition for validity and in which an external manifestation of consent has no effect due to the presence of a lack of required form, or of defect of consent, or of a diriment impediment. It is called *putative* (*putativum*) if it has been celebrated in good faith by at least one party, until both parties become certain of its nullity. There is the appearance of a true marriage, although actually null due to some substantial defects, e.g., if celebrated in good faith in complete ignorance of the existence of a forbidden degree of consanguinity. An invalid marriage entered into in bad faith by one or both parties is called an attempted marriage, e.g., a civil ceremony by one bound by the canonical form or a diriment impediment.[12]

A promise of marriage, whether unilateral or bilateral, is called an engagement. It may be regulated by laws of the Conference of Bishops. It is not the basis for a process to require the celebration of the marriage but may found the obligation of reparation of damages.[13]

### 4. ESSENTIAL PROPERTIES OF MARRIAGE

The essential properties of marriage are unity and indissolubility, which in Christian marriage acquire a distinctive firmness in virtue of the sacrament.[14]

The unbaptized, together with the baptized, are subject to the prescriptions of the natural and the divine law regarding the essential properties of the contract of marriage: unity and indissolubility. These properties are even more firmly attached to Christian marriage, since the sacramental union more perfectly reflects and signifies the perfect and lasting union of Christ with his Church. Thus as the woman gives herself wholly and perpetually to the one man, so equally the man should give himself to the woman.

The unity of matrimony, which is the union of one man with one woman to the exclusion of all other persons, is called monogamy. To this unity is opposed plurality or polygamy, whether simultaneous or successive.

The property whereby marriage even as an institution of nature cannot be dissolved is called indissolubility or unbreakableness. Because of its intrinsic and inviolable firmness the conjugal *bond* should be lasting and stable and not be dissolved. Although this firmness certainly belongs to the natural bond, it is more strongly present in a sacramental marriage, in which the indissoluble union of Christ with his Church is more perfectly represented and signified, and thus it is called the good of the sacrament. This property is called firmness inasmuch as the intimate nature itself of marriage requires an indivisible bond; it is called indissolubility, since no human cause or agency can divide or break the *bond*. "What God has joined together, let *no man* put asunder." Thus marriage is said to be indissoluble as diseases are said to be incurable, i.e., not excluding the power of God to interfere.

Matrimony cannot be dissolved by an intrinsic cause, such as the mutual consent of the parties themselves, and thus it is said to be intrinsically indissoluble. The primary precepts of the natural law would be violated; one of the principal ordinations of marriage, the procreation and education of offspring, could not be realized if at any time and at their own pleasure the parties themselves were able to sever the conjugal bond. The contractants in a marriage contract do not of themselves stipulate or determine the terms of the contract; these have already been instituted by nature and by divine law. Thus the terms of marriage are not proposed by the parties but to the parties, by God, the third and interested and authoritative party to every marriage. The parties are free to enter or not into the marital contract, but they assume the contract as stipulated, i.e., with the properties of unity and indissolubility. They are then bound by the marital bond contracted and are not free of themselves to change or sever it.[15]

The marriage *bond* cannot be dissolved by any human authority outside the parties themselves, even by those holding the supreme natural civil power or by those endowed with highest supernatural power simply as head of a supernatural society; it is thus said to be extrinsically indissoluble. To dissolve the bond by an extrinsic authority does not appear to be absolutely contrary to the purpose of the natural law but opposed to the secondary precepts. However, the prohibition of the natural law has been reinforced by that of divine law. Although marriage could sometimes be dissolved by a bill of divorce (*libellus repudii*) under the Mosaic law (and the relaxation probably extended to the Gentiles), Christ in the New Law recalled marriage to its original indissolubility, so that no marriage by anyone can be dissolved henceforth by any human authority or power or for any cause but only in certain cases by the divine power itself. God can dissolve any marriage bond whatsoever (which exceptions are rare and special), either by direct action or by granting the power to dissolve the bond to men, either the spouses themselves (as in the case of the Pauline privilege), or to the Supreme Pontiff, dispensing in a divine and natural law not as head of the supernatural society with the general mandate to rule the faithful but by an extraordinary and vicarious power (the so-called Petrine power or privilege of the faith) as successor of St. Peter as the Vicar of Christ on earth.[16]

The altogether adequate reason for the indissolubility of marriage as an office of nature and as a sacrament is very probably the positive will or precept of God. However, nature itself indicates the exigency. Every marriage, especially when consummated, is indissoluble by at least the secondary precepts of the natural law. Absolutely speaking, the primary purpose of marriage can in certain cases be achieved without perpetual indissolubility. However, notwithstanding this, marriage is of itself ordered to a primary purpose, which is protected and fostered by the properties of unity and indissolubility, even though the purpose cannot be actually realized, as in the cases of a sterile union or where the education of offspring is providable outside of the union; in the generality of cases the achievement of this purpose is impeded or made very difficult and far less perfect if the bond is held to be dissoluble. The other purposes cannot be enjoyed without this property. Dissolubility would cause the greatest inequality between man and woman, to the detriment of the woman. Mutual help in domestic partnership of itself ought to endure for life; love itself tends to perpetuity, since the total giving should be mutual and irrevocable. Nature intends the education and care of the offspring for his whole life; the possibility of separation with a new marriage and the fragile union of peace endanger this. The concord of domestic and civil society is imperiled, and strife and the corruption of morals are given entrance.

## II. PASTORAL CARE AND WHAT MUST PRECEDE CELEBRATION OF MARRIAGE

"The pastoral intervention of the Church in support of the family is a matter of urgency. Every effort should be made to strengthen and develop pastoral care for the family, which should be treated as a real matter of priority, in the certainty that future evangelization depends largely on the domestic Church. . . The Church's pastoral action must be progressive, also in the sense that it must follow the family, accompanying it step by step in the different stages of its formation and development. . . The Church must therefore promote better and more intensive programs of marriage preparation, in order to eliminate as far as possible the difficulties that many married couples find themselves in, and even more in order to favor positively the establishing and maturing of successful marriage.''[17]

The local Ordinary has the responsibility to see to it that proper pastoral assistance in all its aspects is duly provided in his diocese by all those entrusted with pastoral care regarding marriage.[18] The latter should consult the canons of the Code on marriage, be familiar with pertinent diocesan norms and directives, and carefully complete all required marriage forms.

Pastors of souls have the obligation to provide all necessary assistance, not only in promoting the Christian character of the marriage state, but in the preparation for, the celebration of, and the pastoral care after marriage.[19] This assistance includes:

### 1. PREPARATION FOR MARRIAGE

Preaching and instruction in the meaning of Christian marriage and the roles of Christian spouses and parents, the obligations to be assumed and the holiness to be sought in the married state by persons entering marriage;[20] the pre-marital instructions and time interval before the celebration of the marriage required in the diocese, especially the regulations affecting mixed marriages.

"More than ever necessary in our times is preparation of young people for marriage and family life. In some countries it is still the families themselves that, according to ancient customs, ensure the passing on to young people of the values concerning married and family life, and they do this through a gradual process of education or initiation. But the changes that have taken place within almost all modern societies demand that not only the family but also society and the Church should be involved in the effort of properly preparing young people for their future responsibilities. Many negative phenomena which are today noted with regret in family life derive from the fact that, in the new situations, young people not only lose sight of the correct hierarchy of values but, since they no longer have certain criteria of behavior, they do not know how to face and deal with the new difficulties. But experience teaches that young people who have been well prepared for family life generally succeed better than others.

"This is even more applicable to Christian marriage, which influences the holiness of large numbers of men and women. The Church must therefore promote better and more intensive programmes of marriage preparation, in order to eliminate as far as possible the difficulties that many married couples find themselves in, and even more in order to favor positively the establishing and maturing of successful marriages.

"Marriage preparation has to be seen and put into practice as a gradual and continuous process. It includes three main stages: remote, proximate and immediate preparation.

"*Remote preparation* begins in early childhood, in that wise family training which leads children to discover themselves as beings endowed with a rich and complex psychology and with a particular personality with its own strengths and weaknesses. It is the period when esteem for all authentic human values is instilled, both in interpersonal and in social relationships, with all that this signifies for the formation of character, for the control and right use of one's inclinations, for the manner of regarding and meeting people of the opposite sex, and so on. Also necessary, especially for Christians, is solid spiritual and catechetical formation that will show that marriage is a true vocation and mission, without excluding the possibility of the total gift of self to God in the vocation to the priestly or religious life.

"Upon this basis there will subsequently and gradually be built up the *proximate preparation*, which — from the suitable age and with adequate catechesis, as in a catechumenal process — involves a more specific preparation for the sacraments, as it were a rediscovery of them. This renewed catechesis of young people and others preparing for Christian marriage is absolutely necessary in order that the sacrament may be celebrated and lived with the right moral and spiritual dispositions. The religious formation of young people should be integrated, at the right moment and in accordance with the various concrete requirements, with a preparation for life as a couple. This preparation will present marriage as an interpersonal relationship of a man and a woman that has to be continually developed, and it will encourage those concerned to study the nature of conjugal sexuality and responsible parenthood, with the essential medical and biological knowledge connected with it. It will also acquaint those concerned with correct methods for the education of children, and will assist them in gaining the basic requisites for well-ordered family life, such as stable work, sufficient financial resources, sensible administration, notions of housekeeping.

"Finally, one must not overlook preparation for the family apostolate, for fraternal solidarity and collaboration with other families, for active membership in groups, associations, movements and undertakings set up for the human and Christian benefit of the family.

"The *immediate preparation* for the celebration of the sacrament of Matrimony should take place in the months and weeks immediately preceding the wedding, so as to give a new meaning, content and form to the so-called premarital enquiry required by Canon Law. This preparation is not only necessary in every case, but is also more urgently needed for engaged couples that still manifest shortcomings or difficulties in Christian doctrine and practice.

"Among the elements to be instilled in this journey of faith, which is similar to the catechumenate, there must also be a deeper knowledge of the mystery of Christ and the Church, of the meaning of grace and of the responsibility of Christian marriage, as well as preparation for taking an active and conscious part in the rites of the marriage liturgy."[21]

### 2. CELEBRATION OF MARRIAGE

A fruitful liturgical celebration of marriage makes it clear that the spouses manifest and share in the mystery of the unity and fruitful love between Christ and the Church.[22]

"Christian marriage normally requires a liturgical celebration expressing in social and community form the essentially ecclesial and sacramental nature of the conjugal covenant between baptized persons.

"Inasmuch as it is a *sacramental action of sanctification*, the celebration of marriage — inserted into the liturgy, which is the summit of the Church's action and the source of her sanctifying power — must be *per se* valid, worthy and fruitful. This opens a wide field for pastoral solicitude, in order that the needs deriving from the nature of the conjugal covenant, elevated into a sacrament, may be fully met, and also in order that the Church's discipline regarding free consent, impediments, the canonical form and the actual rite of the celebration may be faithfully observed. The celebration should be simple and dignified, according to the norms of the competent authorities of the Church. It is also for them — in accordance with concrete circumstances of time and place and in conformity with the norms issued by the Apostolic See — to include in the liturgical celebration such elements proper to each culture which serve to express more clearly the profound human and religious significance of the marriage contract, provided that such elements contain nothing that is not in harmony with Christian faith and morality.

"Inasmuch as it is a *sign*, the liturgy celebration should be conducted in such a way as to constitute, also in its external reality, a proclamation of the word of God and a profession of faith on the part of the community of believers. Pastoral commitment will be expressed here through the intelligent and careful preparation of the Liturgy of the Word and through the education to faith of those participating in the celebration and in the first place the couple being married.

"Inasmuch as it is a *sacramental action of the Church*, the liturgical celebration of marriage should involve the Christian community, with the full, active and responsible participation of all those present, according to the place and task of each individual: the bride and bridegroom, the priest, the witnesses, the relatives, the friends, the other members of the faithful, all of them members of an assembly that manifests and lives the mystery of Christ and his Church. For the celebration of Christian marriage in the sphere of ancestral cultures or traditions, the principles laid down above should be followed.

"Precisely because in the celebration of the sacrament very special attention must be devoted to the moral and spiritual dispositions of those being married, in particular to their faith, we must here deal with a not infrequent difficulty in which the pastors of the Church can find themselves in the context of our secularized society.

"In fact, the faith of the person asking the Church for marriage can exist in different degrees, and it is the primary duty of pastors to bring about a rediscovery of this faith and to nourish it and bring it to maturity. But pastors must also understand the reasons that lead the Church also to admit to the celebration of marriage those who are imperfectly disposed.

"The sacrament of Matrimony has this specific element that distinguishes it from all the other sacraments: it is the sacrament of something that was part of the very economy of creation; it is the very conjugal covenant instituted by the Creator 'in the beginning.' Therefore the decision of a man and a woman to marry in accordance with this divine plan, that is to say, the decision to commit by their irrevocable conjugal consent their whole lives in indissoluble love and unconditional fidelity, really involves, even if not in a fully conscious way, an attitude of profound obedience to the will of

God, an attitude which cannot exist without God's grace. They have thus already begun what is in a true and proper sense a journey towards salvation, a journey which the celebration of the sacrament and the immediate preparation for it can complement and bring to completion, given the uprightness of their intention.

"On the other hand it is true that in some places engaged couples ask to be married in church for motives which are social rather than genuinely religious. This is not surprising. Marriage, in fact, is not an event that concerns only the persons actually getting married. By its very nature it is also a social matter, committing the couple being married in the eyes of society. And its celebration has always been an occasion of rejoicing that brings together families and friends. It therefore goes without saying that social as well as personal motives enter into the request to be married in church.

"Nevertheless, it must not be forgotten that these engaged couples, by virtue of their Baptism, are already really sharers in Christ's marriage Covenant with the Church, and that, by their right intention, they have accepted God's plan regarding marriage and therefore at least implicitly consent to what the Church intends to do when she celebrates marriage. Thus, the fact that motives of a social nature also enter into the request is not enough to justify refusal on the part of pastors. Moreover, as the Second Vatican Council teaches, the sacraments by words and ritual elements nourish and strengthen faith: that faith towards which the married couple are already journeying by reason of the uprightness of their intention, which Christ's grace certainly does not fail to favor and support.

"As for wishing to lay down further criteria for admission to the ecclesial celebration of marriage, criteria that would concern the level of faith of those to be married, this would above all involve grave risks. In the first place, the risk of making unfounded and discriminatory judgments; secondly, the risk of causing doubts about the validity of marriages already celebrated, with grave harm to Christian communities, and new and unjustified anxieties to the consciences of married couples; one would also fall into the danger of calling into question the sacramental nature of many marriages of brethren separated from full communion with the Catholic Church, thus contradicting ecclesial tradition.

"However, when in spite of all efforts engaged couples show that they reject explicitly and formally what the Church intends to do when the marriage of baptized persons is celebrated, the pastor of souls cannot admit them to the celebration of marriage. In spite of his reluctance to do so, he has the duty to take note of the situation and to make it clear to those concerned that, in these circumstances, it is not the Church that is placing an obstacle in the way of the celebration that they are asking for, but themselves.

"Once more there appears in all its urgency the need for evangelization and catechesis before and after marriage, effected by the whole Christian community, so that every man and woman that gets married celebrates the sacrament of Matrimony not only validly but also fruitfully."[23]

### 3. PASTORAL CARE AFTER MARRIAGE

Assistance should be given to those already married so that, by faithfully observing and protecting their conjugal covenant, they may day by day come to lead a holier and fuller family life.[24]

"The pastoral care of the regularly established family signifies, in practice, the commitment of all the members of the local ecclesial community to helping the couple to discover and live their new vocation and mission. In order that the family may be ever more a true community of love, it is necessary that all its members should be helped and trained in their responsibilities as they face the new problems that arise, in mutual service, and in active sharing in family life.

"This holds true especially for young families, which, finding themselves in a context of new values and responsibilities, are more vulnerable, especially in the first years of marriage, to possible difficulties, such as those created by adaptation to life together or by the birth of children. Young married couples should learn to accept willingly, and make good use of, the discreet, tactful and generous help offered by other couples that already have more experience of married and family life. Thus, within the ecclesial community — the great family made up of Christian families — there will take place a mutual exchange of presence and help among all the families, each one putting at the service of the others its own experience of life, as well as the gifts of faith and grace. Animated by a true apostolic spirit, this assistance from family to family will constitute one of the simplest, most effective and most accessible means for transmitting from one to another those Christian values which are both the starting-point and goal of all pastoral care. Thus young families will not limit themselves merely to receiving, but in their turn, having been helped in this way, will become a source of enrichment for other longer established families, through their witness of life and practical contribution.

"In her pastoral care of young families, the Church must also pay special attention to helping them to live married love responsibly in relationship with its demands of communion and service to life. She must likewise help them to harmonize the intimacy of home life with the generous shared work of building up the Church and society. When children are born and the married couple becomes a family in the full and specific sense, the Church will still remain close to the parents in order that they may accept their children and love them as a gift received from the Lord of life, and joyfully accept the task of serving them in their human and Christian growth."[25]

### 4. CAUTIONS

Pastors of souls, and others who supply for them in any way, should take care, before the celebration of marriage, that:

(a) it is evident that nothing stands in the way of a valid and lawful marriage;[26]

(b) the parties have proper canonical residence and validly received Baptism; in danger of death, if other proofs are not available, it suffices, unless there are contrary indications, to have the affirmation of the parties, even under oath or if the case warrants it, that they have been baptized and are free of any impediment;[27]

(c) the norms on mixed marriages in the diocese are observed;[28]

(d) the banns of marriage are published as required;[29]

(e) the diocesan norms are observed regarding documentation and testimony when the parties are of different parishes in the diocese or from different dioceses or rites;

(f) the sacrament of Confirmation is received, when lacking, if it can be done without serious inconveniences, and also the sacraments of Penance and the Eucharist, unless the case indicates otherwise;[30]

(g) young people are dissuaded from entering marriage before the age customarily accepted in the region;[31]

(h) the Church's teaching is explained and all pastoral care exercised regarding irregular situations: trial marriages, free unions, Catholics in civil marriage, separated or divorced persons whether unmarried or married again;[32]

(i) the document certifying the results of the investigations of the parties to be married is sent as soon as possible to the proper pastor.[33]

### 5. FORBIDDEN ASSISTANCE

Assistance at a marriage is forbidden to anyone, except in case of necessity, without the permission of the local Ordinary, in the following cases:[34]

(a) a marriage of those without a fixed residence (*vagi*);

(b) a marriage which cannot be recognized or celebrated in accord with the norm of civil law;

(c) a marriage of a person who is bound by natural obligations toward another party or toward children, arising from a previous union;

(d) a marriage of a person who has notoriously rejected the Catholic faith; the local Ordinary is not to give permission unless, with the proper adjustments, the norms governing the conditions for a mixed marriage have been observed;

(e) a marriage of a person who is under censure;

(f) a marriage of a minor whose parents are either unaware of it or are reasonably opposed to it;

(g) a marriage to be entered by means of proxy.

### 6. DOCUMENTATION

Documentation will be more or less required of the priest or deacon according as the individual marriage case requires and diocesan law or practice may indicate. The following list may assist.

(1) Transcript or summary of the dossier of documents.

(2) Certificate of the priest of the freedom of each party to marry.

(3) Prenuptial questioning or inquiry form properly signed and annotated are necessary.

(4) Formula of oaths or affidavits (supplementary or suppletory oaths) (a) of witnesses to prove freedom to marry, (b) of the party intending marriage regarding freedom from all impediments when direct

proof is lacking,   (c) of parents or guardians of their lack of objection to the marriage of a minor.

(5) Baptismal certificate including Confirmation and other notation duly issued within six months.

(6) Certificate of publication of the banns or of the Ordinary's dispensation.

(7) Death certificate of a previous spouse executed by competent authority according to diocesan regulations.

(8) Authentic record of a papal dissolution, decree of nullity (whenever marriage has been attempted), Pauline privilege or a privilege of the faith.

(9) Civil divorce decree with date and place of issuance.

(10) Ordinary's decision regarding any previous marriage.

(11) Promises or guarantees (*cautiones*) required in mixed marriages and properly executed in the form prescribed.

(12) Civil certificate of marriage in a case of revalidation with place and date of issuance.

(13) Dispensations from impediments.

(14) Parental consent for the marriage of minors.

(15) Delegation for valid assistance at the marriage; also when another rite is involved.

(16) Permission for lawful assistance at the marriage; also in the case of another rite.

(17) Permission of the local Ordinary for

    (a) person of no fixed residence (*vagi*) or emigrants.

    (b) apostates, public sinners or persons under censure.

    (c) a lawful condition to be attached to the marital contract.

    (d) minors to marry without parental consent.

(18) Curial testimonial of the *nihil obstat*.

(19) Assurance received of registration in the marriage and baptismal registers.

(20) Civil license with date and place of issuance.

## III. DIRIMENT IMPEDIMENTS IN GENERAL

### 1. AUTHORITY OVER IMPEDIMENTS

A diriment impediment renders a person incapable of contracting a marriage validly.[35] It is a circumstance present in one or both parties on account of which marriage, by disposition of law either divine or natural or ecclesiastical (or even civil) cannot be validly celebrated. Even though an impediment exists on the part of one party only, it affects the right of both parties, disqualifies them. It directly affects a marriage inasmuch as it is a contract and only consequently as a sacrament. Although some other cause may render a marriage null or invalid, e.g., fear, error, lack of jurisdiction, only recognized by law as diriment impediments are canonical impediments.

Only the supreme authority in the Church can authentically declare when the divine law prohibits or invalidates a marriage; likewise, it alone has the right to establish other impediments for those who are baptized. The local Ordinary, and those equivalent in law, can, in a particular case, forbid the marriage of his own subjects wherever they are staying and of all persons actually present in his own territory, but only for a time, for a serious reason, and while that reason persists. Only the supreme authority in the Church can attach an invalidating clause to a prohibition of marriage.[36]

It is at least theologically certain that the government of Christian marriage, i.e., between two baptized persons, pertains exclusively to the Church and is not possessed cumulatively with the civil power. It is commonly held that a marriage between a baptized and an unbaptized person is governed by the law of the Church.

Civil authority, for the good of society, can and ought to make just laws (which bind in conscience) for the temporal effects of marriage, the separable civil effects, e.g., inheritance, dowries, social status, titles, registration, union and administration of goods, as long as they are not evil in themselves nor expressly proscribed by the Church. Inseparable civil effects exclusively reserved to the Church in the case of the baptized are, e.g., legitimacy of children, the right of parties to mutual marital relations, questions affecting or depending on the validity of marriage.

The Church does not have authority directly over marriages of unbelievers. However, all marriage is governed by the divine law. The Church as the one authentic interpreter of the natural and divine law may speak on all marriage by her Teaching Authority. She alone can give a judgment as to what natural marriage is valid before God. It is most common teaching that the marriage of unbelievers is governed not only by natural and divine law but also by civil law exclusively and properly. The practice of the Church confirms this. Thus the civil power probably may establish both diriment and prohibitive impediments for their unbeliever subjects, as long as they are not contrary to natural or divine positive law (although it is sometimes not clear which quality of impediment the lawgiver intended). However, there can be no perfect divorce or dissolution of the natural bond granted, as this is forbidden to all by positive divine law in the New Testament. Marriage between unbelievers is a juridic fact with consequent effects even for the faithful inasmuch as it constitutes an impediment of existing bond. The civil power may justly regulate espousals or betrothal, the valid form of celebration, civil effects, recognize and define causes of nullity, etc. In mission territories care and consideration must be given to the various kinds of marriage possible or current in the area, such as unions entered into according to tribal customs, according to the marriage statutes of the government, or in other ways, and the effects obtained by various acts placed. The mission law of the territory must be consulted; nullity of a legitimate marriage contracted contrary to tribal or civil law is to be referred to the local Ordinary.

## 2. TYPES OF IMPEDIMENTS

An impediment is said to be public, when it can be proved in the external forum; otherwise, it is occult.[37] An occult *impediment* refers to the possibility of proof in the external forum; an occult *case* refers to the lack of notoriety of an impediment, whether it is known or not by others. Thus an impediment may be public by nature, i.e., which is customarily evident, e.g., age, sacred orders, consanguinity by legitimate birth; or by nature occult, i.e., which is customarily secret, e.g., crime, consanguinity by illegitimate birth. An occult impediment may become known in fact or remain a secret; a public impediment may not be known in fact and thus remain in certain circumstances classed as an occult case; it may be known by only a very few discreet people who will keep it a secret. It may be public in one place, e.g., where the impediment was contracted, but occult in another, e.g., where the marriage is celebrated; or public at one time and becoming later occult, e.g., after ten years. To determine how many people must be in the know in order to render a case no longer occult, the common rule of thumb is four or five people in a town and eight to ten in a city, which numbers may increase or lessen as these individuals are discreet, hostile, garrulous, etc. For an impediment to be by nature public, it is not necessary that it be known as an impediment but only that the fact be public, e.g., uxorcide.

An impediment is absolute if it prevents marriage from being contracted with any person whatsoever, e.g., sacred orders, absolute impotency; or relative if forbidding marriage with a certain person, while permitting it with others, e.g., consanguinity, affinity, relative impotency. It is perpetual if it always endures unless there is room for dispensation, e.g., consanguinity; or temporary, if it ceases with lapse of time, e.g., age. An impediment is indispensable, from which the Church cannot or customarily does not dispense, e.g., absolute impotency, episcopate; otherwise, it is dispensable.

### 3. DISPENSATION FROM IMPEDIMENTS

#### a. *Apostolic See*

The impediments whose dispensation is reserved to the Apostolic See are:

1° the impediment arising from sacred orders or from a public perpetual vow of chastity in a religious institute of pontifical right;

2° the impediment of crime mentioned in Canon 1090.[38]

#### b. *Local Ordinary*

The local Ordinary can dispense his own subjects wherever they are residing, and all who are actually present in his territory, from all impediments of ecclesiastical law, except for those whose dispensation is reserved to the Apostolic See. A dispensation is never given from the impediment of consanguinity in the direct line or in the second degree of the collateral line.[39]

The local Ordinary in this case also includes Vicars General and Episcopal Vicars. Since it is ordinary power, it is delegatable, both for a single act and for all cases.[40]

### c. *Danger of death*

#### *Local Ordinary*

Whenever danger of death threatens, the local Ordinary can dispense his own subjects wherever they are residing, and all who are actually present in his territory, both from the form prescribed for the celebration of marriage, and from each and every impediment of ecclesiastical law, whether public or occult, except the impediment arising from the sacred order of the priesthood.[41]

#### *Pastor and others*

In the same circumstances, but only for cases in which not even the local Ordinary can be reached, the same faculty of dispensation is possessed by the pastor, by a properly delegated sacred minister, and by the priest or deacon who assists at the marriage in the absence of the one competent to assist. The local Ordinary is considered unable to be approached if he can be reached only by telegram or by telephone.[42]

#### *Confessor*

In danger of death a confessor possesses the faculty to dispense from occult impediments for the internal forum, whether within the act of sacramental confession or outside it.[43]

### d. *Imminent celebration*

Whenever an impediment is discovered after everything has already been prepared (*omnia sunt parata*) for the wedding and the marriage cannot without probable danger of great harm be postponed until a dispensation is obtained from the competent authority, the power to dispense from all impediments, excepting those of sacred orders, a perpetual vow of chastity in a religious institute of pontifical right, and crime, is possessed by the local Ordinary and, provided the case is occult, by the pastor and others as permitted and described in the conditions for danger of death.[44]

The same power applies also to the celebration of a marriage when there is the same danger in delay and no time to have recourse to the Apostolic See or to the local Ordinary in the case of impediments from which he can dispense.[45]

### e. *Record of dispensation*

The pastor and others empowered to dispense impediments in danger of death or of imminent celebration are to inform immediately the local Ordinary of a dispensation granted for the external forum and see that it is recorded in the marriage register. But, unless a rescript from the Sacred Penitentiary states otherwise, a dispensation from an occult impediment granted in the internal non-sacramental forum is to be recorded in the secret archives of the diocese. However, if later on the occult impediment becomes public, no other dispensation for the external forum is necessary.[46]

### 4. REASONS FOR DISPENSATIONS

There must be reasons or causes which justify the granting of a dispensation. The priest or deacon who submits a petition is bound in conscience in each case to verify the real existence and the objective gravity of the cause or reason cited. The reason should be proportionate to the nature of the impediment from which the dispensation is sought. A primary, final or motivating reason (*causa motiva*) is one that of itself suffices for the granting of the dispensation; a secondary, persuasive or subordinate reason (*causa impulsiva*) does not of itself suffice but together with others may suffice. Canonical reasons are those which are ordinarily accepted by the Roman Curia or by the diocesan curia; otherwise they are non-canonical and may be accepted in an extraordinary case. Due consideration should be given to the possible effects of the circumstances on the proposed marriage.

## IV. DIRIMENT IMPEDIMENTS SPECIFICALLY

### 1. LACK OF AGE

A man before he has completed his sixteenth year, and a woman before she has completed her fourteenth year, cannot validly enter marriage. The episcopal conference may establish an older age but only for the lawful celebration of marriage.[47] Where the conference or the diocesan bishop has established a minimum age, the parties must obtain the local Ordinary's permission to marry.

Marriages of non-Catholic baptized and of the unbaptized in which at least one party had entered marriage below the canonical or the civil legal age should be referred to the local Ordinary.

Assurance for the achievements of the purposes of marriage, its fruitfulness and stability, the health of the spouses, the maturity needed for offspring and family life are protected by this law of the Church and by diocesan regulations. Although marriages of the young are discouraged,[48] too great a disparity of age in the couples to be married is not recommendable, but is not an impediment. The impediment of nonage in civil law must be considered.

A civil birth certificate is acceptable proof of age, a baptismal certificate will indicate only the maturity of the party, if the birth date is missing. The impediment of nonage normally ceases with the attainment of the required age; it is rarely dispensed. In doubt of the fact of the age the local Ordinary is to be consulted. A marriage invalid due to nonage requires for validation a renewed act of consent according to the prescribed form of marriage.[49]

### 2. ANTECEDENT AND PERPETUAL IMPOTENCE

#### a. *Nature and types of impotency*

*impotency and sterility.* The human action as such is the only action over which the human individual has control and thus responsibility, and consequently the only action which can be made the object of the marital contract. In the process which leads to generation of offspring in marriage the specifically human act is the conjugal act. Thus, those things which pertain to copulation alone are within the control of the individual and not subsequent acts which are solely of nature itself. For this reason the parties in marriage mutually transfer the rights to those acts which *of themselves* are *apt* for generation; the action of nature itself in the process of generation or procreation is neither included nor excluded. The impediment of impotency is therefore the inability to copulate (*impotentia copulandi*), the incapacity for normal, sexual intercourse.

Anything which is extraneous or accidental to copulation itself and which frustrates the passage of the seed of generation is a lack of fertility or sterility (*impotentia generandi*). It is a failure in some phase of the natural process of the physiological functions that operate independently of the human will and control, e.g., the movement of the semen within the female organism, the descent of the ovary, the fecundation of the same, the fertility of the male sperm itself. Thus the inability of nature itself to accomplish its purpose where copulation is not impeded is the defect of sterility and not of impotency.

*types of impotency*:

*as to time*:   impotency may be antecedent, if it existed prior to or at the time of the marriage contract; *subsequent*, if it arose after a valid and indissoluble contract was entered into.

*as to extent*:   it may be *absolute*, i.e., extending to marriage with any person; *relative*, i.e., limited only to marriage between particular individuals but not others.

*as to origin*:   impotency is *natural*, if it is from nature or has existed from birth; *artificial* or *accidental* if it has been acquired from an accidental cause, such as surgery, disease, accident.

*as to certainty*:   it is *certain*, if its existence or presence can be certified or proven with at least moral certainty; otherwise it is *doubtful*.

*as to duration*:   impotency is *temporary*, if it will cease in time or can be overcome by human effort, e.g., surgery; *perpetual*, if in the prudent judgment of experts it will never cease or if it cannot be cured without danger to life or be removed by lawful means. Perpetuity is usually unlikely in cases of functional impotence.

*as to cause*:   impotency is *organic*, mechanical or anatomical, if it arises from an anatomical defect in the genital organs themselves, when either the organs are lacking or are inept for perfect copulation; it is *functional*, when due to some lack of stimulation preventing normal functioning, or due to some organic defect or abnormality in another part of the body or to some disease of the nervous system, or due to some psychical cause arising from the purely mental or psychological makeup of the person, e.g., homosexuality, ejaculatio praecox, vaginism.

### b.  *Canonical impediment of impotency*

By the natural law itself a marriage is rendered invalid by *antecedent* and *perpetual* impotency on the part of either the man or the woman, whether known to the other party or not, whether it is absolute or not. If the impediment of impotency is doubtful because of either a doubt of law or a doubt of fact, the marriage is not to be hindered. Sterility neither invalidates marriage nor renders it unlawful.[50]

There must be real and true impotency which is both antecedent and perpetual and which must be proved with moral certainty. The presumption is in favor of the power to copulate until the contrary is proved. It is difficult to prove antecedent and perpetual impotency, especially if arising from a psychic cause. It is not necessary that it actually existed or was evident before marriage but that the proximate causes of the impediment existed then and thus it was virtually antecedent.

In the case of persons who have undergone vasectomy and other persons in similar conditions marriage is usually not prohibited, because certain proof of impotency is not present. In practice, in such cases, the priest will consult the local Ordinary about the application of the impediment.[51]

Sterility neither forbids nor invalidates a marriage.[52] Fecundity is not absolutely necessary for the community of life to which marriage is ordered nor does it impede sexual intercourse. However, unless it is known to the parties before marriage, it may affect the marriage partnership itself. If fraudulently concealed, it may indicate a case of defect of consent by reason of error or fraud.[53] A sterile partner is bound to reveal this defect to the other party, whether discovered before or after the marriage is celebrated; also in the case of subsequent impotency.

### c. *Pastoral care*

The pastor or confessor does not usually inquire about impotency. If he becomes aware of it and the parties are in good faith, he should not immediately warn them, since it is usually very difficult to separate and material sins may become formal ones. A dispensation from at least an unconsummated marriage will be petitioned (if there is a doubt of the fact of the impotency being antecedent or perpetual and irreparable). Only in a rare and exceptional case will an arrangement to live as brother and sister be admitted. When certain and antecedent impotency is discovered after marriage the parties lose all right to the marital act; they may exercise their right until the impediment becomes certain or nullity declared. A woman is bound to submit to surgery to remedy an impediment, if the operation is relatively easy and ordinary, but not if it is truly dangerous. Separation is not urged as long as there is reasonable hope of substantial fulfillment of the marital act; if there is no hope, acts are permissible which do not expose either party to the proximate danger of pollution.

Medical science and civil law are not always in accord with canon law regarding the definition of impotency and the consideration of cases. In almost all the American States impotency is grounds for annulment or divorce (but not double vasectomy). Concealment of sterility is often treated as impotency, but knowledge by the innocent party of the other's defect often precludes judicial action.

### 3. PREVIOUS BOND

One who is bound by the bond of a previous marriage, even though it was not consummated, attempts marriage invalidly. Even though the former marriage is invalid or dissolved for any reasons whatsoever, it is not therefore allowable to contract another marriage before the nullity or dissolution of the previous one has been established in accordance with the law and with certainty.[54]

The freedom of a party from a previously existing bond of marriage, even though it is certainly known to be invalid, must be canonically certified.[55] This applies also to validation. Where the previous spouse is deceased, the death must be proved by authentic document.[56] The testimony of the surviving spouse is of no value. The authentic death certificate (normally from the pastor of the place of burial) should be compared with the certificate of the first marriage to insure that the same party is involved and that there is no prohibited degree of consanguinity. Mere lapse of time and the presumptions of civil law (or of military authorities or an insurance company, etc.) are canonically insufficient proofs, unless other evidence and indications, in the judgment of the local Ordinary, warrant a declaration of freedom.

Whenever it is discovered that a party has at any time possessed marital status, even only civilly, and the death of the previous spouse is not authentically certified, the case must be referred to the local Ordinary, who will proceed according to the norms of law. Petition for a declaration of freedom or decree of nullity should be made according to the forms or procedures required in the diocese, with the collection of baptismal certificates pertaining to the previous marriage, impediments dispensed, divorce decrees, record of convalidation or affidavit of non-convalidation, marriage certificates, affidavits of the three parties in the two marriages. Where the previous bond has been dissolved by papal dispensation, the authentic document to this effect must be obtained, or the certification on the baptismal certificate. A second marriage or convalidation cannot be allowed until there is moral certainty of the absence or the removal of the impediment of ligamen, as well as assurance of the non-convalidation of the union. Investigation of the possible existence of the impediment of crime must always be made and dispensation *ad cautelam* may be necessary.

The impediment of marriage bond may also be present in the case of a common law marriage. From the viewpoint of the Church this type of informal marriage implies that two parties — neither of whom are bound to the canonical form of marriage — have exchanged true marital consent effective of a valid marriage according to the natural law, but without any religious or civil ceremony. Civil law in some State and U.S. jurisdictions recognizes common law marriage as valid, but not in others. When both parties to the union are unbaptized, the validity or invalidity will be regulated by the law of the particular civil jurisdiction. If at least one party is validly baptized (as a non-Catholic), the local Ordinary must decide on the validity of the common law union, regardless of the attitudes of the civil law. A common law marriage of baptized non-Catholics enjoys the presumption of validity. In common law marriage in general the assumption of marital status as indicative of true marital consent is presumed, until proven otherwise, when the parties themselves live as man and wife, are publicly considered as married, perform public acts as a married couple, e.g., joint bank account or income tax return, registration for voting, housing, etc.

If it becomes morally certain during the second marriage that the first spouse is still alive, the second marriage is invalid, but the children are considered legitimate inasmuch as they are born of a putative marriage. A doubt about the death of the first spouse arising after the second marriage must be carefully investigated. Meanwhile the doubting party, being a possessor in bad faith, must refrain from requesting the debt but may render it. If both parties are in doubt, both must abstain. If the existence of the first spouse becomes certain, the parties must separate from bed and also from cohabitation, if the case is public. If the doubt persists after careful investigation, the present partners are considered to be possessors in good faith and thus may continue fully as spouses in a presumed valid marriage, until the second marriage is declared null by an ecclesiastical tribunal because of a positive and insoluble doubt of the validity of the first marriage, or until the existence of the first partner becomes certain.

### 4. DISPARITY OF WORSHIP

#### a. *Impediment*

Marriage between two persons, one of whom is baptized in the Catholic Church or has been received into it and has not left it by means of a formal act, and the other of whom is non-baptized, is invalid.[57]

No baptized person has an unrestricted right to marry an unbaptized party. The divine law itself prohibits (but does not invalidate) such a union when there is any danger of perversion to the spouse or offspring. From this law there is no dispensation. The impediment of ecclesiastical law is diriment, nullifying a marriage, whether the danger of perversion is present or not. Lacking the danger, the impediment is dispensable.

If at the time the marriage was contracted one party was commonly understood to be baptized, or the person's Baptism was doubtful, the validity of the marriage is to be presumed until it is proven with certainty that one party was baptized and the other was not.[58] If the doubt about the Baptism of the non-Catholic party arises before the marriage, it must be resolved and a dispensation requested, at least *ad cautelam*. If the doubt arises after the marriage, the marriage is presumed to be valid until the contrary can be proven with certainty and a validation requested. A doubtfully baptized Catholic should be rebaptized conditionally.

### b. *Those bound by the impediment*

One of the parties must be unbaptized. The other party must be baptized in the Catholic Church. Thus, the impediment is drawn in the present law in a restricted sense. It binds only those Baptism (or conversion) binds or aggregates to the external communion of the Catholic Church, as acknowledged members of the Catholic Church. This is determined in an adult Baptism by his own intention, in an infant Baptism by the intention of the parents or guardians or the minister in lieu of either (a Catholic baptizes an infant in danger of death in the Catholic Church, even against the wishes of the parents). Thus, the impediment does not bind validly baptized Protestants who remain unconverted to the Catholic Church when marrying the unbaptized. On the other hand, non-Catholic or separated (Orthodox) Orientals are bound by this impediment.[59] Likewise bound were those who were born of non-Catholic parents but baptized in the Catholic Church and raised outside the Church, although they formerly were not bound by the canonical form of marriage, unless they were baptized unlawfully.[60]

Catholics who do not practice their faith but still consider themselves at least nominal Catholics and not anything else are bound by the impediment. They are not bound who have left the Church by a formal act of separation, that is a formal act of embracing another sect or an anti-Catholic organization, abjuring the faith, or some other clear practice or action providing basis for judging that membership in the Catholic Church has been abandoned.

### c. *Conditions for dispensation*

The requirements of just and serious reasons for seeking a dispensation, the obtaining of the declarations and sincere promises or guarantees, and the prohibition of any other marriage ceremony, must be strictly observed, as in the case of mixed marriages, for the validity of the dispensation.[61]

### 5. SACRED ORDERS

Those who are in sacred orders invalidly attempt marriage.[62] Sacred Orders in the Latin Church are episcopacy, priesthood, and diaconate.[63] The impediment is of ecclesiastical origin. The ordination must be free and valid; ignorance, force and fear would be difficult to prove juridically today because of the oath taken before the diaconate.[64]

Single men in receiving the diaconate are obliged to perpetual celibacy and married men who receive the permanent diaconate, in the event they are widowed or receive an ecclesiastical annulment, may not validly marry again.[65]

Laicization does not necessarily bring with it a dispensation from celibacy, which must be distinctly granted. When a process has declared that sacred orders have been invalidly received, the impediment ceases to exist.[66]

### 6. PUBLIC PERPETUAL VOW OF CHASTITY

Those who are bound by a public perpetual vow of chastity in a religious institute invalidly attempt marriage.[67] An indult to leave the institute, lawfully granted and notified to the member, brings with it a dispensation from the vow. In an institute of pontifical right, that is, one approved by the Apostolic See, this indult is reserved to the latter. In an institute of diocesan right, that is, one approved by the diocesan bishop, this indult is reserved to the latter. However, if the member is a cleric, the indult is not granted until he has found a bishop who will incardinate him or at least receive him there on probation. By lawful dismissal from a religious institute, which must be confirmed by the Apostolic See, the vow ceases.[68]

### 7. ABDUCTION

No marriage can exist between a man and a woman who has been abducted, or at least detained, with a view to contracting a marriage with her, unless the woman, after she has been separated from her abductor and established in a safe and free place, chooses marriage of her own accord.[69]

For the impediment to be present it must be a woman who is abducted or kidnapped; the man purposing to marry her must abduct her himself or through an agent acting under his orders; the abduction must be precisely for the purpose of marriage; the abductor must remove the woman from one place to another which is morally distinct, even though close by; the abductor must use violence, either physical force or threats or fraud and deceit; the woman must not have consented to the abduction or at least to its purpose of marriage; the woman must be under the power of the abductor in the place where she is taken. For the impediment to be present in the case of violent retention (*sequestratio*) of the woman all the above conditions must be verified, with the exception of removal to another place. The impediment binds only the baptized, and it suffices that one party is baptized.

The above conditions establish the matrimonial *impediment* of abduction. This latter is of wider scope, including the kidnapping of a woman for lustful purposes and the elopement with or seduction of a girl who is still a minor and who consents to her removal unknown to or against the will of her parents or guardians. Abduction or kidnapping is also a crime in civil law but not an impediment to marriage.

## 8. CRIME

A person who for the purpose of entering marriage with a certain person has brought about the death of that person's spouse or one's own spouse, invalidly attempts such a marriage. They also invalidly attempt marriage between themselves who have brought about the death of the spouse of one of them by mutual physical or moral action.[70]

The impediment is based upon an actual murder, direct or indirect, and an intention to marry on the part of at least one party, even if the conjugicide is committed against the will of the other. The impediment is present if there is a conspiracy to bring about, or cooperation in, a conjugicide. Even in an occult case, outside of danger of death, the pastor or attending priest should be most prudent in arranging for a dispensation, because of possible future scandal and the reliability of the guilty party or parties in approaching properly a new marriage. Conjugicide has been a diriment impediment of civil law only in Puerto Rico.

## 9. CONSANGUINITY

### a. *Notion*

Consanguinity (*cum sanguine unitas*) or blood relationship is a natural moral bond or relation between persons which is based on carnal generation (legitimate or illegitimate, full-blood or half-blood) and which unites them in blood. Consanguinity exists in the *direct* line if one of the persons is the direct ancestor or progenitor of the other, in the *collateral* or indirect and oblique line if neither person is the direct ancestor of the other but both are descended from a common ancestor or progenitor.

An ancestor in blood relationship is the person — male or female — from whom as from a common stock (*stipes*) or root (*stirpes*) two or more persons descend through carnal generation. A *line* (*linea*) is the series of persons who spring from the common ancestor, either directly or collaterally. The direct line is ascending if the order of the blood relatives is counted back to the common ancestor, e.g., son to father to grandfather; it is descending if the reverse order of compilation is used, e.g., father to son to grandson. When both parents in the common stock are the same progenitors there is only one line; when only one parent is common — in half-blood relationship — each parent must be considered separately in computing lines of relationship, when the respective descendants wish to intermarry.

A *degree* (*gradus*) is the measure of distance between blood relatives and their common ancestor. Degrees are computed in the *direct* line according to the number of persons in the line without counting the common ancestor. In the *collateral* line they are computed according to the number of generations in each branch or according to the number of persons in each line without counting the common ancestor.

In ecclesiastical law consanguinity is reckoned by lines and degrees. In the direct line there are as many degrees as there are generations, that is, as there are persons, not counting the common ancestor. In the collateral line there are as many degrees as there are persons in both lines together, not counting the common ancestor.[71]

It is necessary in *interritual* marriages to know also the impediment as it binds the Oriental party.[72] In the direct line marriage is invalid between all ancestors and descendants, legitimate or not. In the collateral line it is invalid up to the sixth degree inclusively, but the impediment is multiplied as the common ancestor is multiplied. Marriage is never to be permitted while there exists any doubt of blood relationship in any degree of the direct line or in the second degree of the collateral line. In the direct line the degrees are computed according to the number of persons in the line without counting the common ancestor. In the collateral line there are as many degrees as there are persons in *both* branches without counting the common ancestor.

It should be noted that the terms denoting blood relationships in common language usage and in civil law do not always correspond with the canonical terminology respecting the same degrees of relationship. Care should be taken to be aware of civil laws respecting consanguineous marriages.

### b. *Impediment*

Marriage is invalid between those related by consanguinity in *all degrees* of the *direct* line, whether ascending or descending, legitimate or natural. In the *collateral* line, it is invalid up to the *fourth degree* inclusive. The impediment of consanguinity is not multiplied.[73]

### Collateral relationships

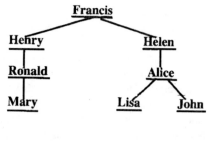

| Henry | - | Helen | 2nd degree |
|-------|---|-------|------------|
| Ronald | - | Alice | 4th degree |
| Ronald | - | Helen | 3rd degree |
| Mary | - | John | 6th degree |
| Ronald | - | Lisa | 5th degree |

### c. *Dispensation*

Consanguinity is an impediment of the divine and natural law certainly to the first degree in the direct line and probably to other degrees, in the collateral line probably to the second degree. The unbaptized are bound by the divine and natural law and by just civil law. Ecclesiastical law states that a marriage is never to be permitted if a doubt exists as to whether the parties are related by consanguinity in any degree of the direct line, or in the second degree of the collateral line.[74] Thus even in a case of doubt the Church, because of the consequences, does not dispense. Blood relationship is a permanent fact and may be dispensed for proportionate reasons only within the forbidden degrees of ecclesiastical origin. It is recommended that a genealogical tree accompany every petition for dispensation. A clear statement of the existing relationship which is an impediment to marriage should be made.

### 10. AFFINITY

### a. *Notion of in-law-ship*

Affinity of in-law-ship is a relationship arising from a *valid* marriage between two persons whereby each party is related to the blood relatives of the other. It is natural *fact* and thus is contracted by the valid marriage of the unbaptized, although it becomes an *impediment* only for the baptized. Affinity arises from a valid marriage, whether ratified only or ratified and consummated, which must now be understood to refer not only to a sacramental union but also to any valid marriage, whether consummated or not; this natural relationship only becomes also an impediment where at least one party is baptized or becomes baptized. Thus the natural foundation or fact of affinity may be placed before or after the reception of Baptism, but the new marriage to which it is an impediment must take place after the Baptism of at least one of the parties.

Affinity is computed in such wise that the blood (even half-blood) relatives of the husband are related by affinity to the wife in the same line and degree as they are related by consanguinity to him, and vice versa. By this reckoning a man is related in the direct line to his mother-in-law, grandmother-in-law, etc., and to his step-daughter, step-grand-daughter (i.e., any children of his wife by a previous marriage), and to his daughter-in-law and grand-daughter-in-law, step-parent or step-grand-parent. In the collateral line he is related to the wives of his brothers, uncles, grand-uncles or great-uncles, nephews and grand-nephews, cousins, and to similar collateral relatives of his own wife.

### b. *Impediment*

Affinity in any degree of the direct line invalidates marriage.[75] Collateral line degrees are no longer forbidden. The purpose of the impediment is to lessen a danger to chastity, to foster mutual reverence among in-laws, and to embrace others in a wider range of charity and friendship through marriage. It, moreover, does not prohibit marriage between the blood relatives of one spouse and those of the other.

For Orientals the common law of affinity places an impediment arising from a valid marriage, whether consummated or not, in all degrees of the direct line and to the fourth degree inclusively of the collateral line. The Oriental computation is followed. The Oriental Code also sanctions two particular laws regarding affinity where they are operative, namely, an impediment of affinity existing between the blood relatives of one spouse and the blood relatives of the other spouse to the fourth degree inclusively (computed by totaling together the degrees of consanguinity on each side); likewise, when two persons successively are married to the same third person and when two persons are successively married to two persons who were blood relatives, to the first degree (unmultiplied).

### c. *Dispensation*

Affinity is an impediment of ecclesiastical law. It is permanent and ceases only by dispensation. Civil laws vary in the degree in which affinity is established as an impediment to marriage, with consequent penalties for incest.

11. PUBLIC PROPRIETY

a. *Impediment*

The impediment of public propriety or public decency (*honestas publica*) arises when a couple live together after an invalid marriage, or from a notorious or public concubinage. It invalidates marriage in the first degree of the direct line between the man and those related by consanguinity to the woman, and vice versa.[76]

One foundation for the impediment is an invalid marriage, due to lack of true consent, to defect of form, or to the presence of a diriment impediment, but with cohabitation. It makes no difference whether consummation took place or whether the union was entered into in good or bad faith (thus a putative marriage incurs the impediment), as long as there is at least an appearance of marriage, an apparent contract. When at least one party is bound by the canonical form of marriage, an attempt at a purely civil marriage, when there is no cohabitation, has not even the appearance of marriage, and consequently does not incur the impediment. Usually public or notorious concubinage accompanies this civil act (or a marriage attempted before a non-Catholic minister), and thus the impediment is incurred.[77]

Concubinage is a *modus vivendi* or relationship between a man and a woman which has a certain semblance of marital life. The parties cohabit as man and wife in sexual intercourse, without necessarily dwelling in the same abode or without necessarily involving financial arrangements, and even though the woman is already married. There must be a certain unity and continuance or permanence in the carnal relations of the man and the same woman, so that a condition of acceptance of the state of relationship exists or an understanding perdures between them to live in an apparently marital fashion. This stability or understanding is thus lacking in the approach to a prostitute or in the frequency of fornication, even with the same woman.

b. *Dispensation*

The degree of relationship is computed in the same way as for consanguinity, but only in the direct line. Being of ecclesiastical law only, this impediment does not bind the unbaptized marrying among themselves. Becoming baptized and remaining in the conditions of the impediment, it begins to bind. The impediment is permanent and thus can be removed only by dispensation.

## 12. LEGAL RELATIONSHIP

Those who are legally related by reason of adoption cannot validly marry each other if their relationship is in the direct line or in the second degree of the collateral line.[78]

There must be a true legal relationship to establish this impediment, whatever other relationship may exist. Ecclesiastical legislation depends on civil law to determine what constitutes or establishes an adoptive relationship. Civil law should be consulted to ascertain if it is also an impediment in civil law. The impediment, which is computed as with consanguinity, does not bind non-Catholics.

## V. MATRIMONIAL CONSENT

### 1. CAPACITY

A marriage is brought into being by the lawfully manifested consent of persons who are legally capable. This consent cannot be supplied by any human power. Matrimonial consent is an act of will by which a man and a woman by an irrevocable covenant mutually give and accept one another for the purpose of establishing a marriage.[79]

The consent must be genuine, true and sincere, an internal act of the will and not falsified or merely theatrical or jocose. If in no way it is expressed explicitly or implicitly, the contract is null. Internal consent is always presumed to be in conformity with the words or signs used in the contracting of marriage. A spouse who falsely gives consent sins seriously against truth, justice, and chastity, and is forbidden the use of marital rights. The innocent spouse may seek or render the debt, since the deception need not be believed until proven in the external forum.

There must be a reciprocal consent and not a unilateral donation and acceptance of rights and obligations; nor does it depend upon the approval of a third party, e.g., parents.

The expression of consent must be made by one capable of a perfectly human act, with the independence required by natural and ecclesiastical law, e.g., as in the case of child marriage in mission areas.

Deliberate consent is required in undertaking such serious obligations, i.e., with full knowledge and will. By the natural law there must be at least a moral simultaneity of mutual consent, so that the consent of one perdures when the other consents, both being present.

The contract must be consented to here and now. A promise of future contract is not marriage but espousals or betrothal (*sponsalia*).

Matrimony as a human contract must be expressed by some human sensible sign; as a sacrament it requires that there be a sensible sign. The spouses are to express their matrimonial consent in words; and if they can speak, it is not lawful for them to employ equivalent signs. Thus the baptized, even non-Catholics, if they can speak, are bound to express their consent in words for lawfulness; for validity it must be expressed in the juridical form by those so bound. Also for validity it is necessary that the parties be present to each other in person or by proxy. This binds baptized non-Catholics as well. Thus consent given by letter, messenger, radio, telephone, telegraph, etc., is invalid for them. The unbaptized are not bound by any specific formalities in the expression or exchange of their consent. It suffices that they abide by what conforms to the natural law and by what is required for validity by the civil law or the estimation of the region.

Ecclesiastical law requires that, for contracting a valid marriage, the parties in giving consent must have:

### a. *Sufficient use of reason*[80]

Those who do not have the use of reason to a sufficient degree to give proper marital consent are incapable. The deficiency, especially if it is temporary, must have existed at the time of the canonical celebration of marriage.

By the natural law all those who are incapable of the use of reason cannot validly enter a matrimonial contract as long as they remain in that state, e.g., infants, the insane, those totally under the influence of intoxicants or drugs, those asleep, etc. The demented or partially insane, i.e., affecting certain matters, may contract marriage but not validly if the matters affected concern the substance of matrimony. Prudence often indicates that such weak-minded parties should be discouraged from marriage at all, also deaf-mutes, unless it is prudently judged they can properly fulfill their marital obligations. In attacking a marriage bond the marriage must be considered valid until the want of reason is proved to have existed at the time the contract was made. Civil law regarding insanity antecedent and subsequent to marriage should be consulted.

### b. *Discretionary judgment*[81]

There must be sufficient discretion of judgment concerning the essential rights and obligations to be mutually given and accepted in the marital covenant. The judgment must not be seriously faulted through lack of information or understanding. There should be the ability to evaluate what is involved in a life commitment of interpersonal relationship, which ability is sufficient to sustain the consequences of the decision to be made in the light of oneself and of one's partner. The lack of due discretion may result from many factors, especially personality disorder.

### c. *Psychological capability*[82]

They are incapable of contracting marriage who, because of causes of a psychological nature, are unable to assume the essential obligations of marriage, mutual help and the procreation of children. The incapacity must be present before marriage. Many afflictions affecting the personality may be of such gravity as to impede the person from assuming a marital interpersonal relationship and its consequences.

### 2. KNOWLEDGE FOR CONSENT

For matrimonial consent to be present it is necessary that the contracting parties be at least not ignorant of the fact that marriage is a permanent partnership between a man and a woman, ordered to the procreation of children through some form of sexual cooperation. This ignorance is not presumed after puberty.[83]

A party invalidly assumes a marital covenant who does not know that marriage is a permanent and self-sacrificing community of life ordered to the good of the spouses and the procreation and education of children. However, a general or vague or implicit knowledge of this necessary bodily cooperation suffices for valid consent. It is more commonly held that, because of the very serious obligations assumed, the matrimonial contract requires greater discretion of judgment than that necessary to commit a serious sin.

Knowledge of the particular manner of procreation or the exact technique of intercourse is not necessary for valid consent; it is sufficient to intend to enter marriage as it is in itself and as practiced by all men and women thus implicitly and deliberately willing all that is connected with marriage. It is not any subsequent and more exact knowledge — even that which, if known at the time of the marriage, would have deterred it — which invalidates, i.e., not the consent which would not have been given but that which actually was given. A false idea about the union of the bodies in marriage, e.g., that it means only kisses, may be a substantial error invalidating the consent.

Knowledge that marriage is a permanent state does not mean a knowledge that it is indissoluble, or an approval of its perpetuity and indissolubility, but rather that it is not a transient or, as it were, a momentary or experimental association (trial marriage), a mere friendly arrangement or sex outlet. It suffices that the parties do not positively exclude the essential properties of marriage, and, since they are inseparable, they are implicitly consented to.

### 3. ERROR

Error about a person renders a marriage invalid.[84] Error is a false judgment, which is substantial in marriage if it affects the very nature or object of the contract, and accidental if it does not. As with ignorance, error which is substantial invalidates marriage, but such an error is not presumed after the age of puberty. Since the will bears upon the object as known, error in the intellect always influences the will, but not every kind of error renders the consent null and invalid.

An error or mistake of *fact* will be about the person with whom the marriage contract is made or about a quality of that person. To be in error about the very identity of the person with whom one contracts marriage is substantial and invalidates the contract by the natural law itself, i.e., to judge that one is marrying the very party intended, whereas it is someone else.

Error about a quality of the person, even though it be the reason for the marriage to come into being in the first place, does not render a marriage invalid unless this quality is directly and principally intended.[85] To be mistaken or in error about some quality of the person with whom marriage is contracted is accidental, e.g., that the person is rich, or healthy, or a virgin, or has a different name, etc., and does not of itself invalidate marriage either by natural law or by positive law of the Church, even though the contract is based on it.[86] Notwithstanding error about the accidental qualities, the substance of the contract remains — consent to contract with the person of the other contracting party. However, error of quality will invalidate if the error as to quality amounts to an error of person. This is most rare, unless in those areas where marriages are arranged with the parties never previously known to or seen by each other or in proxy marriages. Thus the quality must be one that identifies or is most proper and individual to a definite person, e.g., the *first-born* daughter. Similarly, if this accidental quality or characteristic is the necessary condition (*sine qua non*) of the marital consent or at least is implicitly demonstrable from the circumstances, the marriage is invalid, e.g., consent is given *only* on the supposition of condition of the presence of virginity.

Provided it does not determine the will, error concerning the unity or dissolubility or the sacramental dignity of marriage does not vitiate matrimonial consent.[87]

An error of *law* concerns the natural or essential object or properties or sacramental character of the matrimonial covenant, as in the case of ignorance. Thus, a simple error, that is, one that does not determine or move the will, regarding any of the above, even though the motivating reasons for entering into the marriage, does not invalidate matrimonial consent.

A simple error is one which remains in the intellect without a positive act following in conformity with it. Thus, as the essence of matrimony has inseparably attached to it its essential properties, in consenting to marriage as it is in itself, consent is thereby also given to its properties of unity and indissolubility. To know a thing with all its properties and to will a thing differ; one can simply will a thing as it is in itself and not know very well its properties or be mistaken about them. Thus an error about the essential qualities of marriage does not necessarily invalidate it. The general intention to contract marriage as instituted by God prevails over the error. Although many today consider marriage to be dissoluble and not sacramental, e.g., Protestants, Jews, unbaptized, yet they normally will to contract marriage as it is. They probably would positively exclude these properties if they were later *questioned* about them, but they *did not* actually exclude them at the time the consent was given.

If either party or both parties by a *positive* act of the will should exclude marriage itself, or all right to the conjugal act, or any essential property of marriage, he contracts invalidly.[88] This is of the natural law. Thus the error is no longer simple, if it so influences the act of the will that this positive exclusion is made in the matrimonial consent. Such a positive exclusion may be *explicit*, e.g., an agreement made to experiment with the marriage for a while and to break up by divorce if it turns out unhappily, or *implicit*, e.g., while intending to contract a true and proper marriage, one is at the same time deliberately disposed to terminate the contract by divorce in the future, should some special circumstance be verified, such as infidelity of the other party. Nevertheless, every marriage must be held to be valid in the external forum until the contrary can be proved. No general rule of invalidity can be applied, but each individual case must be examined on its own merits, even in mission areas where polygamy and divorce are prevalent. Civil law on fraudulent representation in a marriage contract should be consulted.

### 4. KNOWLEDGE WITH CONSENT

Knowledge of or opinion about the nullity of a marriage does not necessarily exclude matrimonial consent.[89] The knowledge of or probable suspicion of the existence of an invalidating impediment or of the absence of the required formalities does not necessarily exclude matrimonial consent. This is with reference to consent as naturally valid, not as juridically efficacious. If the parties intend to contract marriage insofar as they can or as it depends on their will, consent is valid, although inefficacious. Such consent is presumed to endure until it is proved that it was recalled. This is important for cases involving radical sanation. Each case is to be judged by itself.

The internal consent of the mind is presumed to conform to the words or the signs used in the celebration of marriage. If, however, either or both of the parties should by a positive act of will exclude marriage itself or any essential element of marriage or any essential property, such party contracts invalidly.[90] Simulation of consent is difficult to prove. Only by way of presumptions from words and signs can it be ascertained whether or not evidence is sufficient to judge that the original consent was invalid.

Simulated or feigned consent is present in marriage when, although exteriorly the words expressing matrimonial consent are duly and seriously pronounced, one or both parties withhold internal consent. The intention of the pretender may be not to contract marriage, or to contract it but not to assume its obligation, or not to fulfill its obligation. An intention not to contract marriage excludes consent and nullifies the contract. Likewise, the intention not to assume the obligations of marriage, since without it there cannot be true matrimonial consent. The intention not to fulfill the matrimonial obligations does not invalidate consent, as this does not pertain to the essence of the contract. The intention to *violate* an obligation can exist with the intention to assume the obligation itself.

To feign consent is certainly a serious sin; it is a violation of truth, justice, chastity (if intercourse is intended) and perhaps religion by simulation in the case of the sacrament (although this is not agreed upon). The guilty party is bound to repair the injustice done, even by giving true consent, if this is the only way and it can be done without serious inconvenience. Lack of internal consent is clearly difficult to prove. Civil law in the U.S.A. does not generally admit it as a grounds for nullity.

## 5. DECEPTION BY FRAUD

A person who enters into marriage deceived through a fraud, perpetrated in order to obtain consent, concerning a quality of the other party, which quality of its very nature can seriously disturb the partnership of conjugal life, contracts invalidly.[91]

The deception about the presence or absence of an important quality about himself or herself causes an error on the part of the other party who is deceived and initiates the breakdown and end of the marriage. The capacity to disrupt the partnership seriously is enough to invalidate the marriage. The partnership includes at least reasonably harmonious relationship and mutual give and take assistance. The burden of proof is on the victim.

## 6. CONDITION

Marriage conditioned on a future event cannot be validly contracted. Marriage conditioned on a past or present event is valid or not as the event covered by the condition exists or not; however, such a condition cannot be lawfully imposed unless the Ordinary of the place granted permission in writing.[92]

A condition is a circumstance in marriage upon which one makes his consent depend, so that the consent (if not revoked) takes its effect as the circumstance is verified or not. Thus the contract is consented to *only if* or *when* the condition placed is fulfilled (a *sine qua non*). A condition must thus be distinguished from a mode (*modus*) or prenuptial agreement or stipulation to do or to omit something *after* marriage is validly contracted and realized, e.g., to move to another State, which neither affects the validity of the marriage nor rests the consent on it. Of itself a condition need not be expressed, but a merely internal condition is seldom easy to prove to have existed; it may relate to the past, the present, or the future. The use of a marital right is prohibited until the condition is clearly verified and the marriage is in possession.

If the condition is base and against the substance or properties of marriage, i.e., an intention *not to assume* the obligations, it is destructive of true marital consent and nullifies the contract, since a right to an essential element is not given but rather excluded. Whether the right itself or only the fulfillment of a right is withheld in certain conditions is difficult to ascertain. In the internal forum it depends upon the actual intention of the one placing the condition, in the external forum upon the proof that can be reached with moral certainty from indications and circumstances. Each case must be examined to ascertain whether an excluding condition or merely a stipulation (mode) or agreement was made; the latter is generally presumed until the former is proved and thus the marriage is considered to exist.

Matrimonial consent is valid only when the intention predominates to transfer (and not positively to exclude) the perpetual and exclusive and continual right to natural intercourse. A condition designed to exclude this transference perpetually or for a certain time or after a certain time (e.g., periodic continence or the non-use except on infertile days or the right only to onanistic relations) is contrary to the substance of marriage, vitiates the consent, and invalidates the contract (*contra bonum prolis*).[93] If this right is transferred and the condition implies only the intention to abuse this transferred right, the contract is valid, as the sinful condition is not contrary to the substance of marriage.

If a restriction made on marital intercourse is absolute, without any limit of time, i.e., the marital right and obligation would be perpetually abused, the *presumption* (in the external forum) is that the right itself, i.e., the order to the object of the contract, is excluded and thus no true marital consent and valid contract exists. This is especially true if a pact has been made acceding to this condition. If the condition is not absolute but limited to a certain time when this marital abuse is intended, the *presumption* is that true (although sinful) consent has been given and the marriage is presumed valid. This latter presumption considers that the right to the use was given but the fulfillment restricted. If the restriction is one of perpetual non-use (and not abuse), this is also against the substance of marriage if it implies that the conjugal right is not exchanged. However, such a condition of non-use is less clearly a vitiation of marital consent as is the condition of abuse. It is, moreover, not authoritatively determined nor generally agreed upon whether a condition of perpetual non-use or abstinence is in itself opposed to the substance of marriage. The condition may not be permitted, but a marriage so contracted must be *presumed* in practice to be valid.

A condition against the requisite fidelity or unity of marriage (*contra bonum fidei*) e.g., if you will commit adultery, invalidates the contract, if the intention is to exclude it and not merely not to observe it. A restriction of essential indissolubility (*contra bonum sacramenti*) e.g., only until I find someone more suitable, even though an implicit and hypothetical exclusion, always invalidates, as there can be no distinction between the intention to assume and to fulfill the property of indissolubility.

It is the more common view that a condition which is contrary to the Catholic upbringing of offspring is not one that is opposed to the substance of marriage, although it is sinful and unlawful. Moreover, although in a non-Catholic marriage ceremony or formula a condition contrary to essential indissolubility may be present and thus invalidate it, the marriage itself must not be presumed invalid until an investigation of the individual case proves that the consent itself was vitiated.

Conditions affecting matrimonial consent which are not forbidden may be lawfully placed for a serious cause and with the written permission of the local Ordinary. However, such conditions are discouraged, since the very intention to place a condition may be a sign of lack of commitment, and when allowed should be made before witnesses and recorded in the marriage register (as well as the fulfillment). Civil law in the U.S.A. does not recognize the effect of these conditions.

### 7. FORCE OR FEAR

A marriage is invalid which is entered into out of grave force or fear inflicted externally, even if not intentionally imposed, from which the person has no escape other than by choosing marriage.[94]

Force and fear militate against the free consent of the parties and true marital commitment. The gravity of the force or fear induces the marriage as the lesser evil, as inescapable, even if the one inducing the grave duress had no intention to intimidate or compel. The fear must be inflicted by an external agent and not spring from mere internal anxiety not related to any external cause, in which latter case the consent may not be free due to some grave personality disorder.

Fear is absolutely grave, such as a brave man or one not easily intimidated might experience, e.g., death, exile, loss of all goods, etc.; relatively grave, inasmuch as it is grave for some people and not for others, e.g., because of age or temperament or health or intelligence or other circumstances. Reverential fear is the trepidation of the evil consequences impending as a result of offending a parent or superior. It is not of itself grave, but it may become so from contributing circumstances.

Where there is physical violence or duress forcing an external compliance with the will of the one exercising such pressure, the consent thus manifested is null by natural law as excluding a voluntary act, e.g., forcing a reluctant victim to nod his head or making his hand inscribe his signature. Also by the natural law a fear which is so intense that it removes the control of reason invalidates matrimonial consent. Whether in other cases the impediment of force or fear arises from the natural law, no authoritative declaration has been given, but in practice the Church does not dispense in what is even probably of divine law. It binds certainly a baptized non-Catholic and probably also the unbaptized marrying among themselves, certainly if the civil law declares marriage contracted in fear to be null.[95]

The fear or pressure brought to bear from without may be unjust itself, e.g., threat of an unjust penalty such as to take life or unjustifiably ruin a good name, or unjustly brought to bear, e.g., a just penalty to be inflicted in an unjust manner such as to expel one's relative from one's home unless she marries a certain man. Moreover, one is said to be forced to enter marriage when there appears to be no other alternative to ridding oneself of the fear.[96] The unjust pressure must actually exist at the time of the celebration of the marriage.[97] The party forcing the marriage is bound to repair the unjust damage, and if he is party to the forced marriage and if there is no other means of reparation, he is bound to enter or to convalidate the marriage, if the innocent party or victim so desires.

### 8. PRESENCE

#### a. *In person*

To contract marriage validly it is necessary that the contracting parties be present together, either personally or by proxy. They are to express their consent in words or, if they cannot speak, by equivalent signs.[98] The parties must be present to each other, in person or by proxy, in order to give and to exchange consent in the one ceremony.

#### b. *By proxy*

For a valid proxy marriage it is required that there be a special mandate to contract with a specific person, and that the proxy be designated by the mandator and personally discharge this function. For the mandate itself to be valid (and therefore the marriage), it is to be signed by the mandator, and also by the parish priest or local Ordinary of the place in which the mandate is given or by a priest delegated by either of them or at least by two witnesses, or it is to be drawn up in a document which is authentic according to civil law.[99]

Marriage in which marital consent is exchanged by proxy is permitted when one or both spouses cannot be present to one another, usually when there is urgent need without delay. The proxies may be of either sex. Civil law acceptance of the use of a proxy must be first considered; local and state laws and regulations should be known and observed. The spouses may at a later time receive the nuptial blessing.

### 9. PERDURANCE OF CONSENT

Even if marriage has been entered into invalidly by reason of an impediment or defect of form, the consent given is presumed to persist until its withdrawal has been established.[100] This norm gives the basis for a possible retroactive validation of a marriage on the strength of the consent without necessarily observing once more the external legal requirements.

## VI. THE FORM OF THE CELEBRATION OF MARRIAGE

The natural law requires for validity of the contract no special conditions of the form of entering into the contract or formalities but only that the ministers — the contracting parties themselves — externally manifest deliberate and mutual consent in some way. Divine law likewise has laid down no particular solemnities. Positive civil law is competent to make determinations or validating requirements concerning contracts for the sake of public good and order. This power can be exercised also regarding the matrimonial contract between two unbaptized parties. But, since the marriage of two baptized parties (a sacrament), and where even only one party is baptized, is subject to the competence of the Church, the positive ecclesiastical law can and does lay down certain conditions, formalities or solemnities, which must be observed by those wishing to enter a marital union. This is the canonical or juridical form (or formality) of marriage, rendering the contract juridically public or celebrated in the sight of the Church. Solemnities are substantial when required for validity, accidental when prescribed for lawfulness (to which the liturgical form of marriage pertains).

The first decree *"Tametsi"* establishing a juridical form of marriage was issued by the Council of Trent in 1583, prescribing the presence of the pastor of the parties and witnesses. The form was again regulated by the universal decree of Pius X *"Ne temere"* promulgated in 1908 requiring the presence of the pastor of the place where the marriage was celebrated and witnesses. With minor changes this became also the form prescribed by the 1917 Code and continued in the 1983 Code.

### 1. ORDINARY CANONICAL FORM

Only those marriages are valid which are contracted in the presence of the local Ordinary or the pastor or a priest or deacon delegated by either of them, who assist, and in the presence of two witnesses, according to the pertinent canonical norms. Only that person who, being present, asks the contracting parties to manifest their consent and in the name of the Church receives it, is understood to assist at a marriage.[101]

2. OFFICIAL WITNESS

The official witness is the Ordinary, pastor, or delegated priest or deacon.[102] He must ask for and receive the consent of both parties, such as is provided in the ritual of marriage.

### a. *Territorial*

Within the limits of their territory the local Ordinary and the pastor by virtue of their office validly assist at the marriages not only of their subjects, but also of non-subjects, provided one or other of the parties is of the Latin rite. They cannot assist if by sentence or decree they have been excommunicated, placed under interdict, or suspended from office, or declared to be such.[103] Those who in law are equivalent to a local Ordinary or pastor have the same jurisdiction.

A parochial vicar or assistant priest does not enjoy ordinary power to assist validly at a marriage. Rectors of churches, the rector of a seminary, and chaplains lack power to assist, unless endowed with full parochial power.[104]

A pastor validly assists at marriage only and exclusively in his own territory and not only of his own subjects but also of others. He may not validly witness the marriage of his own subjects outside his own territory without delegation of the pastor of that place. For validity he must ask and receive the consent of the contracting parties without being coerced to do so by force or grave fear, induced either by the contractants or by a third party even without their knowledge.

At least one of the contractants must be of the Latin rite. The pastor may assist at the marriage of two Oriental Catholics or of one Oriental Catholic and a non-Catholic only if the Oriental party has no proper hierarch or pastor and is thus subject to the Latin Ordinary. Otherwise, the pastor needs delegation from the competent Oriental authority.

### b. *Personal*

A personal Ordinary and a personal pastor by virtue of their office validly assist, within the confines of their jurisdiction, at the marriages of only those of whom at least one party is their subject.[105]

Personal parishes are established, where it is useful, on the basis of the rite, language or nationality of the faithful of a certain territory, or on some other basis.[106] Their limits may also be geographical if there is more than one such parish set up for the same purpose. Chaplains of certain groups may fall into this category. U.S. Military Vicariate chaplains validly and lawfully assist at marriages of their (personal) subjects anywhere, which power they share cumulatively with the pastor and local Ordinary of the place of celebration.

### c. *For a Rite*

The marriage of Catholics of different rites is normally celebrated in the rite of the groom and before the pastor of the rite.[107] The local Ordinary (Latin or Eastern, as the case may be) may dispense.[108]

The Holy See grants the dispensation in the following cases: (1) marriage in the Latin rite of an Eastern Catholic with a non-Catholic; (2) marriage in an Eastern rite of a Latin Catholic with a non-Catholic; (3) marriage in an Eastern rite of two Latin Catholics; (4) marriage in the Latin rite of two Eastern Catholics; (5) marriage of two Catholics of a different rite in a third rite.[109]

The Apostolic Nunciature has special faculties to grant such permission. This, however, pertains only to the lawfulness of the ceremony. For validity the witnessing priest must have proper delegation and have secured the necessary dispensations.[110] Where there is no Ordinary of a particular Eastern rite, the Latin Ordinary is the proper Ordinary.[111] Where there is an Eastern rite jurisdiction: Byzantine-Ruthenian, Byzantine-Ukrainian, Byzantine-Romanian, Melkite, Maronite, Chaldean, Armenian, the Eastern rite pastor or hierarch should be approached. The priest lawfully assisting at such marriages must in each case follow his own liturgical rite.[112]

### d. *Delegated*

Those who have the power to assist at marriage because of the office they hold, and as long as they hold the office, can delegate to priests and deacons the faculty, even the general faculty, to assist at marriages within the confines of their territory. For validity this delegation must be given to specific persons; if there is question of a special delegation, it is to be given for a specific marriage (and need not be given in writing, although the fact must be noted in the marriage register); if however there is question of a general delegation, it is to be given in writing.[113]

It is the common opinion, to be followed in practice, that the one delegated must be aware of his delegation and at least tacitly accept it; thus one should not assist at a marriage unless he has a morally certain presumption that delegation has been granted him.

The permission or delegation to assist at marriage must be expressly given to a definite priest or deacon for a definite marriage. Tacit or presumed permission does not suffice for valid marriage delegation. It must be expressed, either explicitly or implicitly, directly or indirectly conceded, made orally or in writing.

It is explicit when it is given clearly in so many words; implicit when contained in another act, e.g., in the appointment as administrator of a parish. The delegation need not be made personally but may be transmitted to the delegated priest through a third party. It is more desirable that the delegation be given in writing but it may be given orally and even by telephone, telegraph or radiogram.

Delegation must be granted to a specific priest or deacon who is designated by name or by office, e.g., the present chaplain of such-and-such convent. The permission thus must be so granted that it clearly designates who the individual priest or deacon is; otherwise it is invalid. Delegation may not be given to the priest or deacon who will later be designated by the nupturients or by a religious superior. Several may be delegated for the same marriage, as long as it is clear that definite individuals are designated, e.g., in a case where it is not certain that a certain priest or priests will be free to perform the marriage on the date set. The one delegated need not be known by the delegator, but a substantial error by the latter as to the identity of the one delegated renders the permission invalid.

A specific marriage must be the object of the delegation. The marriage to be performed must be designated by the names of the parties or their office or in some way to individualize or identify the couple to be married for which delegation is given. Delegation can be given for the marriages on an itemized list but not merely for the time and place of a marriage without further identification. It should be kept in mind that a temporary supply priest (e.g., weekend, few weeks, summer), needs specific delegation for specific marriages, since he usually enjoys not even the status of a parochial vicar. A substantial error in the designation of the parties to be married invalidates the delegation.

Those who have general delegation may subdelegate another priest or deacon to witness the marriage for which they have delegated authority, but only to a specific priest or deacon and for a specific marriage. The one who is subdelegated may not again subdelegate another priest or deacon validly unless the competent delegator so states.[114]

Before a special delegation is granted, provision is to be made for all those matters which the law prescribes to establish freedom to marry, as part of the marriage preparation. One who assists at a marriage acts unlawfully unless he has satisfied himself of the parties' freedom to marry in accordance with the law and, whenever he assists by virtue of general delegation, has satisfied himself of the pastor's permission, if this is possible.[115]

### 3. OTHER WITNESSES

These are the ordinary or common witnesses prescribed in addition to the priest or deacon who acts as qualified or authorized witness of the contract. They must be at least two in number, more being permissible. For *validity* alone they may be of either sex, of any age, even separated Christians or the unbaptized, as long as they enjoy the use of reason and are capable of witnessing.[116] Thus those who are asleep, drunk, etc., deaf and blind (but not if only deaf or only blind) may not validly act as witnesses. They may use an interpreter in order to make aware when consent is requested and given. They must be physically present and attentive to the exchange of consent, even if their presence is induced by constraint or fraud or is accidental. It suffices that they are present and can testify to the contract; they need not expressly intend to be witnesses but merely know from what transpires that marriage is being contracted. It is commonly maintained that for validity they need not have been designated beforehand by the contractants or the assisting priest. Civil law regarding witnesses should be consulted, e.g., if it is required that they sign a civil register or marriage certificate. Their names are, however, inscribed in the parish marriage register.

### 4. THOSE BOUND BY THE ORDINARY FORM

The ordinary canonical form for marriage is to be observed if at least one of the parties contracting marriage was baptized in the Catholic Church or received into it and has not by a formal act defected from it; the local Ordinary may dispense from this form in an individual instance of a mixed marriage.[117] In certain circumstances a Catholic may not be bound by the ordinary juridical form but by the extraordinary form of marriage.[118]

Baptism is not received in the Catholic Church necessarily by the fact that it is administered by a Catholic priest. It is by the expressed or tacit intention of being aggregated externally to the Church as manifested by himself in the case of an adult or in the case of an infant by his parents, legitimate guardians or in default of all these by the minister himself. One can be baptized in the Catholic Church even if the parents (or the minister) are non-Catholic. Infants who are validly baptized in heresy or schism, if subsequently reared in the Catholic Church by their parents who have become converts, are considered as converts to the Catholic faith. Converts from unbelief or Judaism become immediately subject to the law of the canonical form by the reception of Catholic Baptism.

The following are not bound for validity to the canonical form of marriage:

All non-Catholics, whether baptized or not, when they contract marriage among themselves.[119]

Before Jan. 1, 1949[120] persons born of non-Catholic parents, even though baptized in the Catholic Church, who have grown up from infancy in heresy or schism or unbelief or without any religion, when they contracted with a non-Catholic party; or with a Catholic Oriental who was not bound to any form. The parents may be two non-Catholics or only one non-Catholic, even if the promises were made, or two apostates, and probably even one apostate. The exemption does not apply to the children of non-practicing Catholic parents. It is often not easy to determine in the individual case the absence or presence of a Catholic upbringing. The practice in the diocese for sufficient certification should be consulted and observed.

Before May 2, 1949[121] Oriental Catholics when married among themselves, or with the baptized or the unbaptized who are not bound to a form, unless by the law of their own Rite they were bound by a canonical form.

Whenever Catholics, either Oriental or Latin, contract marriages with faithful who are non-Catholic Orientals, the canonical form of celebration for these marriages is of obligation only *for lawfulness*; *for validity* the presence of a sacred minister is sufficient, observing all the other requirements of law.[122]

### 5. EXTRAORDINARY CANONICAL FORM

If one who, according to law is competent to assist, cannot be present or be approached without grave inconvenience, those who intend to enter a true marriage can validly and lawfully contract in the presence of witnesses only: 1° in danger of death; 2° apart from danger of death, provided it is prudently foreseen that this state of affairs will continue for a month. In either case, if another priest or deacon is at hand, he must be called upon and, together with the witnessess, be present at the celebration of the marriage, without prejudice to the validity of the marriage in the presence of only the witnesses.[123]

The danger of death may be from any internal or external source, as long as there is true danger of death prudently estimated. It must be at least a probable danger in the normal judgment of prudent people who consider that in the serious danger delay would prohibit the contract from taking place until an authorized priest or deacon could be reached or become available. The motive for entering the marriage may be varied, e.g., legitimation of offspring, to convalidate an invalid union, repair scandal, etc.

The impossibility or morally serious inconvenience of securing qualified assistance may be absolute, e.g., there is no time remaining, or relative, e.g., the inability to bear the expenses. The serious difficulty or danger may affect both spouses or either of them or a third person such as the pastor, even if it is due to a prohibition of the civil law. The serious inconvenience must be real and proportionate to the non-observance of the ordinary juridical form and the real danger of serious scandal. The consent of the contracting parties must be expressed in the presence of at least two competent witnesses.

If any priest or deacon can be easily had, he must be called to assist together with the witnesses, but not under penalty of nullity of the marriage if this is not done for any reason. It is required only for lawfulness. Probably excepted is one who is under sentence of censure. The assisting priest or deacon would enjoy the faculties of dispensation of c. 1079. He should ask and receive the consent of the contracting parties.

In every case of the use of the extraordinary form it is presupposed that the parties are free to marry, not bound by a diriment impediment (the use of this form does not include an implicit dispensation), intend to enter a valid marriage in the circumstance, and are capable of sustaining a marital covenant.

In the exact same impossibility of the assistance of an authorized priest or deacon but outside a case of danger of death, *and* when it is prudently foreseen that this condition of affairs will last for a month, marriage may be celebrated before witnesses alone. This is at times applicable in mission fields or in areas of persecution of the Church.

There must be a continued and complete month which need not have already expired but is prudently foreseen will expire before the opportunity of contracting a qualified priest arises. The validity is not affected if the authorized priest or deacon appears suddenly and unforeseen after the contract has been made, or even if the parties waited until it would be impossible for the priest to be present. The serious inconvenience or impossibility is the same as noted above.

A normal prudent presumption and not a scrupulous inquiry of the pastor's absence suffices, although a mistaken conviction made in good faith that an authorized priest was absent whereas in reality he was available will not make the marriage valid. However, the mere fact of the pastor's absence is not sufficient but moral certainty is also necessary, based either on common knowledge or on inquiry, that for one month the pastor will neither be available nor accessible without serious inconvenience. The pastor must be physically absent or, although materially present in the place, is unable because of serious inconvenience to assist at the marriage asking and receiving the consent of the contracting parties.

### a. *Lawfulness*

Even an unauthorized priest should be called in, if this can be easily done, as in the previous case. He enjoys the faculties of c. 1080. There are no formalities prescribed in this and the previous extraordinary case, except that the priest who assists ought to follow the ritual for marriage realizing that the asking and receiving of consent of the parties does not pertain to validity. There is no serious obligation to supply later the ceremonies and solemnities of marriage. However, the spouses, witnesses, and the priest and deacon are bound *in solidum* to see that the marriage is recorded as soon as possible in the matrimonial and baptismal registers of the parish or diocese of the place of celebration.

### 6. LITURGICAL FORM

Apart from a case of necessity (e.g., danger of death), in the celebration of marriage those rites are to be observed which are prescribed in the liturgical books approved by the Church, or which are acknowledged by lawful customs.[124] The obligation of rite must be respected. The ceremonies concerning consent placed by the official witness are essential and for validity. The complete omission of the liturgical ceremonies outside of necessity is a serious sin, but their suppliance when omitted in necessity is not certainly of obligation.

Whenever marriage is celebrated within the Mass, the Mass for spouses is said and white vestments used, except on Sundays and solemnities when the Mass of the day is used with the nuptial blessing and, where appropriate, the special final blessing. On the Sundays of the Christmas season and throughout the year, in Masses which are not parish Masses, the wedding Mass (*pro sponsis*) may be used without change. When a marriage is celebrated during Advent or Lent or other days of penance, the parish priest should advise the couple to take into consideration the special nature of these times.[125]

It is not strictly necessary to apply the Mass for the spouses, unless they have contracted for the same, i.e., given a stipend. A pastor or his delegate may assist at a marriage and another priest designated by either may celebrate the Mass and impart the solemn blessing. Confession and Communion are not obligatory but are to be strongly urged upon the spouses by the pastor.

In the celebration of a mixed marriage the liturgical form, if taken from the Roman Ritual, is from the *Rite of Celebration of Marriage*, whether it is a question of a marriage between a Catholic and a baptized non-Catholic or of a marriage between a Catholic and an unbaptized person. If, however, the circumstances justify it, a marriage between a Catholic and a baptized non-Catholic can be celebrated, subject to the local Ordinary's consent, according to the rites for the celebration of marriage within Mass, while respecting the prescription of general law with regard to Eucharistic Communion, which is to be considered when plans are being made to have the mixed marriage at Mass or not.[126]

The celebration of marriage before a Catholic priest or deacon and a non-Catholic minister, performing their respective rites together, is forbidden; nor is it permitted to have another religious marriage ceremony before or after the Catholic ceremony, for the purpose of giving or renewing consent.[127]

With the permission of the local Ordinary and the consent of the appropriate authority of the other church or community, a non-Catholic minister may be invited to participate in the Catholic marriage service by giving additional prayers, blessings, or words of greeting or exhortation. If the marriage is not part of the Eucharistic celebration, the minister may be also invited to read a lesson and/or to preach.

In the case where there has been a dispensation from the Catholic canonical form and the priest has been invited to participate in the non-Catholic marriage service, with the permission of the local Ordinary and the consent of the appropriate authority of the other church or communion, he may do so by giving additional prayers, blessings, or words of greeting and exhortation. If the marriage service is not part of the Lord's Supper or the principal liturgical service of the Word, the priest, if invited, may also read a lesson and/or preach.[128]

### 7. PLACE OF MARRIAGE

Marriages are to be celebrated in the parish in which either of the contracting parties has a domicile or quasi-domicile or a month-long residence or, if there is question of those without fixed residence (*vagi*), in the parish in which they are actually residing. With the permission of the proper Ordinary or the proper pastor, marriage may be celebrated elsewhere.[129]

A marriage between Catholics or between a Catholic party and a baptized non-Catholic, is to be celebrated in the parish church. By permission of the local Ordinary or of the pastor, it may be celebrated in another church or oratory. The local Ordinary can allow a marriage to be celebrated in another suitable place. A marriage between a Catholic party and an unbaptized party may be celebrated in a church or in another suitable place.[130]

It is most fitting that marriage between Catholics and between Catholics and baptized non-Catholics take place in the parish church, because of the sacramental dimension and the relationship with the community. Marriage between a Catholic and an unbaptized party is a religious event and fittingly takes place in a church. When one party is a non-Catholic the regulations regarding inter-communion must be strictly observed. This should be pointed out in the pre-marital investigation or preparation. Local diocesan regulations should be consulted in all the above circumstances.

### 8. REGISTRATION OF MARRIAGE

The pastor of the place of celebration of the marriage, or whoever takes his place, has the prime responsibility, even when not having assisted at the marriage, to record, as soon as possible after the marriage, in the marriage register the names of the spouses, the official witness, the other two witnesses, and the place and date of celebration, in accordance with diocesan norms. For a marriage celebrated according to the extraordinary form, the priest or deacon, if present at the celebration, or otherwise the witnesses, are bound jointly with the contracting parties to inform the pastor or local Ordinary as soon as possible about the marriage. When a local Ordinary grants a dispensation from the form, he is to see to it that the dispensation and the celebration are recorded in the marriage register both of the curia and of the proper parish of the Catholic party whose pastor carried out the pre-marital investigation. The Catholic spouse is obliged as soon as possible to notify that same Ordinary and pastor of the fact that the marriage was celebrated, indicating also the public forum which was observed.[131] It is the responsibility of the priest or deacon who conducts the pre-marital investigation to see that this is done.

Marriage is also to be recorded in the baptismal register in which the Baptism of the spouses was entered. If a spouse was married elsewhere than in the parish of Baptism, the pastor of the place of celebration is to notify as soon as possible the pastor of the place of Baptism.[132]

Whenever a marriage is declared validated for the external forum, or declared invalid, or lawfully dissolved other than by death, the pastor of the place of celebration must be informed, so that an entry may be made in the registers of marriage and of Baptism. [133]  This will include dissolution by the Pauline privilege, favor of the faith, *ratum et consummatum*, or cases which have received a declaration of nullity. The date, protocol number, and tribunal issuing the document should be noted. Marriages convalidated in the internal forum are registered only in the diocesan secret archives.

## VII.  MIXED MARRIAGES

Mixed marriage refers only to a sacramental union between a Catholic and any baptized non-Catholic. In the 1917 Code it was referred to as marriage of mixed religion. Although the marriage between a Catholic and a baptized non-Catholic is no longer an impediment in law (and no longer penalized when unlawfully contracted), it still is seriously prohibited and warrants the special pastoral care of the Church and the guidance of her law.

The Church in her experience is wisely reluctant to permit such a union, even in a more ecumenical contemporary society, since it is often harmful to the intimacy of the union and the happiness of the spouses, dangerous to the faith and sometimes the morals of the Catholic party and especially to the children because conducive to indifferentism. It is not as such forbidden by the divine law, except where there is true danger of perversion for the Catholic party and the offspring. [134]

### 1.  PROHIBITION

Marriage is prohibited, without the express permission of the competent authority, between two baptized parties, one of whom was baptized in the Catholic Church or received into it after Baptism and has not defected from it by a formal act, the other of whom belongs to a church or ecclesial community not in full communion with the Catholic Church. [135]

The prohibition is pastoral in order to provide a proper pre-marital preparation of both parties for the problems presented by such marriages. Catholics who have formally departed from the Church are not bound by this prohibition when they marry non-Catholics, but Catholics wishing to marry such former Catholics are bound.

The competent authority to give permission for the marriage is the local Ordinary (and his equivalent in law), which authority may be delegated. It may be the local Ordinary of either party, of the place where the Catholic party is staying temporarily, or of the place of celebration.

## 2. PERMISSION

The local Ordinary can grant permission under certain conditions:[136]

### a. *Just and reasonable cause*

The pastor responsible for the pre-marital investigation and preparation basically judges the sufficiency of the reason for seeking the permission to marry: will it provide better for the welfare of this particular couple or be a danger to the faith of the Catholic? Is there sufficient assurance that this couple is aware of and seems capable of coping with the problems and dangers of such a marriage and its implications for each party?

### b. *As to the Catholic party*

The Catholic party declares that he or she is prepared to remove dangers of falling away from the faith and makes a sincere promise to do all in his or her power to have all the children baptized and brought up in the Catholic Church.

The danger of lapsing from the faith must be impressed upon the Catholic party. This may come about through a gradual lessening of the practice of the faith, through the influence of the stronger personality of the non-Catholic, from a desire not to worship apart, an anti-Catholic sentiment or aversion to regular worship on the part of the non-Catholic.

The Church has always insisted on the obligation of the Catholic party to strive in every way possible, short of endangering the marriage itself, to have children baptized and brought up in the Catholic faith. Where this has not been observed in an invalid mixed marriage, the Church insists, when granting a validation, that the obligation be observed at least with regard to future offspring. Since Baptism and raising in the faith are in one continuity the couple to be married may not agree to baptize some children in one faith and some in the other, or to baptize all as Catholics but raise some or all in another faith, or to baptize the children and leave the choice of church to their choice upon reaching maturity. This would bring into question the reliability of the sacramental covenant of marriage and the advisability of its celebration. The understanding, good faith and sincerity of the Catholic party in making the declaration and promise is of first importance.

### c. *As to the non-Catholic party*

The non-Catholic party is to be informed in good time of the promises to be made by the Catholic party, so that it is clear that he or she is truly aware of the promise and obligation of the Catholic party. The non-Catholic, probably early on in the pre-marital meetings, should be given as complete as possible an explanation of the obligation of the Catholic party. No promise or guarantee is required of the non-Catholic, whose good faith and sincerity are important in judging the prospects of the future marriage.

### d. *As to both parties*

Both parties are to be instructed about the purposes and essential properties of marriage, which are not to be excluded by either contractant. As complete an exposition as possible in the case of the Catholic teaching on these points, in the context of marriage viewed in the unity and fidelity of mutual conjugal love until death, should be given, probing especially the convictions of the non-Catholic. The matter of the Church's teaching on family planning is very relevant. An exclusion of the purposes and essential properties would render the marriage null.

### 3. FORM OF CELEBRATION

### a. *Ordinary form*

The ordinary canonical form is to be used in a mixed marriage for validity. It is required for the lawfulness only when a Catholic marries a non-Catholic of an Oriental rite, although for validity the marriage must take place before a sacred minister, presuming all other requirements for a valid marriage.[137] Permission is required; it may be appropriate, though not necessary, to request a dispensation from the form.

b. *Dispensation from form*

If there are grave difficulties in the way of observing the canonical form, the local Ordinary of the Catholic party has the right to dispense from it, having in the meantime consulted the Ordinary of the place of celebration of the marriage; for validity, however, some public form of celebration is required.[138]

A mixed marriage, with dispensation from the form, validly takes place before a non-Catholic minister or civil official who then acts as the official witness and asks and receives consent in a valid formulary. The dispensation from the form does not need the approval, for validity, of the Ordinary of the place of celebration but only that he be consulted. Dispensation is granted only for a marriage between a Catholic and a non-Catholic (baptized or not) but not between two Catholics (granted only by the Apostolic See). Permission is needed for a mixed marriage to take place outside the parish church or in a non-Catholic church or other place.[139]

Types of reasons for granting a dispensation are:   to achieve family harmony or to avoid family alienation, to obtain parental agreement to the marriage, to recognize the significant claims of relationship or special friendship with a non-Catholic minister, to permit the marriage in a church that has particular importance to the non-Catholic. A public form that is civilly recognized for the celebration of marriage is required.[140]

c. *Other celebration*

It is forbidden, either before or after the canonical celebration, that there be another religious celebration of the same marriage for the purpose of giving or renewing matrimonial consent. Likewise, there is not to be a religious celebration in which the Catholic assistant and a non-Catholic minister, each performing his own rite, ask for the consent of the parties.[141] This would imply that at least one of the parties does not recognize its validity.

Another religious ceremony during which a blessing is imparted but without an exchange or renewal of consent, as in a marriage with an Orthodox, may be permitted. Also, where civil law requires it, civil ceremonies prior to religious ceremonies may be allowed, but only the canonical form is accepted by the Church as establishing the marriage.

With the permission of the local Ordinary and the consent of the appropriate authority of the other church or community, a non-Catholic minister may be invited to participate in the Catholic marriage service by giving additional prayers, blessings, or words of greeting or exhortation. If the marriage is not part of the Eucharistic celebration, the minister may also be invited to read a lesson and/or to preach. In the case where there has been a dispensation from the form and the priest has been invited to participate in the non-Catholic marriage service, with the permission of the local Ordinary and the consent of the appropriate authority of the other church or communion, he may do so by giving additional prayers, blessings, or words of greeting and exhortation. If the marriage is not part of the Lord's Supper or the principal liturgical service of the Word, the priest, if invited, may also read a lesson and/or preach.[142]

### 4. PASTORAL CARE

Local Ordinaries and other pastors of souls are to see to it that the Catholic spouse and the children of a mixed marriage are not without the spiritual assistance needed to fulfill their obligations; they are also to assist the spouses to foster the unity of conjugal and family life.[143] Besides the normal pastoral care recommended for after marriage, mixed marriages have a peculiar need. Diocesan practice and programs should be consulted.

What has been indicated about mixed marriages, especially regarding canonical form, celebration and pastoral care apply also to disparity of worship marriages.[144]

## VIII. MARRIAGES SECRETLY CELEBRATED

Although marriage is a public and community event, the Church makes provision, for a grave and urgent reason, for a marriage to be celebrated in secret. Permission must be granted by the local Ordinary whether of domicile or temporary residence of either party or of the place of the celebration of the marriage. All the norms pertaining to marriage (preliminary investigation of freedom to marry, canonical form, instruction, dispensations, etc.) are observed, except that no banns are published and the celebration remains unknown to the public and the community. Secrecy must be kept by the local Ordinary, by whoever is the official witness, by the other witnesses and by the spouses. The marriage is recorded only in a special register kept in the secret archive of the curia. No notification is placed in the baptismal register.[145]

## IX. THE EFFECTS OF MARRIAGE

### 1. FOR THE SPOUSES

#### a. *Common sharing*

From a valid marriage there arises between the spouses a bond which of its own nature is permanent and exclusive. Besides, in a Christian marriage the spouses are by a special sacrament strengthened and, as it were, consecrated for the duties and dignity of their state. Each spouse has an equal obligation and right to whatever pertains to the partnership of conjugal life.[146]

The rights and obligations of the spouses spring from their mutual giving of themselves through marital consent in a covenantal unique way of life. Theirs is a relationship of equality in accordance with their distinct sexes. These rights and duties are affected and expressed differently in various cultures and by varying personalities. Nevertheless, Christian teaching emphasizes what must always characterize the mutual relationships, especially in a Christian marriage.[147]

Married couples owe each other mutual love, mutual help and solace, and a common life or cohabitation. These are obligations which are of themselves serious but allow of lightness of matter, and in certain circumstances and for proportionate causes do not oblige in whole or in part. It would be a sin against charity for one spouse to hold the other in contempt or hatred, or to sadden or anger the other with injurious words or deeds; likewise to deprive the other in any way of those things which are necessary for a decent maintenance of life and respectable condition. They are bound to preserve conjugal fidelity both internally and externally, and to render mutual aid in the carrying out of their respective duties and functions, in bearing the burdens of marriage, especially in times of adversity. Unless a legitimate reason excuses, they are to dwell together and share the same domestic or family life. The wife retains the domicile of her husband and is bound to follow the husband wherever he fixes his residence, unless reasonably excused.

In the society of the family the husband is the head and the woman has been given to him as helpmate and associate, thus owing him due reverence and obedience in all good and lawful things. Husband and wife are absolutely equal as persons with consequent equal rights; also with respect to the marriage contract. But they have different roles to fulfill in the procreation and education of offspring, which roles are interdependent rather than unequal. In these functional differences the headship of the husband is more in terms of the common good of the family unit. He must protect and provide, and in this function he is aided by the wife, just as the wife is aided in her role of maintaining a comfortable home and of supervising the daily rearing of the children. The relationship is a partnership and companionship with each contributing according to ability the best performance of their respective roles for the common welfare, physical, material, spiritual. Patience, forbearance, kindly consideration and even at times substitution in another's role are the hallmarks of conjugal love and fidelity. Both must edify by example and correct by counsel and friendly persuasion. The common goods or fortune as well as individual possessions must not be dissipated or injured, nor domestic peace and comfort disturbed by word or action or negligence.[148]

### b. *Conjugal Act*

Among the mutual rights and duties is the sexual act, which is the most intimate and complete expression of conjugal love and which is uniquely an element of married life. A sufficient understanding of its role is necessary for harmonious marital life.

### *Right*

The procreation of offspring in marriage is achievable by the conjugal act; thus a prime obligation in marriage is the proper use of this act. As a fulfillment or exercise of the marital contract it is an obligation contained in the duty of marital fidelity (*bonum fidei*). In the fullest sense the conjugal act refers to marital intercourse which is of itself apt for generation. In the wider sense of including also the various actions which are accessory to conjugal intercourse which is to take place or which has been performed, it is sometimes called the use of marriage (*usus matrimonii*).

The right and duty of marital intercourse is both a natural institution and of divine law, and its fulfillment or observance may also be meritorious. Marital love is uniquely expressed and perfected through the marital act, which within marriage is noble, worthy, and meritorious when under the influence of charity.[149]

### Obligation

Each spouse has from the very beginning of marriage the equal right and duty with respect to the acts proper to conjugal life. There is an obligation binding in strict and commutative justice to render the marriage debt when it is justly requested.

### Limitations

The right to the marital debt (and the correlative obligation to render it) is not unlimited. The area in which the right is inoperative is often difficult of precise determination because there are often physical, moral or spiritual conditions of individuals involved and even the necessity of medical advice. A graver cause must exist to deny the debt absolutely than to restrict it or to put it off for a period.

### Cautions

Conjugal intercourse as instituted and designed by God for the propagation of the human race is lawful when apt for generation and in accordance with the *bonum prolis* and the *bonum fidei*.[150] Used outside its proper purpose it is not without some moral defect.[151]

A confessor or a priest in the external forum must beware of hasty and minute questions concerning the various ways of accomplishing intercourse and of lawful or unlawful actions between spouses, since they are not always necessary for the integrity of confession or the effectiveness of counselling by the priest and may give rise to scandal. Questioned on such matters he should reply as briefly as possible and by the general principle of moral theology instead of descending to particulars and details. The instruction that is needed in a particular case may indicate that the penitent or spouse be referred to someone else who is prudent and expert or experienced in such matters. A priest or deacon in giving counsel must always explain the teaching of the Magisterium of the Church and not profer his own private views.

### Abuses

Contemporary society witnesses grave abuses or violations of the conjugal act, which at various times have been reprobated by the Church, Mother and Teacher: contraception, artificial insemination in all its forms, withdrawal, various methods of artificial birth control.

### 2. TOWARD THE CHILDREN

Openness to procreation which is essential to marriage is fulfilled by the education of children born to the union. This is a fundamental responsibility of the spouses and may not be forfeited except in the extreme incapacity of the parents. The proper fulfillment of this responsibility also provides a role model for the children.

Parents have the serious duties of teaching their children what is necessary for them, to correct them when necessary or expedient, and to give them good example.[152] The fatherly power or authority (*patria potestas*) over the offspring, which by nature belongs to the father and subordinately to the mother, requires that provision be made for the well-being and rearing of the children. Civil authority may further detail this obligation in regard to its extent and responsibility affecting the public good. It should also supply public aids for the parents in fulfilling their duties and should safeguard the children from parental neglect, but it may not supply for or supplant parental authority or rights. Ecclesiastical authority may further specify the spiritual obligations of the parents toward their children.

The parental duty to care for their children (even illegitimate) so that they might take their proper place as individuals, as citizens of the community, and as sons of God and members of the Church is a serious office. They must provide for the physical, mental, and spiritual life and development of the offspring, certainly until the attainment of maturity and self-sufficiency.

One of the important items in parental responsibility today is to provide an adequate and Christian sex education for their children so that they may be prepared to cope with the problems in this area in contemporary society in a truly Christian attitude and with openness to the Spirit.[153]

Parents are to provide for the future reasonable opportunity of the children to live decently, as children are not for the enrichment of the parents but vice versa.[154] In their choice of state of life, children are free and independent of their parents, although the parents should in all piety and prudence be consulted and their advice respected. According to their capacity and experience parents are bound to counsel their children about their future; they sin if they force a state of life upon them or if without sufficient cause bring about the abandonment of their choice.

### 3. LEGITIMACY

Children are called legitimate or illegitimate inasmuch as the parents from whom they spring are validly joined in marriage or not. Illegitimate children are called *natural*, if no impediment existed which would have prevented their parents from validly contracting marriage; *spurious*, if it is otherwise; *sacrilegious*, if at least one of the parents is bound by religious profession or by a sacred order; *adulterine*, if one of the parents is already validly married; *incestuous*, if the parents are related within the forbidden collateral degrees of consanguinity or affinity; *nefarious*, if within the forbidden degrees of the direct line. *Legitimacy* is a juridical quality conferred on a child born in wedlock; it produces effects in law based upon the natural dignity deriving from the natural law. *Legitimation* is an institution of positive law or a concession of a lawful superior which attributes to a child born out of wedlock at least some, if not all, of the juridical effects of legitimacy; being one of the inseparable effects of marriage, it pertains exclusively to an ecclesiastical tribunal. Permission should be secured in order to approach the civil court for the merely civil effects.

Children who are conceived or born of a valid or of a putative marriage are legitimate. The father is he who is identified by a lawful marriage, unless by clear arguments the contrary is proven. Children are presumed legitimate who are born at least 180 days after the date the marriage was celebrated, or within 300 days from the dissolution of conjugal life.[155]

To prove the contrary it must be clearly demonstrated that intercourse between the husband and wife was impossible during the time period when conception was possible. The admission by the mother of adultery committed is not sufficient proof of illegitimacy of offspring.

Illegitimate children are legitimated by the subsequent marriage of their parents, whether valid or putative, or by a rescript of the Apostolic See. As far as canonical effects are concerned, legitimated children are equivalent to legitimate children in all respects, unless the law expressly provides otherwise.[156] Foundlings and adopted children are presumed legitimate until proven otherwise.

## X. THE SEPARATION OF THE SPOUSES

### 1. DISSOLUTION OF THE BOND

Marriage is of its nature perpetual and indissoluble; by divine institution what God has joined together no man may dissolve. There is no human power or authority which is capable or qualified to dissolve a valid marital bond; this is the prerogative of the divine author and the restorer of the institution of marriage. This authority has been communicated by Christ to his Church in a restricted degree, i.e., with regard to certain types of valid bond and under specific conditions.

### (a) *Sacramental marriage*

A valid sacramental and consummated marriage (*ratum et consummatum*) cannot be dissolved by any human power or for any cause except death.[157] History proves that the Roman Pontiffs have always been conscious of this impossibility, even in face of the direst consequences. This intrinsic and extrinsic indissolubility is thus of divine law. This is certain teaching, as marriage is taught to be indissoluble even in a case of adultery, and consequently for lesser cause. The Church will never grant a dispensation in a marriage case where there is a possibility of its existence as a sacramental and consummated union. Although a consummated marriage is naturally perfect in its firmness inasmuch as it actually achieves the primary end of marital union, it is especially perfect as a sacred sign of Christ's union with his Church.[158]

A non-consummated marriage between two baptized persons or between a baptized party and an unbaptized party can be dissolved by the

Roman Pontiff for a just reason, at the request of both parties or of either party, even if the other is unwilling.[159]

It is Catholic doctrine that the Church can dissolve an unconsummated marriage in which at least one party is baptized. The Roman Pontiffs have for centuries employed their fulness of Apostolic power, i.e., their ministerial or vicarious power,[160] in dissolving such unions, and such constant and general discipline of the Church is regarded as pertaining to the indirect object of infallibility. However, the Holy See does not act in such cases unless there is certified proof that the marriage was really not consummated and that there is a just cause for granting the dispensation. Such dispensation is sparingly granted as an extraordinary remedy to provide for the salvation of souls.

The process for a dispensation from a ratified and non-consummated marriage is set forth in canons 1697-1706. In this process the manner of proof of this fact is carefully regulated by the local Ordinary, normally by competently supervised inspection and the testimony of appropriate witnesses. The woman in the case should never be advised to consult a physician before the case has been submitted to the episcopal curia for consideration and instructions, as this may complicate later findings. The consummation is taken in the canonical sense of true and natural intercourse after the celebration of valid marriage; thus offspring may have been produced before marriage by illicit relations or even after marriage by means of fecundation that canonically cannot be considered certainly as consummation. The consummation of marriage is always presumed until adequate proof is presented to the contrary; non-consummation is usually most difficult of certification, especially if the woman has remarried. A forced or an unconsciously performed conjugal act is nevertheless true consummation. A case is seriously prejudiced and even its continuance as a case jeopardized where it appears that there has been an avoidance of consummation through the practice of onanism for birth prevention.

Frequently a just cause for dispensation is probable impotency, where it cannot be sufficiently determined whether or not the defect antedated the celebration of the marriage, or whether or not it is perpetual. In such cases a second marriage is often forbidden without leave of the Holy See. Other causes are similar to the following examples: the spiritual welfare of one or both parties after separation following an unconsummated marriage, which may include civil divorce and especially another civil marriage; voluntary and too protracted a delay of one spouse in consummating the marriage; extraordinary and implacable conflicts between the spouses; crime which especially results in a long prison term; the claim, which is not sufficiently proved, that the marriage is null through fear or defective consent, together with certainty of non-consummation; disease, especially that which impedes the use of marriage; probable great scandal or family quarrels that will develop.

Since the marriage in question is a valid union, and often sacramental, the efforts of the priest in both forums must be to try to reconcile the parties, to remove the difficulty or ameliorate the problem, especially when the spouses continue to live together and where there are children, even employing the aid of a reputable Catholic physician or expert. If the efforts appear unpromising or even harmful, consideration then can be given to a possible dissolution. This is more indicated when the union has hopelessly foundered and when in addition civil proceedings have been initiated.

The priest or confessor suspecting the elements of a non-consummation case should not enlighten the parties of a possibility of dissolution. Discreet questioning, preferably outside the confessional, will tend to bring out pertinent factors in the case. Assertions and remarks made by the spouses and others at a time when they are not aware of the value and utility of the information are weighty. All information should be carefully recorded. A dispensation is not necessarily granted only in view of another bond to be contracted. It is effective when granted and not upon the entrance into another union. The dispensation is to be noted in the matrimonial and baptismal registers. The case is a chancery or tribunal case and is only pursued under proper instructions.

Since a case of this kind is usually quite involved and the matters it concerns are often not easily susceptible of proof, greatest forethought should precede sponsorship of this type of case. The dispensation is strictly a favor from the Holy See and one to which the parties can lay no claim. The avoidance of any scandal or a consequence of disrespect for the Church or the sanctity of marriage is always to be kept in mind.

### b. *Pauline Privilege*

#### *Terms*

A marriage entered into by two unbaptized persons is dissolved in virtue of the Pauline privilege in favor of the faith of the party who received Baptism, by the very fact that a new marriage is contracted by that same party, provided the unbaptized party departs. The unbaptized party is considered to depart if he or she is unwilling to live with the baptized party, or to live peacefully without offense to the Creator, unless the baptized party has, after the reception of Baptism, given the other just cause to depart.[161]

"But to those who are married, not I, but the Lord commands that a wife is not to depart from her husband, and if she departs, that she is to remain unmarried or be reconciled to her husband. And let not a husband put away his wife. For to the rest I say, not the Lord: If any brother has an unbelieving wife and she consents to live with him, let him not put her away. And if a woman has an unbelieving husband and he consents to live with her, let her not put away her husband. . . But if the unbeliever departs, let him depart. For a brother or sister is not under bondage in such cases, but God has called us to peace."[162]

#### *Conversion*

There must be a true and *valid* marriage contracted when *both* parties are *unbaptized*. When there are several wives or when there have been several marriages, there must be an investigation from the beginning to determine which is the first lawful wife. One spouse must be *converted* to the Christian faith.[163] The privilege does not apply when both parties become baptized at the same time, nor does it apply to a baptized party who contracted marriage with an unbaptized with a dispensation from disparity of worship.[164] The spouse who has been converted from unbelief must not have lapsed again into unbelief or atheism and must be still married to an *unbaptized* partner. The conversion must be through a certainly established Baptism of *water*, thus excluding catechumens. If both spouses should become baptized, even unbeknown to each other, there is no Pauline case. The privilege also does not apply to two doubtfully baptized non-Catholics; recourse to the Holy See must be made in the case of a doubtfully baptized non-Catholic and an unbaptized spouse. The convert spouse without forfeiting the privilege may have lived for some time before conversion and Baptism in marital union with the unbaptized spouse, even consummating the marriage again.

### Departure

The valid cause for the application of the Pauline privilege is the unjust "departure" (physical or moral) of the unbaptized party.

*Physical* desertion on the part of the unbeliever after the Baptism of the convert which takes place for any reason at all is a cause for applying the privilege, *as long as the convert has provided no just and reasonable cause for such departure*, e.g., by adultery. The departure may be either *involuntary*, such as slavery, capture, imprisonment, perpetual insanity of the unbaptized party, etc., which prevent cohabitation, or *voluntary*, such as a refusal of the unbeliever to cohabit or to move to another dwelling place, the contracting of a second marriage which the unbaptized party refuses to or cannot abandon, departure out of hatred of the Christian faith, disappearance in order to avoid the interpellation, etc. In many cases separation and divorce have already occurred prior to a conversion and application of the privilege.

*Moral* departure or desertion takes place when the unbaptized party refuses to cohabit peacefully with the convert without offense to the Creator. Moral desertion is present when danger to the convert of perversion by the unbaptized spouse is present, such as impelling the convert to give up the Catholic faith, or to commit a serious sin, or to impede the convert from practicing the faith or observing the laws of God or the Church or from educating present or future children in the faith. Likewise, when there is offense to the Creator given by the unbaptized party, such as habitual blasphemy, constant ridicule of the Catholic religion and practices, a life of concubinage or habitual adultery. Also, when conjugal servitude is laid upon the convert inasmuch as the common life is made odious and morally intolerable by quarrels, fights, etc., without just cause, by a dissolute manner of life, criminal pursuits, etc. The motive for the departure may be other than the conversion itself of the baptized convert, as long as no just and reasonable cause after Baptism was provided by the latter and conjugal life in practice is impossible.

### Interpellation

Before *validly* contracting a new marriage the convert must ask the questions: (1) whether the unbaptized spouse is also willing to be converted and to receive Baptism, and (2) if not, whether the unbaptized party is willing to dwell peacefully with the convert without offense to the Creator.[165]

The divine law requires proof of the departure of the unconverted spouse if the departure cannot be otherwise made evident; the normal means of certification required for validity of the use of the Pauline privilege is the interpellation. The law of interpellation binds *all* the baptized *always*, unless dispensed.

The interpellation is to be done after Baptism. However, the local Ordinary can for a grave reason permit that it be done before Baptism; indeed he can dispense from, either before or after Baptism, provided it is established, by at least a summary and extrajudicial procedure, that it cannot be made or that it would be useless.[166]

It is sufficient that the interpellation be made once, but out of charity it may be made more than once. The summary judicial form is before the Ordinary of the convert or his delegate, which is seldom done; the summary extrajudicial form is by an authorized delegate of the Ordinary making contact either in person or by offical letter (registered or certified with return receipt requested), which is the usual form.

As a rule, the interpellation is to be done on the authority of the local Ordinary of the converted party. A period of time for a reply is to be allowed by this Ordinary to the other party, if indeed he or she asks for it, warning the person however that if the period passes without any reply, silence will be taken as a negative response. Even an interpellation made privately by the converted party is valid and indeed lawful if the prescribed form cannot be observed. In each case there must be lawful proof in the external forum of the interpellation having been done and of its result.[167]

### Use

The baptized party has the right to contract a new marriage: (1) if the other party has replied in the negative to the interpellation or if the latter has been lawfully omitted; (2) if the unbaptized person, whether already interpellated or not, who at first persevered in peaceful cohabitation without offense to the Creator, has subsequently departed without just cause. All the requirements for the Pauline privilege must be observed.[168] If a new interpellation is not done, the departure nevertheless must be verified. Although the convert acquires in the circumstances the right to enter a second marriage with a Catholic party, the local Ordinary can for a grave reason allow marriage with a non-Catholic party, whether baptized or unbaptized, but in the manner prescribed for a mixed marriage.[169]

In summary form it can be stated that the *right* to the Pauline privilege, i.e., to interpellate, is acquired at the time of the Baptism of the convert; the *cause* for its use is the unjust departure of the unbaptized spouse; the *use* of the privilege is not of obligation nor does it cease by non-use; the *effect* of the privilege, i.e., the dissolution of the natural bond, contracted when both parties were unbaptized, is had upon the valid contracting of the second marriage.

### Caution

Before admitting a prospective convert to instructions, and certainly before any Baptism, an investigation must be made by the pastor, priest or deacon to determine the canonical and civil marital status of the party. A complete course or period of instructions in the Catholic faith as well as a sufficient time in the practice of the faith is a normal requirement (which may be more precisely determined by local regulation). It is a most prudent caution (if not otherwise prescribed) for the pastor, priest or deacon not to baptize a convert in a possible Pauline privilege case (especially a divorced person) before approbation by the local Ordinary or curia verifies the presence of all necessary requisites for the use of the privilege.

A prospective convert who is under instructions, being in this case already validly married, must not keep company with another person, or, if marriage has been attempted a second time, must separate from this new partner. The Catholic must be strongly admonished about the obligations and the dangers involved. If separation is not possible in the circumstances, a petition for a temporary brother-sister arrangement may be made. It should be noted that any intercourse engaged in by the baptized party after Baptism (being adultery), unless condoned, affords the unconverted spouse cause for just departure and renders the Pauline privilege inapplicable. If the party wishing to enter the Church has been baptized in a sect subsequent to the original marriage, conditional Baptism will follow the norms of prudence mentioned above for approbation before the interpellation is sought. Where there has been an attempted marriage with a baptized party, the impediment of crime is to be investigated and dispensation sought. Oftentimes factors in a Pauline privilege case may change the situation into another category of dissolution in favor of the faith (Pauline privilege) or into a sacramental unconsummated marriage case. Likewise it is not a Pauline privilege as such if the prospective convert is the unbaptized party wishing to marry a Catholic and if the original spouse of the prospective convert was subsequently baptized in a sect. In every case, all danger of scandal must be avoided. The pastor, priest or deacon is not to inform a convert of the possibility of a dissolution, Pauline or otherwise, until all the facts are in, or promise any favorable outcome, since such cases often consume much time and investigation.

The Pauline privilege case usually requires such documentation as the following: the formal petition, the certificates of marriage and divorce (if obtained), affidavits or testimonies from the convert and the non-convert parties and from their witnesses to prove the non-Baptism at the time of the marriage and that the convert was not responsible for the departure, the certificate of Baptism if received after the marriage, the answer to the interpellation or the dispensation from it.

### c. *Polygamous and non-reestablished marriages*

When an unbaptized man who simultaneously has a number of unbaptized wives has received Baptism in the Catholic Church, if it would be a hardship for him to remain with the first of the wives, he may retain one of them, having dismissed the others. The same applies to an unbaptized woman who simultaneously has a number of unbaptized husbands. All the usual norms of law must be observed before the canonical celebration of the marriage. The convert, at the instance of the local Ordinary, should make adequate provision in justice and virtue for the first wife or others who have been dismissed (and perhaps any children).[170]

An unbaptized person who, after Baptism in the Catholic Church, cannot reestablish cohabitation with his or her unbaptized spouse by reason of captivity or persecution, can contract another marriage, even if the other party has in the meantime received Baptism, as long as it is not a case of a sacramental consummated marriage.[171]

### d. *Privilege of the faith*

All cases of marriage which are not clearly dissoluble under the terms of the Pauline privilege must then, to be dissoluble, come under the *vicarious and ministerial* or instrumental power, the fullness of Apostolic power, committed to Peter and his successors. Whenever there is question of the Baptism of one of the spouses, the marriage becomes subject to the Church. All instances in which a valid marriage is dissoluble for the purpose of allowing one party either to embrace the Catholic faith or to preserve the same are called "privilege of the faith" or "favor of the faith" cases. This obviously pertains to the Pauline privilege. However, other situations have developed in which valid bonds have been dissolved in favor of the faith and which derive their dissolubility from the supreme vicarious power of the Roman Pontiffs. Authors have not always employed the generic terms "privilege of the faith" and "favor of the faith" in the same way, referring sometimes to the Pauline privilege and at other times to non-Pauline cases and even to both together. For practical purposes the following cases, since they are not, or at least not clearly, contained under the Pauline privilege, are listed under the so-called Petrine privilege. Like the Pauline, the Petrine privilege is a favor and not a right, and thus the Church may impose certain regulations for the granting of the favor — which in every case means the dissolution of a natural bond or non-sacramental marriage.

In a doubtful matter the privilege of the faith enjoys the favor of the law.[172]

A certain juridic preference is granted to contract a new marriage with a Catholic in every case where such a union would result *in favor of the* (Catholic) *faith*, and where, notwithstanding insoluble doubts, it is at least *certain* that the former marriage can be *dissolved* by the ministerial or vicarious power of the Apostolic See. This privilege is applicable when any doubt arises as to whether all the conditions requisite for the Pauline privilege or the other canons or the dissolution of some type of natural bond are fulfilled. However, if the good of the faith of the convert party does not require the dissolution, then the norm of validity of a previous marriage is maintained, i.e., that a marriage is presumed to be valid and that a doubt is to be solved in favor of the validity of a marriage until the contrary is established.

When the Baptisms of both parties to a consummated marriage are in doubt the favor of the faith privilege does not apply. Reserved to the Holy See are cases in which the Baptism of a non-Catholic party in a marriage with an unbaptized person is involved in an insoluble doubt. Recourse is indicated in practice when the Catholic Baptism in a case is doubtful. No impediments to the new marriage, whether certain or doubtful, are removed by this privilege but rather by the prescribed modes of dispensation. Likewise, there can be no sanation or suppliance of consent, but consent must be renewed by the parties themselves in the canonical form.

The doubt respecting the status of the original marriage must be one that is proved to be morally insoluble after diligent investigation, study and consultation have been made, i.e., when moral certainty cannot be attained. The doubt may respect the existence of a marriage contracted in unbelief or its validity, the verification of the conditions for a Pauline privilege, the fact or validity of the Baptism of one party only, the person or identity of the first spouse in a polygamous union, the dissolution of a marriage contracted in unbelief, the sufficiency of the reasons for a departure, the sincerity of a reply to the interpellation or the adequacy of the reasons for dispensing from it, etc.

In certain cases — so-called "*aut-aut*" cases — the insoluble doubt or doubts may present a dilemma each horn of which opens an entirely distinct avenue of dissolution. Such a case may or may not involve the Pauline privilege or the other canons. The doubt regards which authority is to be operated under in the situation as a source for possible dissolution. However, in every case, no matter what the possibility or the elements involved, the existing bond must be from any point of view chosen clearly dissoluble by the power of the Apostolic See.

All things being equal, a marriage entered into between an unbaptized party and a baptized non-Catholic may be dissolved upon the desire of the unbaptized party to embrace the Catholic faith and to marry (or validate a union with) a Catholic, the non-Catholic party having already remarried after civil divorce.

Dissolution of the natural bond is possible likewise in a marriage between a baptized non-Catholic and an unbaptized partner when the non-Catholic party, subsequent to the breakup of the union, now wishes to embrace the faith and marry (or validate a union with) a Catholic person.

Marriage contracted with a dispensation from disparity of worship between a Catholic party and an unbaptized person may be dissolved, upon the breakup of the first marriage, to allow the Catholic spouse (or even the unbaptized party after coming into the Church) to marry anew a Catholic party. The current norms of the diocese and of the Holy See in all natural bond and privilege of the faith cases should always first be ascertained.

Privilege of the faith cases that come under the Petrine privilege follow most of the procedures and observe the caution already noted for Pauline privilege cases, such as securing adequate proofs, witnesses and testimonies or affidavits, promises not to keep company or live as husband and wife, instructions and delay of Baptism. As with a Pauline case, the regulations and procedures laid down by the Ordinary and his curia must be observed. Since it is a privilege or favor that is being sought, there is no *right* to *demand* even a consideration of the case by the Church and thus the latter may establish certain requirements as conditions for accepting a case and pursuing its course. Petrine privilege cases must be sent to the Holy See who judges the facts, especially the proof of non-Baptism. In a successful case the dissolution of the first marriage takes place when the rescript is granted and its conditions fulfilled. A usual condition is that the unbaptized party is to be baptized before the second marriage is contracted.

The pastor or priest handling a case must make an informal investigation to ascertain if there is truly a case present and that the proper certifications can be satisfactorily secured before submitting a case to the local curia. Sound judgment must be made that the unbaptized party is not using entrance into the Church as a means of removing the impediment of bond (*ligamen*) to a prospective union with a Catholic. True sincerity is present usually if the party wishes to enter the Church even though there is given no likelihood (even an unlikelihood) that a new marriage can take place. A case is prejudiced if marriage is attempted nevertheless during the course of instructions or while the case is being considered by the competent authorities. There must be a grave reason for petitioning the favor of dissolution and the absence of scandal or amazement resulting.

## 2. SEPARATION WHILE THE BOND ENDURES

Marriage is defined as "living together in undivided partnership." Thus, married couples are obliged to preserve the common bond of conjugal cohabitation unless a justifying reason excuse them.[173] Normally conjugal life requires and obliges to the habitual sharing of bed, board, and home (*communio tori, mensae et cohabitationis*) for the full attainment of the purposes of marriage. Severance of this conjugal life, saving the bond itself, is called imperfect divorce or *separation*. Separation is total or complete if it includes the threefold sharing; it is partial if it is from bed alone (mutual consent to abstinence from intercourse is not pertinent to this context). The common law of the Church refers only to complete separation.

Complete separation is either of itself *perpetual*, and then there is no obligation to resume the common life, or *temporary* only, which of itself must cease upon the cessation of its cause. The principal and practical ultimate cause for perpetual separation is the adultery of one party. Mutual consent to complete and perpetual separation is seldom permissible because of the danger of incontinence and scandal. Only the Holy See may authorize this in the case of couples desiring a higher life of perfection.

### a. *Perpetual*

The Church urges married parties to strive in every way to overcome mutual difficulties through the exercise of Christian virtue and a serious consideration of the profound values of marriage and the family, and the consequences of separation. Nevertheless, marriages do break down, especially due to marital infidelity.[174] The injured party is earnestly recommended not to refuse to pardon the adulterous party and not to sunder the conjugal life.[175] However, either party by reason of adultery on the part of the other has the right, though the marriage bond remains intact, to terminate the community life even permanently, unless he or she consented to the crime, or was the cause of it, or condoned it expressly or tacitly, or himself or herself committed the same crime. There is a tacit condonation if the innocent party, after learning of the adultery, of his or her own accord receives the other with conjugal affection; condonation is presumed unless the injured party within six months expels or deserts the adulterer, or brings a legal action against the same.[176]

The crime of adultery must be:     (a) *formal* or committed with a free and deliberate will and not through any force, fraud or ignorance;     (b) *consummated* or effected by perfect copulation and not merely attempted or begun by kisses, touches, embraces, etc.; consummated sodomy, bestiality, etc., are equivalent to adultery;     (c) *morally certain*, at least by sufficient signs or presumptions which leave no room for prudent doubt;     (d) committed *after Baptism*, since the sacrament totally wipes away the crime;     (e) *unapproved*, in that consent to the crime has not been given expressly or tacitly, e.g., by not preventing it when this could be done without great inconvenience or difficulty;     (f) *unprovoked* or caused directly and proximately, e.g., by frequent *unjust* refusal of the marital debt, by desertion, failure to provide, etc.;     (g) *uncondoned*, once the crime has become known, e.g., condoned by a request for or by a free rendering of the marriage debt, or by the continuance of a peaceful marital life with display of affection;     (h) *uncompensated*, in that the other party does not commit a similar crime.

The innocent party *may* terminate the conjugal life either in pursuance of an ecclesiastical decree upon proof of the fact or on his or her own private authority, provided that the crime is certain and public, i.e., either commonly known or committed in such circumstances as easily to give rise to such knowledge, or even if it is occult when serious inconvenience or hardship would result. Outside of cases of direct argument, such as admission of guilt, witnesses, etc., the authority of the external forum, i.e., the local Ordinary, should always be involved. A doubtful right to separate is to be submitted to the judgment of the local Ordinary.[177]

When a separation of spouses has taken place, provision is always, and in good time, to be made for the due maintenance and upbringing of the children. The innocent spouse may laudably readmit the other spouse to the conjugal life, in which case he or she renounces the right to separation.[178] However, there is no obligation to readmit the guilty party.

### b. *Temporary*

The reasons which would justify separation of spouses for a time are not taxative or exhaustive but exemplificative or categories of cause. Thus the delinquent spouse gives reason by:     (a) *joining a non-Catholic sect*, which involves a formal adscription to some sect (spiritual adultery), but not if one spouse is a non-Catholic before the marriage took place; (b) *educating the children as non-Catholics*, which is directly against the *bonum prolis* and a kind of spiritual adultery; (c) *living a criminal and ignominious life*, which is to be understood as an habitual state or condition, such as a drunkard, jailbird, homosexual, etc.; (d) *causing serious spiritual or bodily danger to the other spouse*, which danger to the *soul* would be continual or frequent provocation to serious sin, e.g., stealing, adultery, prostitution, (according to many) conjugal onanism, and to the *body* would be serious hatred, serious threats, disease such as is contagious in the use of marriage (e.g., syphilis) or present and immediate danger (e.g., violent dementia), but not other diseases which rather should be occasions for solace and aid than separation; (e) *cruelty*, such as beatings, serious and frequent quarrels, contumelies, squandering of the family funds, denial of sustenance, etc. These and other causes of similar nature are so many lawful reasons for the other party to depart, on the authority of the local Ordinary, or even on his or her own authority, if the grievances are certain and there is danger in delay. Separation must be practically the only way to avoid sin in these cases, especially in the use of marital relations.[179]

In every case when the cause for the separation has ceased to exist, the common marital life is to be restored; but if the separation was decreed by the local Ordinary for a definite or an indefinite period, the innocent party is not bound to the common life unless by another decree of the Ordinary or upon expiration of the period.[180] By a lawful separation granted by sentence of an ecclesiastical judge or by a decree of the local Ordinary, whether for an indefinite time or perpetual, a wife acquires her own proper domicile.[181] The woman and the children have a right to continued support. The civil law must be taken into consideration in each case, as it is not always the same as canon law.

The procedural norms for cases of separation are noted in canons 1692-1696.

Cases of separation should normally be referred to the local Ordinary, or to the diocesan separation court where this exists. Particular diocesan law or regulations may specify further requirements in this matter. If the parties have already separated with or without recourse to civil authority and without ecclesiastical authorization the obligation need not be insisted upon nor the parties disturbed, if they are in good faith and no benefit can be expected from the admonition and if no great scandal exists. Civil separation or separate maintenance (or even civil divorce) may be necessary in a particular case in order to secure certain civil effects for the injured party. Such a process may be instituted only with the permission of the local Ordinary. The civil laws and the civil rights of parties as they exist in each State or civil jurisdiction are to be consulted, at least for the protection of the innocent party and the children. Pastors and confessors should take reasonable caution in separation cases to avoid the danger of a civil suit for alienation of affections being brought against them.

### c. *Civil divorce and marriage*

It is never permitted Christians to seek a perfect civil divorce for the purpose of entering a new marriage while still bound by the impediment of previous marriage bond.[182] For the purpose of setting certain civil effects it may be permitted — because necessary — that Catholics seek a separation or partial divorce, or even a complete divorce, provided that ecclesiastical permission to separate for a canonical cause has been obtained, that there is serious difficulty from which they expect to be freed by seeking such civil divorce, and that there is no other way to remove the hardship or disadvantage. Civil divorce proceedings may be authorized in an individual case as long as it is clear that this is only for maintaining civil effects and to safeguard a party from injury, e.g., to regulate substantial property rights. Sometimes where a dissolution of a previous marriage bond has been granted by competent ecclesiastical authority it will be necessary to seek permission to secure a civil divorce in order that a second marriage in the Church become also recognized in civil law.

Since the marriage cases of Catholics depend solely upon ecclesiastical authority, the permission of the local Ordinary (or the diocesan divorce court) is necessary in order to invoke the civil jurisdictions by a decree of separate maintenance or separation; consequently the ecclesiastical permission to go to civil court will be given only to this extent and not for a complete or perfect civil divorce.

When civil law requires it, it is not forbidden parties to present themselves before a non-Catholic minister acting only as a civil officer, merely for the purpose of performing the civil act of marriage for the sake of the civil effects. However, American civil law everywhere recognizes pastors and qualified ministers of religion as authorized to officiate at marriages which are thus valid in civil law. Some civil jurisdictions require particular formalities, such as registration as an officiating minister, residence, etc., as well as witnessing of the marriage license. There is hardly ever an occasion for parties to a marriage to present themselves to a civil officer or justice of the peace, and still less to go before a non-Catholic minister, in order to secure the civil effects of their marriage. A case could arise — and a merely civil ceremony permitted by the local Ordinary — whereby the original valid marriage, meanwhile dissolved by a civil divorce in the sight of the State, is to be resumed, and thus a new civil ceremony is in order for its civil effects.

## XI. CONVALIDATION OF MARRIAGE

Validation is the process whereby an apparent marriage which is actually invalid is rendered valid in conscience and in the sight of the Church. There must have been some formality or species of a marriage contract entered into, even though it was ineffective; otherwise there would not be an invalid marriage but mere concubinage. The apparent marriage may have been invalid because at least one of the parties did not give true consent, or the canonical form was not observed, or a diriment impediment prevented the contract from being valid. Not all invalid marriages can be subsequently rendered valid. Validation may be effected either by a renewal of consent under certain conditions (simple convalidation) or by a dispensation from the renewal of consent (radical sanation).

### 1. SIMPLE CONVALIDATION

#### a. *Presence of a removable impediment*

The marriage is invalid because at the time it was contracted the parties were bound by a diriment impediment and thus unable to exchange valid consent. Even though the impediment has ceased to exist (e.g., nonage), or has been dispensed, the law requires that for the validity of the marriage consent be renewed. This renewal must be made by at least the party who is aware of the impediment. The original consent (that is, the marital commitment of the spouses to one another despite the lack of ecclesiastical recognition) must not have been revoked. The renewal of consent must be a new act of the will concerning a marriage which the person renewing knows or thinks was null from the beginning.[183] The juridical effects begin from the moment of the renewal of consent and for the future. The pastor or deacon should be satisfied that the parties (or party) are aware of what convalidation means and are properly motivated to enter into a sacramental or natural bond covenant, as the case may be.

If the impediment is public, after dispensation both parties must renew consent in the form prescribed by law,[184] so that the validation might be publicly known and scandal avoided. Usually the essentials of the juridic form are observed, with a dispensation from the banns and without the nuptial blessing or the blessing of the ring. In case the public impediment is actually not known to others, the marriage should take place with all due secrecy; but the fact must be made known if scandal has to be removed. Registration is made in the usual registers.

If the impediment is occult and known to both parties, after dispensation it suffices that both parties give a new consent privately and secretly.[185] Thus, in the external forum the marriage is considered valid and disclosure of invalidity by a public renewal would be apt to raise scandal. Although the parties may express their mutual consent (which need not be simultaneous) without others being aware and without pastor and witnesses, it is recommendable to exchange consent before a priest or deacon and in the usual formula. Consent may be renewed by other signs than by words as long as they are external and the parties mutually realize what is being signified. If one party refuses to make the renewal, a radical sanation may be in order.

If the impediment is occult and known only to one party, after dispensation it suffices for this party to renew consent privately and secretly, provided that the consent of the other party perseveres.[186] The party aware of the nullity may renew consent implicitly, e.g., by carnal intercourse with marital affection, but it is recommendable that the confessor or priest elicit from this party an explicit expression of consent.

If the impediment is occult and unknown to both parties, they should be told so that they might live chastely until validation is effected, or at least one party should be acquainted with the fact so that consent might be renewed. If even this is not possible without foreseeable danger developing, such as marital sins becoming formal, desertion with serious danger to the spouse or the children, etc., they may be left in good faith until a dispensation is obtained or a radical sanation effected.

### b. *Defect of consent*

A marriage that is invalid because of a defect of consent is validated if the party who did not consent now supplies it, provided that the consent given by the other party perseveres. If both parties are cognizant of the lack of consent, it is better that both renew consent. If the defect of consent was merely internal, it is sufficient that consent be now given interiorly, e.g., if unknown to others a wholly simulated consent was given. If the defect of consent was also external (attestable by two witnesses willing and able to testify), it is necessary also to manifest consent externally either in the form prescribed by law, if the defect was public, or in some private and secret manner, if it was occult.[187]

### c. *Defect of form*

A marriage that is invalid because of a defect of the canonical form can be validated only by a renewal of consent in the prescribed form.[188] If one party will not appear for the new celebration either personally or by proxy, or if there would be proportionate danger or scandal in manifesting the nullity, a dispensation from the form or a radical sanation may be petitioned.

### 2. RADICAL SANATION

Radical sanation (*sanatio in radice*) is a retroactive or retrospective validation, a healing in the root, i.e., a healing of the consent, since this latter is the root and basis of marriage. It is the act by which a marriage is validated effecting, besides a dispensation from or a cessation of the impediment, a dispensation from the law requiring renewal of consent and the canonical form, as well as a retroactive reinstatement by a fiction of the law, of the canonical effects of marriage, and dating from the moment when the marital consent was truly but invalidly given.[189]

The validation (and the sacrament, if the parties are baptized) is effected as of the moment when the favor is granted; but its retroactive effect (but not the sacrament) is understood to date from the beginning of the marriage, unless some restriction is expressly stated in the rescript. Dispensation from the law of renewal of consent can be granted even if one or both parties should be unaware of the favor. The principal retroactive effect is to make legitimate and not merely legitimated children, if they were born after the consent given by the parents to the marriage which the radical sanation now validates.

Any marriage entered into with the consent of both which was naturally sufficient but juridically insufficient because of an ecclesiastical impediment or because of defect of canonical form can be radically sanated, provided the consent perseveres. But the Church does not sanate a marriage contracted with an impediment of the natural or the divine law, even if later the impediment ceases, not even from the moment of the cessation of the impediment, although it can, and for special reasons has. If there is a lack of consent in both parties or in one party, the marriage cannot be radically sanated, whether the consent was lacking from the beginning or, if originally given, was later revoked. But if the consent was lacking in the beginning but was later given, the sanation can be granted from the moment when the consent was given.[190] Consent is considered to exist until it is positively revoked, even though the parties knew they could not contract a valid marriage originally, or they intend to separate or have already separated, or one party refuses to renew consent according to the canonical form. The character of consent is judged by what was factually done, not by what would have been done if knowledge, only later acquired, was possessed at the time.

Besides an impediment that is dispensable and a true consent that is perduring, there must also be a serious justifying cause for a radical sanation — a situation that does not allow of the more normal process of simple validation.[191] Thus, if neither party can be informed of the invalidity without serious harm arising, e.g., due to lack of proper jurisdiction in the minister or because the marriage would break up with great injury resulting to the children, or if a non-Catholic spouse will not renew consent according to the canonical form, reason exists to petition a radical sanation. The reason for the sanation must be in addition to that for dispensing an impediment. The clauses of the rescript received must be exactly executed.

Radical sanation can be granted by the Apostolic See. In individual cases it can be granted by the diocesan bishop, even if several reasons for nullity exist in the same marriage and observing the conditions required for mixed marriages. The diocesan bishop cannot grant it, however, if there is present an impediment whose dispensation is reserved to the Apostolic See or if it is an impediment of the natural law or of the divine positive law which has ceased to exist.[192]

### 3. CAUTIONS

Every pastoral minister in the external forum and every confessor in the internal forum is aware that, besides the norms of the common law and the regulations and procedures of a particular diocese, extreme caution and prudence must be employed in matters of marital validation. Haste in validating an invalid marriage sometimes worsens an already bad situation; on the other hand, any factual approval or acceptance of an unlawful union supplies the material for scandal. In these cases, which are often complex and difficult, the common good must be safeguarded, even at the sacrifice of individuals.

When an invalid union is discovered it is lawful to dissimulate or to omit to enlighten and to warn the parties only  (1)  when there is good faith on the part of both parties in that neither is aware of the invalidity, (2) when others are ignorant of the invalidity so that scandal will not arise,  (3) when there is a proportionately grave reason for permitting a material sin, which is still an evil. Under these *certain* conditions such a reason would be present if the marriage is *incurably null* and the parties, although in good faith, probably would not have the courage to make the heroic sacrifice of separation, especially if there are children or financial or other problems.

In some cases the better procedure is separation with a subsequent declaration of nullity. Such instances would exist when the parties certainly are unsuited to each other, or where the Catholic party does not wish to validate the marriage or where validation is not possible in the circumstances, or when divorce has taken place.

If the nullity of the marriage is unknown to both parties, and unknown also to others, and it is prudently judged that they can be beneficially warned of their condition, they should be told and required to separate from bed and to live in such a way that all proximate danger or occasion of sin is removed. Petition made to the local Ordinary for temporary permission to live as brother and sister may be in order. If there is an indispensable impediment, however, the circumstances may recommend procedures of 1 and 2 above or of the brother and sister arrangement as described below. If it is judged that only one party could be profitably informed, but the nullity is incurable, the same approach would be used. If there is a dispensable impediment, the party can be informed after the dispensation has been obtained (in order to avoid formal occasion of sin) and simple validation taken place or a radical sanation sought for sufficient reason without knowledge of the parties.

If the nullity of a marriage is publicly known, then for the avoidance of continued scandal the parties must separate until everything is arranged for the validation. If the nullity is canonically public but factually not known and there is sufficient cause militating against separation, the local Ordinary should be petitioned for a brother-sister arrangement. If the parties desire validation but are not willing to separate to the extent required to avoid the proximate occasion of sin until the marriage is rectified, the local Ordinary should be consulted. If, however, the marriage is incurably null or should not in prudence be validated, separation should take place and a decree of nullity obtained.

If invalidity is known only to one party and not to the other and not to others, either separation must take place and a decree of nullity obtained or a brother-sister arrangement sought, if the marriage is incurably invalid. If the marriage can be validated and sought to be, the party cognizant of the invalidity must neither seek nor render the marital debt, whether or not the other party can be profitably informed of the validity until validation is effected.

When a marriage problem is discovered by the priest in either form, or presented to him, he must act with all deliberate prudence avoiding haste in attempting to validate or precipitateness in informing the parties of the invalidity. No more than a promise to do what he can to help and to investigate the case should be given to the parties, but no hope of satisfactory solution until all the facts and circumstances have been assembled and carefully examined. Simple validation is the normal process to be pursued, with radical sanation as the last resort.

When validation is not possible at all, or when it cannot be effected until such time as all requisite data has been presented to the local curia, petition may be made to the local Ordinary for a temporary or permanent brother-sister arrangement, as the case indicates. Even though a marriage may have been entered into invalidly but cannot be canonically so established, the Church does not allow a second marriage already contracted to be validated.[193] There must be *compelling serious reasons* for allowing continued cohabitation in an invalid union, together with the *absence of danger of incontinence and scandal.* All cases of brother-sister petition which are in any way canonically public, formally or materially, or will become so, should be referred to the local Ordinary alone for decision. Some dioceses have specific regulations and procedures. A confessor in the sacramental forum is restricted by what he can learn of the penitent and from the penitent. Thus, if he has any doubt concerning the public or occult character of the problem, he ought not to permit a brother-sister arrangement but urge that the problem be taken into the external forum. Even if a case before the confessor is *certainly* and *completely occult* (in which situation alone he ought to act), the danger in granting such permission is such that the confessor is cautioned by expert authorities almost never to grant such permission in the confessional.

In whatsoever situation in which parties (Catholic or non-Catholic) exchanged marital consent, it is never permitted for a priest or deacon to assist merely as a civil officer or civil magistrate. [194]

# FOOTNOTES

# FOOTNOTES

## FOREWORD

1  Apostolic Constitution *Sacrae Disciplinae Leges*, Jan. 25, 1983, which came into force on Nov. 27, 1983.
2  c. 842, 2. *Ordo Baptismi Parvulorum, De Initiatione Christiana, Praenotanda Generalia*, 1-2 (S.C. pro Culto Divino, 15 maii 1969). "As members of Christ, all the faithful have been incorporated into him and made like unto him through Baptism, Confirmation, and the Eucharist. Hence all are duty-bound to cooperate in the expression and growth of his Body, so that they can bring it to fulness as swiftly as possible" (Vatican II, Decree *Ad gentes*, 36).
3  Vatican II, Const. *Lumen Gentium*, n. 11.
4  "For from the wedlock of Christians there comes the family, in which new citizens of human society are born. By the grace of the Holy Spirit received in Baptism these are made children of God, thus perpetuating the People of God throughout the centuries." (Ibid.)

## THE SACRAMENTS

1  *Sacrosanctum Concilium*, 59.
2  Cf. cc. 213, 214.
3  c. 837.
4  cc. 840, 841.
5  *Sacrosanctum Concilium*, 11.
6  Cf. Denz.-Schön. 1612; 1617. Vatican II, Decree *Presbyterorum Ordinis*, 5: "God, who alone is holy and bestows holiness, willed to raise up for himself as companions and helpers men who would humbly dedicate themselves to the work of sanctification. Hence, through the ministry of the bishop, God consecrates priests so that they can share by a special title in the priesthood of Christ. Thus, in performing sacred functions they can act as the ministers of him who in the liturgy continually exercises his priestly office on our behalf by the action of the Spirit."
7  Cf. Denz.-Schön. 1611.
8  Alexander VIII (S. Off. 7 Dec. 1690) condemned the proposition: "Baptism is valid when conferred by a minister who observes the entire external rite and the form of baptizing, while he resolves within his own heart: I do not intend what the Church does" (Denz.-Schön. 2328).
9  Cf. Denz.-Schön. 1611.
10  c. 276, 1.
11  c. 916.
12  c. 843, 1.
13  Cf. c. 843.

14 Mt. 7:6; c. 855.
15 *Summa Theol.*, III, q. 80, a. 6, ad 2.
16 c. 528, 1.
17 c. 844. *Unitatis Redintegratio*, 5: "Concern for restoring unity pertains to the whole Church, faithful and clergy alike. It extends to everyone, according to the capacity of each." Cf. also Vatican II, Declaration *Nostra Aetate*; Secr. ad unitatem Christianorum fovendam, 14 May 1967, *Directorium.*
18 S. Off. 17 maii 1916 ad 2; 1 Nov. 1942.
19 cc. 1378, 1399.
20 Innocent XI condemned the proposition: "Urgent grave fear is a just reason for simulation of the sacraments" (Denz.-Schön. 2129).
21 c. 846. In accordance with canon 2 all existing liturgical norms, viz., in liturgical books, papal apostolic constitutions, decrees and instructions of Roman Congregations, etc., retain the force of law, unless contrary to the legislation of the Code, in which case only the Holy See, in doubt of law, can render an authentic interpretation. In certain specific instances the National Conference of Catholic Bishops is competent to legislate in liturgical matters, as also the diocesan bishop (c. 838).
22 Innocent XI (S. Off. 2 Mar. 1679). DS 2101.
23 S. Off. 2 May 1858, to the Vicar Apostolic of Abyssinia, commanded that Baptism be repeated conditionally whenever the formula is pronounced after the water has been poured or vice versa.
24 S.C. Sac. 17 Nov. 1916.
25 Benedict XIV, Const. *Eo quamvis*, 4 May 1745 a. 1.
26 Innocent III (1201): "He who never consents, but entirely contradicts, receives neither the effect (grace), nor the character of the sacrament" (Denz.-Schön. 781). Cf. *Prostremo mense*, Const. Benedict XIV.
27 c. 916.
28 c. 1335.

## _BAPTISM

1 Vatican II, Decree *Unitatis redintegratio*, 22.
2 *Ordo Baptismi Parvulorum*, 3-6.
3 *Unitatis redintegratio*, loc. cit.
4 Vatican II, *Sacrosanctum Concilium*, 7.
5 *Ibid.*, 6.
6 Vatican II, *Lumen gentium*, 7.
7 *Ibid.*, 11.
8 Paul VI, Const. *Divinae consortes naturae*, 15 aug. 1971.
9 c. 849.
10 c. 850.
11 c. 854.
12 c. 97, 2.
13 c. 851, 2.
14 c. 97, 1; c. 863.
15 c. 851, 1.
16 c. 855.
17 c. 849.

18  *Ordo Baptismi Parvulorum, Praenot. Gen.*, 18-20.
19  S. Off. 17 Apr. 1839.
20  *Ordo Baptismi Parvulorum, loc. cit.*, 21.
21  c. 854.  *Ordo Baptismi Parvul., loc. cit.*, 22. Aspersion or sprinkling is no longer used. Only Sacred Oils are to be used. c. 847.
22  S. Off. 8 Nov. 1770; 9 July 1779; 14 Dec. 1789.
23  *Ordo Baptismi Parvul., loc. cit.*, 23.
24  S. Off. 4 Mar. 1679; cf. Denz.-Schön. 2101.
25  Innocent III, 28 Aug. 1206, cf. Denz.-Schön. 788.
26  cc. 856, 859.
27  *Ordo Baptismi Parvul., loc. cit.*, 9.
28  c. 857.
29  c. 860.
30  c. 861, 1.
31  *Ordo Baptismi Parvul., Praenot. Gen.*, 11.
32  c. 863.
33  c. 861, 2.
34  c. 530, 1°.
35  c. 864.
36  c. 865, 1; cf. also c. 869, 3.
37  c. 869, 1.
38  *Ibid.*
39  c. 865, 1.
40  c. 866.
41  S.C.D.F. 20 Oct. 1980, *Instruction on Infant Baptism*, 4-15, Cf. *Ordo Baptismi Parvul., Praenot.*, 2.
42  S.C.D.F., *loc. cit.*, 17-26.
43  c. 867, 1.
44  c. 868.  Lawfully adopted children are considered as being children of the adopting person or persons (c. 110).
45  cc. 867, 2; 868, 2.  Baptism is not necessary unless the child is in proximate, certain, and personal danger of death, when out of charity one must baptize the child (at least secretly). Even in danger of death Baptism must be omitted if hatred of the unbaptized (especially of Moslems) would be aroused and even persecution of the Church incited, e.g., in mission lands. Prudence demands that the benefit of one soul be sacrificed and left to God's mercy for the sake of the common welfare of the Church and of many other souls.
46  c. 868, 1, 2°. Cf. S.C.D.F. 13 July 1970 (*Notitiae* 61, 69-70).
47  c. 870.
48  c. 871.
49  cc. 111; 214.
50  c. 112, 1.
51  S.C. Or. Ch. 7 July 1981 to the Apostolic Delegate.
52  c. 111, 1.
53  *Ibid.*
54  *Ibid.*
55  c. 111, 2. A free choice by such a minor (c. 97, 2) implies his understanding of ritual differences and their obligations.
56  *Ordo initiationis Christianae adultorum*, Appendix 1.
57  Secr. ad unitatem Christianae fovendam, *Directorium*, 9.

58  *Ibid.*, 12.
59  *Ordo initiationis Christianae adultorum*, Appendix 2.
60  *Ibid.*, 5.
61  c. 869, 2-3.
62  *Ordo initiationis Christianae adultorum*, Appendix 7.
63  *Ibid.*, 8.
64  c. 872.  *Ordo Baptismi Parvulorum Praenot. Gen.*, 8; 8-9.
65  *Ordo initiationis Christianae adultorum*, 42; 43. Cf. also 16; 71; 104.
66  c. 873.  *Ordo Baptismi Parvulorum, Praenot.*, 6.
67  c. 874, 1, 5°.
68  c. 874, 1, 1°.
69  *Ordo Baptismi Parvulorum*, 60; 97; 124; 148; *Ordo initiationis Christianae adultorum*,
    220-221; 261-262.
70  c. 874, 1, 2°.
71  c. 874, 1, 3°-4°.
72  c. 874, 2.
73  *Directorium*, 48; 57.
74  cc. 875; 877, 1.
75  c. 877, 2.
76  c. 877, 3.
77  c. 878.
78  c. 876.


—— CONFIRMATION _____

1   c. 879.  *Ordo Confirmationis, Praenotanda*, 1-2 (S.C. pro Cultu Divino, 22 Aug. 1971).
2   Apost. Const. *Divinae consortium naturae*, 15 Aug. 1971. Cf. c. 879.
3   *Catechism of the Council of Trent* (ed. McHugh & Callan), p. 201.
4   Dogm. Const. *Lumen Gentium*, 11.
5   St. Thomas, *IV Cont. Gent.*, c. 60; cf. also *Summa Theol.*, III, q. 72, a. 1.
6   Decr. *Ad gentes*, 11.
7   *Enchiridion Symbolorum*, Denz.-Schòn. 1628; cf. also 860, 1317, 3444.
8   *Ibid.*, 1609; cf. also 1313.
9   *Ordo Confirm., Praenot.*, 3; c. 787.
10  c. 880, 2.  Denz.-Schòn., 1317; *Ordo Confirm., Praenot.*, 9; S.C.C.D., 3 Dec. 1970,
    *Ordo benedicendi oleum catechumenorum et infirmorum ac conficienda chrisma,
    Praenot.*, 3: "Apt material of a sacrament is olive oil or, according to opportunity, another
    plant oil"; 4: "Chrism is made up of oil and spices or fragrant material"; 2: "By sacred
    chrism it is demonstrated that Christians, having been inserted in the Paschal mystery of
    Christ by Baptism, have died, been buried, and risen with him, are sharers in his royal and
    prophetical priesthood, and receive through Confirmation the spiritual unction of the Holy
    Spirit who is given to them."
11  *Ordo Confirm., Praenot.*, 10; *Ordo benedic.*, 9-10.
12  880, 2.  Cf. S.C. Sac. "Spiritus Sancti munera," 14 Sept. 1946; Secr. ad unitatem
    Christianorum fovendam, *Directorium*, 14 May 1967, 38-55, here makes no mention of
    Confirmation in the sharing in liturgical worship.

13 c. 880, 1. *Ordo Confirm, Praenot.*, 9. The anointing with the thumb sufficiently manifests the imposition of the hand (P.C. Interp. Dec. Vat II, 9 June 1972). The right thumb
anoints the forehead with the oil in the sign of the Cross. *Ordo Confirm.*, 27.
14 *Ordo Confirm., Praenot.*, 9.
15 *Ordo Confirm.*, 27.
16 *Divinae consortium naturae.*
17 c. 881. *Ordo Confirm., Praenot.*, 13.
18 c. 881.
19 c. 888.
20 c. 882.    It is of faith that only a consecrated bishop is the ordinary minister of Confirmation
(Denz.-Schön. 1630; cf. c. 782, 1) by the very power of ordination itself and not any special
papal commission.
21 *Ordo Confirm., Praenot.*, 7.
22 c. 886.
23 c. 885, 1.
24 Cf. cc. 882-884.
25 c. 883.
26 Territorial prelate; territorial abbot; vicar apostolic; prefect apostolic; apostolic administrator; diocesan administration. Cf. cc. 368; 381, 2; 427.
27 c. 884.
28 *Com. Vat. II Interp.* 21 Dec. 1979.
29 cc. 885, 2; 887.
30 c. 889, *Ordo Confirm., Praenot.*, 12.
31 *Ordo Confirm., Praenot., ibid.*
32 c. 866.    *Ordo initiationis christianae adultorum*, 34; 227-234; 266-270; 293; 361-365;
*Ordo Confirm.*, 11; 53.
33 c. 890.    *Ordo Confirm., loc. cit.: Ordo initiationis christianae adultorum*, 19.
34 *Ordo Confirm., loc. cit.*
35 *Ibid.*
36 *Ordo Confirm.*, 52, 53. However, when it is necessary to confer all the sacraments in
danger of death in one continual rite, Confirmation is conferred immediately before the
blessing of the oil of the Infirm (S.C.D., 7 Dec. 1972, *Ordo unctionis infirmorum
eorumque pastoralis curae*, 117, 124, 136-137).
37 c. 891. *Ordo Confirm., Praenot.*, 11.
38 *Ibid.*; also 52. Cf. *Ordo Baptismi Parvulorum, Praenot.*, 22. *Ordo Confirm., Praenot.*, 52.
39 *Ordo Confirm., Praenot.*, 13.
40 c. 892. *Ordo Confirm., Praenot.*, 5.
41 c. 893, 2. *Ordo Confirm., Praenot., ibid.*
42 cc. 893, 1; 874.
43 *Ordo Confirm.* 21.
44 cc. 893, 1; 874.
45 *Ordo Confirm., Praenot.*, 26; 43.
46 c. 895. *Ordo Confirm., Praenot.*, 14.
47 c. 896. *Ordo Confirm., Praenot.*, 15.
48 c. 894.

## ___ THE MOST HOLY EUCHARIST _____

1   c. 897. John Paul II, enc. *Redemptor Hominis* (4 Mar. 1979), 20; *Lumen Gentium*, 11; *Presbyterorum Ordinis*, 5: "The other sacraments, as well as every ministry of the Church and every work of the apostolate, are linked with the Holy Eucharist and are directed toward it. For the most blessed Eucharist contains the Church's entire spiritual wealth, that is, Christ himself, our Passover and living bread."

2   Vat. II. Const. *Sacrosanctum Concilium*, 47; John Paul II, *loc. cit.*

3   Paul VI, enc. *Mysterium Fidei* (3 Sept. 1965), 15; *Lumen Gentium*, 11; Decree *Unitatis redintegratio*, 2; 7; 50; John Paul II, Letter on *The Mystery and Worship of the Holy Eucharist* (24 Feb. 1980), 6:" 'By this love you have for one another, everyone will know that you are disciples'. The Eucharist educates us to this love in a deeper way; it shows us, in fact, what value each person, our brother or sister, has in God's eyes, if Christ offers himself equally to each one, under the species of bread and wine. If our Eucharistic worship is authentic, it must make us grow in awareness of the dignity of each person. The awareness of that dignity becomes the deepest motive of our relationship with our neighbor."

4   c. 898. John Paul II, enc. *Redemptor Hominis*, 20; Vat. II Const. *Dei Verbum*, 26; *Sacrosanctum Concilium*, 10; *Gaudium et Spes*, 38.

5   Cf. I Cor 11:24; Jn 6:32, 35, 51; Ac 2:42; I Cor 10:16; 11:20, 23-24; agape, consecration, mystery of faith, sacred mystery, etc.

6   *Summa Theol.*, III, q. 73, a. 4.

7   Jn 6:52; c. 897; Trent, Denz-Schön. 1636-1638; 1651-1652.

8   Trent, Denz.-Schön. 1653-1654; cf. S.C.D.F., 2 May 1972, *de fragmentis eucharisticis*; cf. *Summa Theol.*, III, q. 76, aa. 2-3; q. 65, aa. 1,3; q. 73, a. 1, ad 1; a. 3; q. 79; Jn 6:48-59; I Cor 10:16 sq.; Trent, Denz.-Schön. 1638; 1655.

9   cc. 898; 899. John Paul II, Letter, *loc. cit.*, 8.

10   *Missale Romanum, Inst. Gen.*, II, 7: S.C. Rit., Instr. *Eucharisticum mysterium*, (25 May 1969) 42; *Lumen Gentium*, 10:  "Though they differ from one another in essence and not only in degree, the common priesthood of the faithful and the ministerial or hierarchical priesthood are nonetheless interrelated. Each of them in its own special way is a participation in the one priesthood of Christ. The ministerial priest, by the sacred power he enjoys, molds and rules the priestly people. *Acting in the person of Christ*, he brings about the Eucharistic Sacrifice and offers it to God in the name of all the people. For their part, the faithful join in the offering of the Eucharist by virtue of their royal priesthood."

11   Instr. *Eucharisticum mysterium*, 43.

12   cc. 900, 1; 1024; S.C.D.F., Declaration *Inter insigniores* (15 Oct. 1976), on the question of the admission of women to the ministerial priesthood; *Lumen Gentium*, 17; cf. Trent. Denz-Schön. 1752; 1771. Cf. *Summa Theol.*, III, q. 82, aa. 1, 3. "Though all the faithful can baptize, the priest alone can complete the building up of the Body in the Eucharistic Sacrifice."

13   cc. 900, 2; 901; 903.

14   c. 904. Instr. *Eucharisticum mysterium*, 44.

15   S.C.C.D., *Instr. Tertia, Liturgicae instaurationes*, 1 (5 Sept. 1970):  "Liturgical reform is not at all synonymous with so-called desacralization and is not intended as an occasion for what is called secularization. Thus the liturgy must keep a dignified and sacred character." *Ibid.*, 3:  "The liturgical texts composed by the Church also deserve great respect. No one may make changes, substitutions, additions, or deletions in them." Instr. *Eucharisticum mysterium*, 45: "In the celebration of the Eucharist above all, no one, not even a priest, may on his own authority add, omit, or change anything in the liturgy. Only the supreme

authority of the Church and, according to the provisions of law, the bishop and episcopal conferences, may do this. Priests should therefore ensure that they so preside over the celebration of the Eucharist that the faithful know that they are attending not a rite established on private initiative, but the Church's worship, the regulation of which was entrusted by Christ to the Apostles and their successors.'' S.C.C.D., 15 May 1969: ''In our day and age there are those who think that they are up-to-date only when they can show off novelty, often bizarre, or devise arbitrary forms of liturgical celebrations. Priests, religious and diocesan, considerate of the true welfare of the faithful, realize that only in a generous and unyielding fidelity to the will of the Church, expressed in its directives, norms, and structures, lies the secret of a lasting and sanctifying pastoral success.''

16 c. 916.
17 c. 919.
18 c. 904. Instr. *Eucharisticum mysterium*, 44.
19 cc. 906; 907. Altar girls are strictly forbidden: ''In conformity with norms traditional in the Church, women (single, married, religious), whether in churches, homes, convents, schools, or institutions for women, are barred from serving the priest at the altar'' S.C.C.D., *Liturgicae instaurationes*, 7 (5 Sept. 1970): ''There are, of course, various roles that women can perform in the liturgical assembly: these include reading the word of God and proclaiming the intentions of the prayer of the faithful. Women are not however permitted to act as altar girls'' S.C.Sac. *Inaestimabile donum*, 18 (3 Apri. 1980).
20 c. 905.
21 c. 902.
22 S.C.C.D. Declaration *In celebratione Missae* (7 Aug. 1972); *Missale Romanum, Instit. Gen.*, 153-158.
23 cc. 910; 230, 3. Those ministers who distribute Holy Communion outside of Mass, to the sick and to the dying, are to follow the liturgical norms (cf. c. 918).
24 S.S. Sacr. Instr. *Immensae Caritatis* (29 Jan. 1973); S.C. Sacr. et Cult Div., Instr. *Inaestimabile donum*, 10 (3 Apr. 1980): ''The faithful, whether religious or lay, who are authorized as extraordinary ministers of the Eucharist may distribute Communion only when there is no priest, deacon or acolyte, when the priest is impeded by illness or advanced age, or when the number of the faithful going to communion is so large as to make the celebration of Mass excessively long. Accordingly, a reprehensible attitude is shown by those priests who, though present at the celebration, refrain from distributing Communion and leave this task to the laity.'' To administer the Eucharist to non-Catholic Christians the norms laid down for the reception of Communion by non-Catholic Christians are to be followed (cf. c. 844).
25 Cf. c. 918.
26 c. 911.
27 cc. 912; 915.
28 Cf. *Summa Theol.*, III, q. 79, a 7.
29 c. 844. Sec. for Christian Unity, Instr. *In quibus rerum circumstantiis* regarding admission of non-Catholic Christians to Holy Communion (1 June 1972).
30 c. 916.
31 ''Since 'it is clear that the frequent or daily reception of the most blessed Eucharist increases union with Christ, nurtures the spiritual life more richly, forms the soul in virtue, and gives the communicant a stronger pledge of eternal happiness, pastors, confessors, and preachers will frequently and zealously exhort the Christian people to this devout and salutary practice.' '' S.C.R. Instr. *Eucharisticum mysterium*, 37.
32 c. 913.

33 c. 914. SS.CC. Sacr. et Cult. Div. et Clero, *Declaration on putting the sacrament of penance before First Communion* (24 May 1973); *Confession before First Communion* (31 Mar. 1977 and 20 May 1977); S.C. Clero, *First Communion before Confession: End of Experimentation in the U.S.A.* (20 June 1973).

34 c. 919, 1, 3. Infirmity in the wide sense of the word is the weakening or the deficiency or the absence of health and thus is much broader than the notion of sickness or disease. In the context of the Eucharistic fast the notion of infirmity is based upon the sound and common estimation of men, who on their well-balanced judgment do not regard every indisposition or weakness as infirmity. Infirmity may be serious or light, chronic or acute, passing or enduring, requiring confinement or not, painful or painless, evident or hidden, more or less somatic or psychic, etc. In a case of doubt an indisposition or weakening of strength can be regarded as an infirmity. It suffices that a person of sound judgment and right conscience judges with true and positive probability that the particular case verifies the notion of infirmity.

35 cc. 918; 923.

36 c. 917.

37 c. 921.

38 c. 920. Cf. Jn 6:54; Trent, Denz.-Schön. 1638; 1659; 1730; 1734.

39 cc. 928; 929.

40 c. 930.

41 S.C.D.F., Reply (29 Oct. 1982). Priests, having an indult, may continue to use *mustum* in celebrating Mass.

42 S.C.E.O., *Facultates Legatis R.P. Concessae*, n. 7; Circular Letter of NCCB, 25 May 1971. Cf. c. 846, 2.

43 NCCB, *loc. cit.*

44 cc. 924; 926; Florence, Denz.-Schön. 1320; *Missale Romanum, Inst. Gen.* 281-285; S.C. Sac. et Div., Instr. *Inaestimabile donum* (3 Apr. 1980), 8: "Faithful to Christ's example, the Church has constantly used bread and wine mixed with water to celebrate the Lord's Supper. The bread for the celebration of the Eucharist in accordance with the tradition of the whole Church, must be made solely of wheat, and, in accordance with the tradition proper to the Latin Church, it must be unleavened. By reason of the sign, the matter of the Eucharistic celebration should appear as actual food. This is to be understood as linked to the consistency of the bread, and not to its form, which remains the traditional one. No other ingredients are to be added to the wheaten flour and water. The preparation of the bread requires attentive care, to ensure that the product does not detract from the dignity due to the Eucharistic bread, can be broken in a dignified way, does not give rise to excessive fragments, and does not offend the sensibilities of the faithful when they eat it. The wine for the Eucharistic celebration must be of 'the fruit of the vine' (Lk 22:18) and be natural and genuine, that is to say not mixed with other substances."

45 A priest may not consecrate hosts from which the gluten has been removed in order to provide Communion for one who must abstain from consuming any gluten. S.C.D.F. (29 Oct. 1982).

46 c. 924, 1. Cf. Trent, Denz.-Schön. 1748; Florence, *ibid.*, 1320; *Summa Theol.*, III, q. 74, a. 6.

47 If the priest notices after the consecration or when he receives Communion that water was poured into the chalice instead of wine, he is to pour the water into another container, then pour wine with water into the chalice and consecrate it. He says only the part of the narrative for the consecration of the chalice, without consecrating bread again (*Missale Romanum, Inst. Gen.*, n. 286).

48  The local Ordinary may permit Communion under the species of wine alone for those faithful who must abstain from all gluten, as is present in wheaten flour. S.C.D.F. (29 Oct. 1982).

49  On the other hand, S. Off. (23 May 1957): "**Q.** Do several priests validly concelebrate the Sacrifice of the Mass, if only one of them pronounces the words '*Hoc est corpus meum*' and '*Hic est sanguis meus*' over the bread and wine, and the others do not quote the words of the Lord, but, with the knowledge and consent of the celebrant, have and manifest the intention to make his words and actions their own? **R.** In the negative, because, by the institution of Christ, he alone celebrates validly who pronounces the words of consecration."

50  In a concelebrated Mass how near the hosts and wine must be to the celebrant to be morally present is left to the judgment of prudent men, the practice of the Church, the position and amount of the hosts and wine, etc.

51  c. 927.

52  c. 931.

53  c. 932. Cf. S.C.C.D., Instr. on *Masses for Special Gatherings* (15 May 1969).

54  c. 933.

55  Cf. *Summa Theol.*, III, q. 79, aa. 5, 7 ad 2; Pius XII, ency. *Mediator Dei* (20 Nov. 1947).

56  Alexander VII, (24 Sept. 1665), prop. 8 condemned (Denz.-Schön. 2028): "A priest can lawfully accept a twofold stipend for the same Mass by applying to the petitioner even the most special part of the fruits appropriated to the celebrant himself, and this after the decrees of Urban VIII."

57  Pius VI, (28 Aug. 1794) (Denz.-Schön. 2630).

58  cc. 945, 1; 946; Paul VI, motu proprio, *Firma in traditione* (13 June 1974): "There has been a strong tradition in the Church that the faithful, led on by a religious and ecclesial awareness, should conjoin a kind of sacrifice of themselves, as it were, with the Eucharistic sacrifice in order that they might more actively participate in it. In this way, they, on their part, provide for the needs of the Church, and especially for the support of her minister. This is done in keeping with the spirit of our Lord's words: *The laborer deserves his wages* (Lk 10:7), which the Apostle Paul calls to mind in his first epistle to Timothy (5:18) and in his first epistle to the Corinthians (9:7-14).

"This practice whereby the faithful associate themselves more closely with Christ offering Himself as victim and thereby reap a more abundant supply of fruits, has not only been approved by the Church but also promoted by it since the Church looks upon that practice as a sign of the union of the baptized persons with Christ, as well as of the member of the faithful with the priest who performs his ministry for the benefit of the said faithful.

"However, in order that this kind of awareness may always be preserved intact and may be protected from any possible change for the worse, apt norms have been established down through the course of the centuries. They have in view that the worship which the faithful liberally wish to render to God, may actually be celebrated with no lessening of observance and generosity. On the other hand, because of unusual circumstances of times and human social conditions, it is sometimes morally impossible — and, therefore, less than with full justice — to discharge in their entirety obligations which have been sought out and accepted. In these cases the Church, of necessity, is forced to revise those obligations in an appropriate way. At the same time, however, she strives to be consistent in this matter and to keep faith with the donors."

59  cc. 947; 945, 2. Only if the stipend would be considered as the price of the Mass and as though the priest would not celebrate the Mass if the stipend were not forthcoming would there be the aspect of simony (cf. c. 1380).

10-The Sacraments and Their Celebration

60  cc. 948; 949; 950.
61  c. 952.
62  c. 951.  Although a priest may not accept a stipend for a second Mass when he binates, when he has already discharged an obligation in justice in the first Mass, he may, however, apply his second Mass gratuitously or in charity for the intention of a person who offers him a stipend for the application of that Mass, and then discharge the justice obligation of the stipend on a subsequent day. Thus, if a donor cannot be put off to another day for the celebration of the Mass or it is not expedient to do so, the priest may choose thus to apply two Masses for the same intention, the bination Mass, out of gratitude or charity and another Mass on a subsequent day as the stipend Mass, all of which more than satisfies his obligation to the donor.
63  cc. 953; 955, 2. S.C. Council (24 Feb. 1947):  "The series of 'Gregorian Masses,' when it is unexpectedly interrupted by an impediment (e.g., by illness) or for other reasonable cause (e.g., the celebration of a funeral or wedding Mass), by dispositive action of the Church continues to have the effects of suffrage for the deceased which the practice of the Church and the piety of the faithful have hitherto attributed to it, but the priest-celebrant remains obliged to complete the celebration of the thirty Masses as soon as possible. The Ordinary, however, is to take opportune safeguards that no abuses creep into a matter of such great importance." The S.C. for the Clergy may also permit an interruption for other reasons, also in the cases of novenas and tridua of Masses (Paul VI, *Firmiter in traditione*).
64  c. 534.
65  c. 955, 1.
66  cc. 956; 954; 955, 3.
67  cc. 955, 4; 958; 957.
68  Paul VI, *Firmiter in traditione; motu proprio Pastorale munus* (30 Nov. 1963), 11-12. These faculties permit bishops to reduce, but not to extinguish, the obligation of funded Masses which has culpably in the past not been satisfied, bearing in mind as far as possible the will of the founders or offerers (Pont. Com. Decretis Conc. Vat. II Interp., resp. I, (1 July 1972).
69  Paul VI, *Firmiter in traditione*.

## ____ PENANCE ____

1  John Paul II, enc. *Redemptor Hominis* (4 Mar. 1979), 20:  "The Christ who calls to the Eucharistic Banquet is always the same Christ who exhorts us to penance and repeats his 'Repent'. Without this constant ever renewed endeavor for conversion, partaking in the Eucharist would lack its redeeming effectiveness and there would be a loss or at least a weakening of the special readiness to offer God the spiritual sacrifice in which our sharing in the priesthood of Christ is expressed in an essential and universal manner." Letter on *The Mystery and Worship of the Holy Eucharist* (24 Feb. 1980), 7:  "It is not only that Penance leads to the Eucharist, but that the Eucharist also leads to Penance. For when we realize who it is that we receive in Eucharistic Communion, there springs up in us almost spontaneously a sense of unworthiness, together with sorrow for our sins and an interior need for purification."
2  Trent, Denz.-Schön. 1668; 1670; S.C.C.D. *Rite of Penance* (2 Dec. 1973), 1, 3-5.
3  Cf. Ezk 18:30; Lk 13:3; Ac 2:38; Trent, Denz.-Schön. 1525-1526; 1553; *Summa Theol.*, III, q. 85, aa. 1, 3; *Suppl.*, q. 16, aa. 1, 3; Paul VI, Apost. Const. *Poenitemini*, on Christian Penance (17 Feb. 1966):  "All the faithful are obliged by divine law to do penance."
4  Trent, Denz.-Schön. 1669; 1667-1678:  Imperfect contrition or attrition springs from a consideration of the malice of sin or from the fear of hell and its punishments. It excludes the

will to sin and hopes for pardon; thus it does not make a man a hypocrite or a greater sinner but is a gift of God and an inspiration of the Holy Spirit, not as already dwelling in the soul but as merely giving an impulse that helps the penitent make his way toward justice. Necessary as *means* for salvation signifies that without it salvation cannot be obtained; necessary by *precept* means required inasmuch as it is prescribed.

5  Ec 5:8-9; Rm 2:4-5. Cf. *Summa Theol.*, II-II, 1, 14, a. 2; *Suppl.*, q. 6, a. 5; *IV Sent.*, d. 17, q. 3, a. 1, qcla. 4.

6  Trent, Denz.-Schön. 1670; 1672; 1674; 1677-1678; 1706. Paul VI, Address on *The ministerial aspect of the sacrament of Penance* (12 Mar. 1975): "This personal reconciliation of the sinner with God is possible at all times and in cases of emergency suffices to obtain the revivifying pardon of grace through an act of perfect contrition, as the catechism teaches. But we must remember that an act of perfect contrition must include, at least implicitly, the resolve to seek out, as soon as possible, the authorized ministry of the priest, endowed with the awesome power to forgive sins and to reconcile with God and with the living community of the Church those who have been unfaithful." Cf. *Rite of Penance*, Introd. 2. Interior penance or sorrow for sin committed must last a lifetime, as sin must always be displeasing. The external signs of this sorrow will last for a determined time in proportion to the sin. Penance must be habitually continual (the act itself must necessarily be interrupted) by doing nothing contrary to Penance and resolving to maintain displeasure of past sins.

7  c. 989. Cf. *Rite of Penance*, 7.

8  Trent. Denz.-Schón. 922; 1542-1543; 1580; 1672; 1674-1675; 1712; 3670. *Rite of Penance*, Introd. 5: "Penance always entails reconciliation with our brothers and sisters who are always harmed by our sins."

9  Trent, Denz.-Schón. 1671-1672; 1709.

10  c. 960.

11  c. 960. Cf. John Paul II (30 Jan. 1981), *Necessity of Sacramental Confession*; Apostolic Exhortation *Reconciliatio et Paenitentia* (2 Dec. 1984), 30-32.

12  Cf. Florence, Denz.-Schón. 1323; Trent, 1673; *Summa Theol.*, III, q. 84, a. 3.

13  *Rite of Penance*, 19; 21.

14  *Ibid.*, 46.

15  *Ibid.*, Appendix I.

16  *Ibid.*

17  c. 961. S.C.D.F. *Sacramentum Poenitentiae*, Pastoral Norms regarding General Absolution (16 June 1972); *Rite of Penance*, 31-35; 60-63; John Paul II, *Reconciliatio et Paenitentia*, 33.

18  c. 961, 1, 1°.

19  c. 961, 1, 2°.

20  c. 961, 2. Paul VI, Address to N.Y. Bishops on the Sacrament of Penance (20 Apr. 1978): "Ordinaries are not authorized to change the required conditions, to substitute other conditions, for those given, or to determine grave necessity according to their personal criteria, however worthy."

21  Pastoral Norms, *loc. cit.*; S.C.D.F. (20 Jan. 1978), *General Absolution*; Letter on *General Absolution* to N.C.C.B. (14 Jan. 1977).

22  *Ibid.*

23  *Ibid.*; cc. 962; 963.

24  c. 964; *Rite of Penance* 13. Face-to-face option for cloistered nuns is celebrated in such a way that the confessor remains outside the enclosure and the penitential rite not interfere with or be at variance with the law of enclosure (S.C. Rel., Reply, 4 Dec. 1978).

25 cc. 965; 966. Trent, Denz.-Schön. 1684; 1710; cf. *Summa Theol.* Suppl. q. 8, a. 1; q. 19, 1. 4; *Rite of Penance*, 9.

26 Trent, Denz.-Schön. 1686: *Summa Theol.* Suppl. q. 8, a. 4.

27 Cf. cc. 129-143.

28 cc. 867, 1-2; 968, 1.

29 cc. 968, 2; 967, 3.

30 Cf. cc. 129-143.

31 cc. 969; 972.

32 cc. 970; 971; 973.

33 c. 974.

34 cc. 967, 3; 974, 4.

35 cc. 975; 976; 144. Common error in the sacrament of Penance is a false judgment by which a priest is believed to be in possession of the jurisdiction necessary here and now to hear a confession and grant absolution, although in reality he does not. If the error is commonly held or if the situation would lead to a commonly held error, the Church, in order to safeguard the pastoral and juridical welfare of the faithful, supplies the needed jurisdiction for the moment. Likewise, the Church supplies such necessary jurisdiction in the case of a doubt of laws regarding the existence, extent or the meaning of a law respecting confessional jurisdiction in a particular situation or a doubt of fact regarding the existence of the conditions required by a law as it applies to a particular case.

36 c. 977.

37 cc. 1387; 982. There is a *latae sententiae* penalty for a false denunciation of a confessor (c. 1390, 1).

38 c. 983. Interpreters and others who receive confessional knowledge, and who violate the secret, are to be punished with a just penalty not excluding excommunication (1388, 2).

39 c. 1388, 1.

40 Lateran IV, Denz.-Schön. 814; *Rite of Penance*, 10d.

41 It thus differs from a purely natural secret. The violation of a natural secret, unlike the seal, is not a sacrilege, and it admits of lightness of matter; the obligation even of a committed secret can cease in certain instances, but the seal allows of no exception whatsoever; the obligation of the seal, unlike that of the secret, binds even toward the penitent or person who committed the sin.

42 c. 984. The director of novices and his assistant, and the rector of a monastery of any educational institution, are not to hear the sacramental confessions of their students living in the same house, unless in individual instances the students of their own accord request it (c. 985).

43 c. 978.

44 Cf. c. 279 on the continuing education of priests.

45 c. 987, 2. The confessor should be conversant with the Church's teaching on sexual ethics: pre-marital sex, homosexuality, masturbation, the reality of serious sin in moral acts (cf. S.C.D.F., *Declaration on Certain Questions concerning Sexual Ethics*, 29 Dec. 1975); euthanasia, painkillers, extraordinary means (cf. *ibid., Declaration on Euthanasia*, 5 May 1980); abortion (cf. *ibid., Declaration on Procured Abortion*, 18 Nov. 1974); sex education (cf. S.C. pro Inst. Catholica, *Educational Guidance in Human Love*, 1 Nov. 1983).

46 c. 986.

47 c. 980. However, absolution may not be imparted to the divorced and remarried; likewise in the case of Christians living together in an irregular union. Cf. John Paul II, Apostolic Exhortations *Familiaris Consortio*, 79-83, and *Reconciliatio et Paenitentia*, 34.

48  cc. 979; 981.  Cf. Thomas Aquinas, *Questiones quodlibetales* 3, q. 13, a. 28.: "It seems quite right that the priest not burden a penitent with the weight of a heavy penance. A small fire would be quickly put out if many logs were piled onto it; so too it might happen that the small spark of contrition just kindled in a penitent would be put out because of the heaviness of a penance and the sinner might fall into complete despair. Thus it is better for the priest to point out to the penitent what a heavy penance ought to be imposed for his sins, but then in fact to impose something that the penitent is capable of bearing. From performing this the penitent may learn to perform the greater works of penance that the priest would not attempt to impose. The expiation of the penitent over and above what has been expressly enjoined acquires greater value in atoning for past sins by reason of that general charge the priest expresses in the words: 'May whatever good you do profit you for the remission of sins.' Thus it is a praiseworthy practice that many priests use these words of the longer form of absolution."

49  cc. 1311; 1312.

50  Cf. cc. 1313-1320.

51  c. 1314.

52  cc. 1331-1333.

53  Cf. cc. 1321-1330.

54  c. 1367.

55  c. 1370, 1.

56  c. 1382; cf. also c. 1383: a person who has received a sacred order from a bishop without the lawful dimissorial letters is automatically suspended from the order received.

57  c. 1378, 1.

58  c. 1388, 1.

59  c. 1364, 1.

60  c. 1370, 2.

61  c. 1378, 2.

62  c. 1390, 1.

63  c. 1394.

64  c. 1398.

65  cc. 876; 1357, 3.

66  c. 1355, 2.

67  *Ibid.*, 1.

68  c. 1357, 1-2.  Confessors who are religious and canonically recognized as Regulars or Mendicants, when they hear confessions within the diocese for which they have confessional faculty, may absolve, but in the internal forum, from the automatically incurred (*latae sententiae*) reserved by the common law to the local Ordinary. The same confessors may dispense their penitents from irregularities *ex delicto occulto*, except in a case of voluntary homicide or a successful abortion or in a case which is before a judicial court. Restricted to the sacramental forum but not to more urgent cases, this faculty may be used to permit the penitent to receive Orders and to exercise Orders already received. (Cf. Ralph V. Shuhler, O.S.A., *Privileges of Regulars to Absolve and Dispense*, Washington, 1943, CUA Canon Law Studies, no. 186, pp. 169-170). These privileges are still operative (cf. canon 4.).

69  Vatican II, *Lumen Gentium*, 11.

70  c. 987.

71  *Rite of Penance*, 11. Cf. Paul VI, Addresses on the conditions for receiving the sacrament of Penance (5 Mar. 1975); on the ministerial aspect of the sacrament of Penance (12 Mar. 1975); on Penance as the "sacrament of resurrection and peace" (23 Mar. 1977).

72 Trent, Denz.-Schön. 1673; 1675; 1704; 1685; 1462; 1709. Cf. *Summa Theol.*, III, q. 84, a. 1, ad. 1; a. 2; q. 86, a. 6; 1. 90, a. 1, a. 2, ad 2.
73 Trent, Denz.-Schön. 1678; 1705.
74 *Ibid.*, 1679; 1706-1707.
75 *Ibid.*, 1683.
76 c. 990.
77 Trent, *loc. cit.*, 2158.
78 Innocent XI, Denz.-Schön. 2159.
79 Trent, *loc. cit.*, 1689-1691; 1693; 1712-1715.
80 *Ibid.*, 1692; 1715.
81 c. 988.
82 c. 989.
83 c. 991.
84 Trent, *loc. cit.*, 1679-1682; 1706-1707.
85 Alexander VII, Denz.-Schön. 2045.
86 c. 914. Cf. SS.CC. Sacr. et Cult. Div. et Clero, *Declaration on putting the sacrament of Penance before First Communion* (24 May 1973); *Confession before First Communion* (31 Mar. 1977 and 20 May 1977); S.C. Clero, *First Communion before Confession. End of Experimentation in the U.S.* (20 June 1973); *General Catechetical Directory, Addendum* (11 Aug. 1971).
87 Paul VI, Ap. Const. *Indulgentiarum Doctrina* (1 Jan. 1967), 1; S.C.D.F., *Pastoral Norm XII on general confession* (16 June 1972).
88 *Rite of Penance*, 7b. Cf. Pius XII, enc. *Mystici Corporis* (29 June 1943) 18. Cf. c. 988, 2.
89 Sec. for Christian Unity, *Ecumenical Directory* (14 June 1967), 46.

## ___ ANOINTING OF THE SICK _____

1 John Paul II, Apostolic Letter *On the Christian Meaning of Suffering*, (11 Feb. 1984). *Ordo unctionis infirmorum eorumque pastoralis curae*, nn. 1-3, S.C.C.D., (7 Dec. 1972).
2 c. 988. Vat. II, Const. *Lumen Gentium*, 11. This sacrament has usually been called Extreme Unction, because it is normally the last of the holy oils to be administered in life (cf. Const. *Sacrosanctum Concilium*, 73). From its matter it is sometimes called "holy oil" or "prayer with oil," or "oil of the sick" or "sacrament of the dying" from its recipient.
3 *Ordo unctionis infirmorum eorumque pastoralis curae*, n. 7.
4 Cf. Trent, Denz.-Schön. 1694; 1696.
5 *Ibid.*, 1695; cf. 1716. Apost. Const. *Sacram unctionis infirmorum*, (30 Nov. 1972): "The Catholic Church professes and teaches that the Sacred Anointing of the Sick is one of the seven Sacraments of the New Testament, that it was instituted by Christ, and that it was 'alluded to in Mark (6:13) and recommended and promulgated to the faithful by James the Apostle and Brother of the Lord.' "
6 Apost. Const. *Sacram unctionem infirmorum*: "This reality is in fact the grace of the Holy Spirit, whose anointing takes away sins, if any still remain to be taken away, and the remnants of sin; it also relieves and strengthens the soul of the sick person, arousing in him a great confidence in the divine mercy whereby, being thus sustained, he more easily bears the trials and labors of his sickness, more easily resists the temptations of the devil 'lying in wait' (Gn 3:15), and sometimes regains bodily health, if this is expedient for the health of the soul." Cf. Denz.-Schön. 1696; 1717.
7 *Ordo unctionis infirmorum eorumque pastoralis curae*, n. 6.

8  c. 1001.
9  c. 999. *Ordo unctionis infirmorum eorumque pastoralis curae*, nn. 20-21; 75.
10  *Ibid.*, n. 21.
11  *Ibid.*, n. 22.
12  *ibid.*, n. 23. Particular Rituals in the future may provide for additional unctions (*ibid.*, n. 24).
13  c. 1000.
14  c. 1002.
15  Apost. Const. *Sacram unctionem infirmorum; Ordo unctionis infirmorum eorumque pastoralis curae*, n. 25.
16  c. 1003, 1-2. *Ordo unctionis infirmorum eorumque pastoralis curae*, n. 16.
17  c. 1003, 2. *Ordo unctionis infirmorum eorumque pastoralis curae*, n. 18. It belongs to the local Ordinary to regulate those celebrations where the sick from different parishes or homes for the sick are brought together to be anointed (*ibid.*, n. 17).
18  Cf. Pius XII, Discourse "The Foundations and Norms of Christian Morality for the 'Exercise of the Mission of Health.' " (12 Nov. 1944).
19  *Ordo unctionis infirmorum eorumque pastoralis curae*, nn. 13; 17.
20  *Ibid.*, n. 19.
21  c. 1003, 3.
22  ·Vat. II, Const. *Sacrosanctum Concilium*, n. 73; *Ordo unctionis infirmorum eorumque pastoralis curae*, n. 8.
23  c. 1006. *Ordo unctionis infirmorum eorumque pastoralis curae*, n. 14.
24  *Ibid.*, n. 12.
25  c. 1005. Cf. Pref. S.C. Cult. Div., reply, (July, 1970).
26  c. 1004, 1. *Ordo unctionis infirmorum eorumque pastoralis curae*, n. 8; cf. Pius XI, Litt. Apost. *Explorata res*, (2 Feb. 1923) (AAS 15 [1923], 103-107). "The sacrament may be administered only to a person who is gravely ill through sickness or old age. Really serious senile debility or sickness already constitute a sufficient danger of death; or may be said to be dangerous. When there is prudent doubt about the gravity, the sacrament may be administered. But *any* chronic disease is not sufficient." Pref. S.C. Cult. Div., reply, (July, 1970).
27  *Ordo unctionis infirmorum eorumque pastoralis curae*, n. 10.
28  *ibid.*, n. 11. In arranging for communal celebration of this sacrament those who minister to the sick should not simply set an age as the sole determinant of who may be anointed. Other conditions should be considered in addition to the age chosen. A condition present in one person may not be as serious or dangerous as in another. However, in an elderly person chronic, debilitating diseases or conditions weaken and can place that person in a dangerous situation. Prudent judgment in arranging for the celebration is needed, based on the norms of this sacrament and the seriousness of the condition of the candidates. It would, moreover, be an abuse of the sacrament for those who minister to the sick or take part in a communal celebration, and who are themselves in good health, to be anointed to demonstrate a sense of solidarity with the sick. Adequate preparation and proper explanation by the minister previous to a celebration will usually obviate imprudences. Cf. also c. 1002.
29  Vat. II, Decree *Orientalium Ecclesiarum*, n. 27; Secr. ad unitatem Christianorum fovendam, *Directorium*, (14 May 1967), nn. 42, 44.
30  *Directorium*, n. 55.
31  *Ordo unctionis infirmorum eorumque pastoralis curae*, nn. 30; 115-116.
32  c. 1004, 2. *Ordo unctionis infirmorum eorumque pastoralis curae*, n. 9.
33  c. 1007.

THE SACRAMENTS AND THEIR CELEBRATION

34  c. 1005.
35  c. 921. *Ordo unctionis infirmorum eorumque pastoralis curae*, 32-37; 42-45.
36  *Ibid.*, nn. 46-48; 56; 62; 95.  Communion under both species may be given to the sick person who is being anointed and to those present only when the Eucharist either as Communion or as Viaticum is administered at a Mass celebrated in a church or lawfully in a home of a sick person or in a rest home. (*Missale Romanum. Instr. Gen.*, n. 242; *Ordo unctionis infirmorum eorumque pastoralis curae*, nn. 80; 82; 99).
37  *Ibid.*, nn. 49-63.
38  *Ibid.*, nn. 26-27; 93-114.
39  *Ibid.*, n. 29.
40  *Ibid.*, nn. 115; 122.
41  *Ibid.*, nn. 30; 116.
42  c. 883, 3°.
43  *Ordo unctionis infirmorum eorumque pastoralis curae*, nn. 117; 136-137.
44  *Ibid.*, nn. 138-151.

___ HOLY ORDERS _____

1  c. 1008.
2  John Paul II, Address to the clergy of Rome (9 Nov. 1978); Vat. II, *Lumen Gentium*, 10.
3  John Paul II, *Novo incipiente*, Letter to all priests of the world on Holy Thursday (8 Apr. 1979), 4.
4  *Lumen Gentium*, 20-21; 28; *Christus Dominus*, 2; 15-16; c. 1009: the orders are the episcopate, the presbyterate, and the diaconate, each of which is conferred by an imposition of hands and the prescribed prayer of consecration.
5  *Lumen Gentium*, 28-29; *Presbyterorum Ordinis*, 2-3; 6; 9; 12.
6  Florence, Denz.-Schón. 1326; Trent, Denz.-Schón. 857; 959-960; 1609; 1764; 1766-1771; 1773-1774; 1776; *Lumen Gentium*, 10; Pius XII, Ap. Const. *Sacramentum Ordinis* (30 Nov. 1947); *Presbyterorum Ordinis*, n. 2:  "Therefore, while it indeed presupposes the sacraments of Christian initiation, the sacerdotal office of priests is conferred by that special sacrament through which priests, by the anointing of the Holy Spirit, are marked with a special character and are so configured to Christ the Priest that they can act in the person of Christ our Head."
7  *Summa Theol.*, *Suppl.*, q. 35, a. 1, ad 3. Cf. Pius XI, enc. *Ad Catholici Sacerdotii* (20 Dec. 1935); Pius XII, enc. *Mediator Dei* (20 Nov. 1947); John Paul II, *Novo incipiente, op. cit.*
8  c. 1010.
9  c. 1011.
10 c. 1012. It makes no difference for validity if the bishop is heretical, schismatic, excommunicated, degraded, etc. Anglican ordinations were declared invalid (Leo XIII, Const. *Apostolicae curae*, 13 Sept. 1896) because the Anglican rite lacked the essential form, did not express the Catholic teaching on sacrifice and priesthood, and lacked the intention of conferring a properly priestly power. Ordinations conferred by dissident Oriental bishops, Jansenists, and Old Catholics, are generally valid, because of a validly consecrated hierarchy (cf. Pius IX, Enc. *Etsi multa*, 21 Nov. 1873).
11 c. 1015, 1. Dimissorial letters (*litterae dimissoriae*) are those by which a superior releases (*dimittere*) or sends his own subject to another bishop with the faculty of receiving orders from him. They differ from testimonial letters by which is given merely an authentic attestation of birth, age, character, doctrine, etc., of the one to be ordained.
12 c. 1015, 3.

13  c. 1016.
14  Paul VI, *motu proprio, Ministeria quaedam* (15 Aug. 1972), IX.
15  S.C. Sacr. et Cult. Div., Reply (15 Nov. 1979).
16  c. 1019.
17  cc. 1020-1021. Dimissorial letters, which must be clearly proven to the ordaining bishop to be genuine, may be restricted or revoked by the grantor or his successor, but are operative even when the authority of the one granting them ceases (cc. 1022-1023).
18  S.C. Sacr. et Cult. Div., Reply (20 Apr. 1980).
19  c. 1024; S.C.D.F. (15 Oct. 1976) *Declaration on the admission of women to the ministerial priesthood*; Paul VI, *motu proprio, Ministeria quaedam* (15 Aug. 1972), VII.
20  c. 1025, 1-2. The bishop ordaining his own subject who is destined for service in another diocese must be certain that the ordained will be assigned to the other diocese (c. 1025, 3).
21  *Ministeria quaedam, op. cit.*; c. 910, 2; NCCB (15 Nov. 1972).
22  Paul VI, *motu proprio, Ad pascendum* (15 Aug. 1972); *motu proprio, Sacrum Diaconatum Ordinem* (18 June 1967); NCCB (15 Nov. 1972).
23  cc. 1037; 1087.
24  *Sacrum Diaconatus Ordinem, op. cit.*, n. 22.
25  cc. 1026-1029.
26  cc. 1031, 1; 1032, 1-2. A dispensation from more than one year of age is reserved to the Apostolic See (c. 1031, 4).
27  cc. 1026-1029. A candidate should have won the respect of the clergy and faithful by having lived a truly Christian life for a long time, by his upright character, and by showing that this nature and disposition are inclined toward the ministry. Married men should have lived as spouses for a number of years and have shown themselves to have been good heads of their homes and whose wives and children lead a truly Christian life and have a good reputation. The wives should not only consent but also have the Christian moral character and attributes which will neither hinder their husband's ministry nor be out of keeping with it (*Sacrum Diaconatus Ordinem*, III).
28  c. 1031, 2. The conference of bishops may require an older age for the permanent diaconate, but for an age lower than one year recourse must be had to the Apostolic See (*ibid.*, 3-4).
29  c. 1032, 3; *Sacrum Diaconatus Ordinem*, n. 16; *Ad pascendum*, VI; c. 1044, 1, 3°.  It is not the practice of the Apostolic See to allow remarriage, unless in very exceptional cases.
30  Cf. *Presbyterorum Ordinis*, 1-2; *Lumen Gentium*, 10; Paul VI, enc. *Sacerdotalis caelibatus* (24 June 1967); John Paul II, *Novo incipiente, op. cit.*; S.C.D.F., Declaration *Mysterium Ecclesiae* (24 June 1973), 6.
31  cc. 1026-1029; 1031, 1, 4. The episcopal conference may set a later age for the priesthood and permanent diaconate (c. 1031, 3).
32  cc. 1030; 1038.
33  cc. 1033; 1035.
34  cc. 1034; 1036.
35  c. 1037. Cf. also Paul VI, *Sacerdotalis caelibatus, op. cit.*
36  c. 1039.
37  St. Pius X, *Sacrorum Antistitum* (1 Sept. 1910).
38  Cf. *Summa Theol.*, II—II, q. 184, a. 6; q. 189, a. 1, ad 3.
39  c. 1040.
40  The faithful are bound to reveal to the Ordinary, before the ordination, any impediments to sacred orders they may know about (c. 1043).
41  cc. 1041; 1047.

42 The delinquent need not have belonged to a sect; the irregularity refers to past or present separation or apostasy from the Catholic Church.

43 cc. 1042; 1047.

44 Those things forbidden to clerics are listed in cc. 285-286.

45 cc. 1044, 1; 1047.

46 cc. 1044, 2; 1047.

47 cc. 1047, 1; 1049, 3.

48 cc. 1045-1046.

49 c. 1048. Confessors who are Regulars or Mendicants with jurisdiction from the local Ordinary can dispense their penitents from irregularities arising from an occult offence, except in cases of voluntary homicide or effectively procured abortion or those before a judicial forum. Restricted to the internal forum but not to more urgent cases, this faculty may be used to permit the penitent to receive a sacred order or to exercise an order already lawfully received.

50 c. 1049, 1-2.

51 c. 1052.

52 c. 2053.

53 c. 1054.

## MARRIAGE

1 Cf. cc. 1055, 1; 1057; Vatican II, *Apostolicam Actuositatem*, 11; *Gaudium et Spes*, 48; John Paul II, Apostolic Exhortation, *Familiaris Consortio* (22 Nov. 1981), 3; "Willed by God in the very act of creation, marriage and the family are interiorly ordained to fulfillment in Christ and have need of his graces in order to be healed from the wounds of sin and restored to their 'beginning', that is, to full understanding and the full realization of God's plan."

2 Paul VI, Address *Tout d'Abord* (4 May 1970).

3 Cf. Gn 1:27; 2:3, 18; Mt 19:3-6; Mk 10:2-9; Trent, Denz.-Schön. 1797-1799.

4 Cf. *Summa Theol.*, *Suppl.*, 1, 41, aa. 1. 3; III *Cont. Gent.*, c. 122; Denz.-Schön. 206; 461; 1012.

5 I Cor 7:9; cf. *Summa Theol.*, II-II, q. 152, a. 2, ad 1; *Suppl.*, q. 41, aa. 2, 3; III *Cont. Gent.*, c. 136; *Gaudium et Spes*, 49; Leo XIII, enc. *Arcanum Divinae Sapientiae* (10 Feb. 1880), 19.

6 *Gaudium et Spes*, 48-49. John Paul II, *Familiaris Consortio*, 11: "Sexuality, by means of which man and woman give themselves to one another through the acts which are proper and exclusive to spouses, is by no means something purely biological, but concerns the innermost being of the human person as such. It is realized in a truly human way only if it is an integral part of the love by which a man and a woman commit themselves totally to one another until death. The total self-giving would be a lie if it were not the sign and fruit of a total personal self-giving, in which the whole person, including the temporal dimension, is present: if the person were to withhold something or reserve the possibility of deciding otherwise in the future, by this very fact he or she would not be giving totally." The right (as distinguished from the use) to the acts of themselves apt to procreate is essential; if the right is not transferred (in the sense of being intended and not excluded) or if the party is not apt to generate, there can be no marital contract or union. Marriage bespeaks an order to carnal copulation, although the latter does not pertain to its essence but to its integrity.

7 Paul VI, enc. *Humanae Vitae* (25 July 1968), n. 8: "Marriage . . . is the wise institution of the Creator to realize in mankind his design of love. By means of the reciprocal personal gift of self, proper and exclusive to them, husband and wife tend towards the communion of their beings in view of mutual personal perfection, to collaborate with God in the generation and education of new lives."

*Gaudium et Spes*, nn. 48-49; 50: "But in fact marriage is not instituted merely for procreation. The indissoluble character of the personal pact and the good of the children themselves demand that mutual love should be properly shown between a married couple, that it should progress and mature. Even therefore if children, often so much desired, are lacking, marriage persists as a lifetime comradeship and keeps its value and indissolubility."

There are certain goods or benefits or effects which follow from a validly and lawfully contracted marriage, substantial or essential goods which cannot be intentionally excluded and which safeguard the validity of marriage. Inasmuch as they accrue to the spouses they are called goods or benefits or blessings; inasmuch as they attract or move men to contract marriage they are called ends or goals. They compensate for the difficulties and trials of married life. They are: (1) the benefit or blessing of *offspring*, which founds the rights and obligations regarding the use of marriage and the rearing and formation of the offspring; (2) the good of *faith*, i.e., conjugal fidelity or mutual faithfulness of the spouses as regards bodily rights and what is conducive to leading a stable family life; (3) the *sacrament* or the hallowedness or sacredness of every marriage bond and the inseparableness of the spouses as a sign of the indivisible union of Christ with his Church — which is confirmed and strengthened in a marriage which is also a sacrament.

John Paul II, *Familiaris Consortio*, 3: "The Church is deeply convinced that only by the acceptance of the Gospel are the hopes that man legitimately places in marriage and in the family capable of being fulfilled"; cf. also n. 12.

8 *Familiaris Consortio*, 13.
9 c. 1055, 2; Ep 5:22-32; Trent, Denz.-Schön. 1797-1801; Pius XI, enc. *Casti Connubii* (31 Dec. 1930); *Gaudium et Spes*, 48; *Apostolicam Actuositatem*, 11; *Familiaris Consortio*, 13.
10 c. 1055, 2; only the legitimately manifested consent between two persons capable in law to give consent brings a marriage into being (c. 1057).
11 cc. 1058-1060.
12 cc. 1061; 1117.
13 c. 1062.
14 c. 1056; *Familiaris Consortio*, 19-20.
15 Cf. Paul VI, Address *"Tout d'Abord"*; *Summa Theol.*, *Suppl.*, q. 67, a. 1; *III Cont. Gent.*, c. 123.
16 Mt 5:31-33; 19:3-12; Mk 10:2-12; Lk 16:18; I Cor 7:10-11; Rm 7:2-3; Trent, Denz.-Schön. 1805; 1807; Pius VII, Denz.-Schön. 2705-2706; Pius IX, Denz.-Schön. 2967; Pius XII, *Allocution to the Rota* (3 Oct. 1941).
17 *Familiaris Consortio*, 65-66.
18 c. 1064.
19 c. 1063.
20 *Ibid.*, 1°; 2°.
21 *Familiaris Consortio*, 66.
22 c. 1063, 3°.
23 *Familiaris Consortio*, 67-68.
24 c. 1063, 4°.

25   *Familiaris Consortio*, 69.
26   c. 1066.   Before the celebration of the marriage all who know about any impediments are bound to reveal them to the pastor or local Ordinary (c. 1069). The pastor, before assisting at the marriage, must observe the norms laid down by the episcopal conference concerning questions to the parties, inquiries to be made, banns to be published (c. 1067).
27   cc. 1115; 1068.
28   Cf. Paul VI, motu proprio *Matrimonia Mixta* (31 Mar. 1970); NCCB, *Implementation in the USA* (16 Nov. 1970).
29   Cf. c. 1067.
30   c. 1065; cf. *Familiaris Consortio*, 57.
31   c. 1072.
32   *Familiaris Consortio*, 79-85.
33   c. 1070.
34   c. 1071.
35   c. 1073.
36   cc. 1075; 1077; 134.   This power to prohibit may be delegated, e.g., to ecclesiastical judges who may issue prohibitions following marriage annulment trials. A custom which introduces a new impediment, or is contrary to existing impediments, is to be reprobated (c. 1076). Cf. Trent, Denz.-Schön. 1804; Leo XIII, enc. *Arcanum*; Pius XI, enc. *Casti Connubii*; Pius XII, Allocution to the Rota (6 Oct. 1946).
37   c. 1074.
38   c. 1078, 2.
39   cc. 1078, 1, 3; 134.
40   cc. 131; 134, 2; 137.   The power to delegate should follow the norms of cc. 85-93, especially c. 90, 1, regarding a just and reasonable cause for the validity and lawfulness of the dispensation. The general norms for rescripts (cc. 59-75) are valid for the manner of dispensations.
41   c. 1079, 1.   The danger may be intrinsic, e.g., serious illness, or extrinsic, e.g., impending critical surgery, imposed death sentence.
42   *Ibid.*, 2, 4.   There must be a prudent judgment or at least a serious probability of death ensuing. The local Ordinary is considered available if he can be reached by mail or in person within a reasonable period of time.
      The pastor may dispense in the circumstances from the canonical form required for the validity of marriage. Thus he may dispense from his own presence and/or that of one or both qualified witnesses. He may not dispense from the obligation of giving or renewing consent.
      When there is question of a dispensation from mixed religion or from disparity of religion the declaration and promise of the Catholic party must be given even in danger of death, which in an extreme case may be given at least implicitly.
43   *Ibid.*, 3.   This includes a case in which one of the parties is conscious of an occult impediment but wishes it to remain confidential. The confessor, who may exercise this power even outside sacramental confession, need not have recourse to the local Ordinary or inform him of the dispensation. If both public and occult impediments are present, the attending priest may, acting as a confessor, dispense from occult impediments and also from public impediments if recourse to the local Ordinary is impossible.
      The confessor cannot dispense from the obligation of consent. When he judges it prudent to dispense in the internal forum from the canonical form, he must have the penitent renew marital consent and notify his partner that consent must be renewed by both parties. This he may allow the penitents to do privately and secretly, i.e., externally but

without the canonical form and without others knowing about it. If the requisite circumstances are present and he judges it to be prudently expedient, the confessor may urge that he be approached outside the sacramental forum and act as the assisting priest of canon 1116, 2.

44    c. 1080, 1.    The discovery of the impediment is made by the priest or deacon, even if the impediment was concealed in bad faith (in which case the reason for the concealment should be carefully examined in view of the good of the projected marriage). The pastor and others may dispense only in occult cases (as distinct from occult impediments), i.e., when there is an impediment public by nature but in fact secret from most persons. The harm that may be present is, for example, loss of reputation of the parties, notable family quarrels, deportation. The undelegated priest of canon 1116, 2 may dispense in occult cases.

45    *Ibid.*, 2.    Assistance at or convalidation of a marriage in danger of death should be approached with great caution. In an urgency of the condition or danger of death the preparation of the soul of the dying person by right dispositions for the sacraments is paramount. A promise to do what is necessary to straighten out the invalid marriage situation would suffice. Dispensation would be given from impediments and from the canonical form (if indicated), absolution imparted from sins and censures, marital consent asked for and received or renewed.

46    cc. 1081; 1082.

47    c. 1083.

48    cc. 1071, 1, 6°; 1072.

49    cc. 1156; 1157.

50    c. 1084.

51    Cf. S.C.D.F. (13 May 1977); S.C. Sacr. (R Aug. 1972); S.R. Rota *Decisiones* (22 Feb. 1963).

52    c. 1084, 3.

53    Cf. cc. 1097; 1098.    *Familiaris Consortio*, 14: "It must not be forgotten however that, even when procreation is not possible, conjugal life does not for this reason lose its value. Physical sterility in fact can be for spouses the occasion for other important services to the life of the human person, for example, various forms of educational work, and assistance to other families and to poor or handicapped children."

     The Holy See has condemned as contrary to the natural law direct sterilization, e.g., Pius XI, enc. *Casti Connubii; S. Off.* (21 Mar. 1931); and artificial insemination, e.g., S. Off. (26 Mar. 1897; 24 iul. 1929); Pius XII, Allocutions (29 Sept. 1949); 29 Oct. 1951); Paul VI enc. *Humanae Vitae*, n. 14 (25 July 1968); Vat. II Const. *Gaudium et Spes*, n. 51.

54    c. 1085.

55    A petitioner may wish to convalidate a subsequent union and thus be declared free of the bond of the previous marriage because of the death of the previous partner or because of a defect or impediment in the first marriage. On the other hand, the petitioner may have married a divorced person and now wishes to be freed on the basis of the latter's previous valid and extant bond, or the petitioner has married a second time — the first partner dying after this second marriage was entered into — and now desires freedom from the second marriage. The cases concerning nullity of a previous marriage, dissolution of a prior marriage, are considered in cc. 1141-1150; 1671-1691; 1697-1706.

56    c. 1707.

57    c. 1086, 1.

58    *Ibid.*,3.    There must be certainty also that the marriage has not been validated or sanated. S. Off. (28 Dec. 1949): "Whether, in adjudicating matrimonial cases, Baptism con-

ferred in the sects of the Disciples of Christ, the Presbyterians, the Congregationalists, the Baptists, the Methodists, when the necessary matter and form were used, is to be presumed invalid because of the lack of the requisite intention on the part of the minister to do what the Church does or what Christ instituted, or whether such Baptism is to be considered valid, unless the contrary is proved in the particular case. In the negative to the first part; in the affirmative to the second part.''

59   Cod. Or. c. 60, 1.   The impediment existed also prior to the present Oriental Code of 2 May 1949 (cf. S. Off. 18 May 1949; 17 Apr. 1950).

60   PCI 29 apr. 1940; c. 1099, 2 (1917 Code).   An infant of non-Catholic parents, who is baptized by a Catholic priest or layman contrary to the law (c. 868, 1, 2°) outside the danger of death and who is educated outside the Church, is probably not bound, but the local Ordinary should be consulted in practice.

61   c. 1086, 2; cc. 1125; 1126.

62   c. 1087.

63   The present Oriental Code (c. 62) extends this same impediment also to the subdiaconate, although in the Oriental Church (with the exception of the Armenians) it is not a sacred or major order.

64   Motu proprio *Ad Pascendum* (15 Aug. 1972), V. Previously an oath was taken before subdiaconate. This oath still perdures for those who took it.

65   c. 1037; *Sacrum Diaconatus Ordinem*, n. 16; *Ad Pascendum*, VI; c. 1044, 1, 3°.

66   cc. 290-292; 1078, 2, 1°.

67   c. 1088.

68   cc. 691-693; 700-701.

69   c. 1089.

70   c. 1090.

71   c. 108; Cod. Or., *Crebrae allatae*, 66.

72   Cod. Or. c. 66.

73   c. 1091, 1-3.

74   c. 1091, 4.

75   c. 1092.

76   c. 1093.

77   The impediment does not arise from non-sacramental or sacramental non-consummated marriages which are canonically dissolved, since they are valid marriages.

78   c. 1094.

79   c. 1057.

80   c. 1095, 1°.

81   *Ibid.*, 2°.

82   *Ibid.*, 3°.

83   c. 1096.

84   c. 1097, 1.

85   *Ibid.*, 2.

86   However, it may be that, in an individual case, such an error is substantial.

87   c. 1099.

88   S. Off. (11 Mar. 1886):   "Marriages are valid which are entered into when the contractants are solely in error that the bond of consummated marriage can be dissolved in the case of adultery or for other causes. However, if they are entered into under this expressed condition, they are to be considered as invalid.''

89   c. 1100.

90   c. 1101.

91  c. 1098.

92  c. 1102.  Baptized Orientals are forbidden to contract marriage lawfully with any condition whatever (Cod. Or. c. 83).

93  There is a question here not of a desire or pupose of maintaining temporary or perpetual continence but of a *condition* whereby (especially when there is a mutual pact) the parties to the marriage intend to bind themselves in justice not to seek to render the natural marital debt. Pius XII, *Allocution to Italian Midwives* (26 Nov. 1951): "If at the time of the marriage at least one of the couples intended to restrict the marriage right, not merely its use, to the sterile periods, in such a way that at other times the second party would not even have the right to demand the act, this would imply an essential defect in the consent to marriage, which would carry with it invalidity of the marriage itself, because the right deriving from the contract of marriage is a permanent, uninterrupted, and not intermittent right of each of the parties, one to another. On the other hand, if the act be limited to the sterile periods insofar as the mere use and not the right is concerned, there is no question about the validity of the marriage."

94  c. 1103.

95  Because of the uncertainty of the invalidity springing from ecclesiastical law alone or also from natural law, fear present in the contracting of marriage between two unbaptized persons doubtfully invalidates and must be submitted to the tribunal of the local Church.

96  Cod. Or. c. 78, requires that the unjust pressure be induced precisely to extort marital consent.

97  This must be distinguished from the reluctance or resistance which, in some mission areas, is shown by the bride as part of the ritual or ceremonial of marriage.

98  c. 1104.  Marriage can be contracted through an interpreter, but the pastor may not assist at such a marriage unless he is certain of the trustworthiness of the interpreter (c. 1106).

99  c. 1105, 1-2.  If the mandator cannot write, this is to be recorded in the mandate and another witness added who is also to sign the document; otherwise, the mandate is invalid. If the mandator revokes the mandate, or becomes insane, before the proxy contracts in that person's name, the marriage is invalid, even though the proxy or the other contracting party is unaware of the fact (*ibid.*, 3-4).

100  c. 1107.

101  c. 1108.  Exceptions are in regard to lay persons as official witness, the extraordinary form of marriage, the power of the local Ordinary to dispense from the form (cc. 1112, 1; 1116; 1127, 2-3.  In the case of common error or of positive and probable doubt of law or of fact as to legitimate assistance, the Church supplies the power of assistance for the internal and external forums, (c. 144) e.g., if the one to be married requests a particular priest to assist at his marriage, since he judges — as most of the parish would — that he has (since he has had) the faculty to do so; or if an assisting priest thinks he is in his proper territory or that he has been properly delegated or that as parochial vicar he is empowered to supply in all things, etc. From the circumstances it will be judged whether the error was common or private, whether the cause of the common error is certain in that the public fact founding it is disposed to result with a certain constraint in the error. Common error in the form of marriage is not easily proved. More common teaching maintains that in the case of such an error or doubt regarding a priest who habitually assists at marriages, e.g., as a curate, or frequently helps out in this capacity, he receives the suppliance of the Church in these circumstances; not, however, in the case of a priest who habitually is not engaged in marriage assistance, for a single marriage. The practice of the Rota is and has been to declare as null a marriage where the delegation — not otherwise habitually enjoyed by the priest — is absent in the particular case.

102 Where there are no priests or deacons, the diocesan bishop can delegate lay persons to assist at marriages, if the episcopal conference has given its prior approval and the permission of the Holy See has been obtained. A suitable lay person is to be selected, capable of giving instruction to those who are getting married, and qualified to conduct the marriage liturgy properly (c. 1112).

103 c. 1109.

104 cc. 262; 558; 566, 1.

105 c. 1110.

106 c. 518.

107 *Crebrae allatae*, c. 88, 3.

108 Oriental Code Commission, 3 May 1953 (*CLD* IV, p. 17); S.C. Doc. Faith, 1 Feb. 1967 (*CLD* IV, pp. 411-412); S.C. Or. Ch., 13 Dec. 1968 (*CLD* VII, pp. 8-9, 752-753); NCCB, 8 Mar. 1967.

109 S.C. Or. Ch., 30 May 1979.

110 Thus an Eastern rite pastor does not validly assist in his territory at the marriage of two Latin faithful or a Latin rite pastor at the marriage of two Eastern faithful (CIC, c. 1095, § 1, 2°; *Crebrae allatae*, c. 88, § 1, 2°; Pont. Or. Commission, 3 May 1953; *CLD* IV, p. 16). An Eastern rite pastor within the confines of his territory validly and lawfully assits at the marriage of the faithful of his rite in places which are exclusively of another rite, provided there be the express consent of the Ordinary or pastor or rector of the aforesaid places (Pont. Or. Commission, 8 July 1952; *CLD* III, p. 32). It should be noted that in the case of Catholics, either Eastern or Latin, contracting marriage with a faithful of non-Catholic Eastern churches, the canonical form of celebration for these marriages is of obligation only for lawfulness; for validity, the presence of the sacred minister is sufficient, observing the other requirements of law (Decree *Crescens matrimoniorum*, S.C. Or. Ch., 22 Feb. 1967; *CLD* VI, pp. 605-606; CIC, c. 1127, 1 in the revised Code).

111 Oriental Code Com., 8 Jan. 1953; *CLD* VI, pp. 14-15. "All the Orientals, who do not have an Ordinary of their own and who are outside the Patriarchate of the East, are subject to the local Latin Ordinary in all respects. Therefore, the local Latin Ordinary has, with respect to the clergy and laity of an Oriental rite resident in his jurisdiction, the same powers he has over the clergy and faithful of the Latin rite" (S.C. Or. Ch., 3 Aug. 1959; *CLD* V, p. 12).

112 c. 846, 2; *Cleri sanctitati*, c. 2, 1.

113 c. 1111.

114 c. 137, 3-4.

115 c. 1114.

116 Cf. Sec. ad unit. fov. *Directorium* (14 May 1957), 49; 58.

117 cc. 1117; 1127, 2. A blessing is also required for validity in the form for Orientals (Cod. Or. cc. 85; 90).

118 c. 1116.

119 c. 1117; Cod. Or. c. 90, 2; even if they belong to an atheistic sect (PCI 30 July 1934). Also exempted are those baptized in a non-Catholic or dissident Oriental sect (S.C. Conc. 28 Mar. 1908).

120 The effective date of the motu proprio Decretum Ne Temere of Pius XII (1 Aug. 1948) abrogating the second comma of c. 1099, 2. It should be noted that these same persons were still bound by the impediment of disparity of worship when they married an unbaptized party (PCI 29 Apr. 1940). PCI 20 iul. 1929; 25 July 1931; 17 Feb. 1930. S. Off. 7 Jan. 1947.

121 The effective date of the motu proprio *Crebrae allatae* of Pius XII (22 Feb. 1949) establishing the Oriental Code on marriage. It had already been declared that a Latin rite woman who in virtue of c. 98, 4 declared she wished to transfer *in matrimonio ineundo* to the Oriental rite of the man, was still bound to the form for the celebation of marriage (PCI 29 apr. 1940; c. 1099, 1, 3°); thus the observance of the form preceded the change of rite.

122 S.C.D.E. Decree *Crescens Matrimoniorum*, 22 Feb. 1967. It should be noted that Vat. II Decree *Orientalium Ecclesiarum* stated that, when Eastern Catholics marry baptized Eastern non-Catholics, the canonical form obliged only *for lawfulness*; for *validity* the presence of a sacred minister sufficed, observing the other prescriptions of law. (The decree became effective in the USA on 21 Jan. 1965). The sacred minister referred to is taken to mean any sacred minister, including a deacon, accepted as validly ordained by the Eastern Orthodox and used by them to bless marriages. The other requirements of the law to be observed (for lawfulness) are: dispensation from the canonical form for lawfulness, prenuptial investigation, promises, dispensation from mixed religion, etc. The local Ordinary who grants the dispensation from the impediment of mixed religion is the one who may dispense from the canonical form for lawfulness (Decree *Crescens Matrimoniorum*); he may be either the Ordinary of the Catholic party or the Ordinary of the place of the marriage. If the former, as is customary, the latter should be informed beforehand. Marriages of Latins which took place before an Orthodox minister before 25 Mar. 1967 (the effective date of *Crescens Matrimoniorum*) would require a renewal of consent before a sacred minister (Catholic or Orthodox) or a radical sanation if the Orthodox party refuses. Cf. c. 1127, 1.

123 c. 1116.

124 c. 1119.

125 S.C. Rit., 19 Mar. 1969, *Ordo Celebrandi Matrimonium*, n. 11 (U.S.C.C., *Rite of Marriage*). Cf. nn. 12-18 for adaptations within the competence of episcopal conferences.

126 Motu proprio *Matrimonia Mixta*, 31 Mar. 1970, n. 11; *Rite of the Celebration of Marriage*, nos. 39-54, 55-66, 1938; Sec. ad unit. Christ. Fovendam *Directorium*, n. 39; NCCB, *Implementation of the Apostolic Letter on Mixed Marriages*, 16 Nov. 1970, n. 17.

127 Motu proprio, *Matrimonia Mixta*, n. 13.

128 NCCB, *Implementation*, nos. 16-17. Cf. *Directorium*, 56.

129 c. 1115.

130 c. 1118.

131 c. 1121.

132 c. 1122.

133 c. 1123.

134 Cod. Or. cc. 50-54; Pius XI, enc. *Casti Connubii*; Paul VI, motu proprio *Matrimonia Mixta* (31 Mar. 1970); NCCB, *Implementation* (16 Nov. 1970); Paul VI, motu proprio *Causae Matrimoniales* (28 Mar. 1971); John Paul II, Apostolic Exhortation *Familiaris Consortio* (22 Nov. 1981), 78 ff.

135 c. 1124.

136 c. 1125. The regulations of the local diocese and any statutes of the episcopal conference are to be followed (c. 1126). Cf. also *Familiaris Consortio*, 28 ff., on the transmission of life.

137 c. 1127, 1.

138 *Ibid.*, 2. The norms in the diocese or from the episcopal conference are to be followed.

139 cc. 933; 1118; NCCB, *Implementation*, 19.

140 NCCB, *Implementation*, 10, 11.

141 c. 1127, 3.

142 NCCB, *Implementation*, 15; 16.
143 c. 1128.
144 c. 1129. Cf. *Familiaris Consortio*, 78.
145 cc. 1130; 1131; 1133. The local Ordinary is freed from their secrecy if from its observance a threat arises of grave scandal or grave harm to the sanctity of marriage; the parties are made aware of this fact before the marriage (c. 1132).
146 cc. 1134-1135.
147 Vatican II, *Gaudium et Spes*, 47-52; *Familiaris Consortio*; cf. also *The Vatican Charter of the Rights of the Family* (24 Nov. 1983).
148 Cf. Gn 2:18; Mt 19:5; Ep 5:25, 31; 1 Tm 2:15; Col 3:18; 1 Cor 11:3; Leo XIII, enc. *Arcanum divinae sapientiae*; Pius XI, enc. *Casti Connubii*; Vat. II, *Gaudium et Spes*, 49-50; *Apostolicam Actuositatem*, 11; Paul VI, enc. *Humanae Vitae*, 9.
149 1 Cor 7:3-5; Heb 13:4; Pius XI, ency. *Casti Connubii*; Vat. II, *Gaudium et Spes*, 49; *Summa Theol., Suppl.*, q. 41, a. 4.
150 Cf. Gn 1:28; 1 Cor 7:3; Paul VI, ency. *Humanae Vitae*.
151 Innocent XI (S. Off. 4 Mar. 1679) condemned the proposition: "opus conjugii ob solam voluptatem exercitum omit penitus caret culpa ac defectu veniali". Denz.-Schón. 2109. Cf. also *Summa Theol, Suppl.*, q. 49, aa. 406.
152 Cf. Dt 11:19; Ec 7:25; Pr 13:13-14, 24; 22:6; Ep 6:4; Col 3:21; *Gaudium et Spes*, 52.
153 Cf. S.C. for Catholic Education, *Educational Guidance in Human Love* (1 Nov. 1983); John Paul II, Apostolic Exhortation, *Catechesi Tradendae* (16 Oct. 1979), 35-39; *Familiaris Consortio*, 36-41.
154 Cf. 2 Cor 12:14; *Summa Theol.* II-II,.q. 101, a. 2, ad 2.
155 cc. 1137-1138.
156 cc. 1139-1140.
157 c. 1141. Cf. Florence, Denz.-Schón. 1327; Trent, Denz.-Schón. 1805, 1807; Pius XI, enc. *Casti Connubii*. Cf. Vatican II, Const. *Gaudium et Spes*, n. 48; Decree *Apostolicam Actuositatem*, n. 11.
158 *Summa Theol., Suppl.*, q. 61. a. 2, ad 1: "Before consummation marriage signifies the union of Christ with the soul by grace, which is dissolved by a contrary spiritual disposition, namely, mortal sin. But after consummation it signifies the union of Christ with the Church, as regards the assumption of human nature into the unity of Person, which union is altogether indissoluble." *Ibid.*, q. 2, ad. 3: "Although indissolubility belongs to the second intention of marriage as fulfilling an office of nature, it belongs to its first intention as a sacrament of the Church. Hence, from the moment it was made a sacrament of the Church, as long as it remains such it cannot be a matter of dispensation, except perhaps by the second kind of dispensation" (or miraculous dispensation).
159 c. 1142.
160 Cf. S.C. Sac. 7 May 1923; S. Off. 12 June 1942; Pius VII (Brief, 8 Nov. 1803) Denz.-Schón. 2705-2706; Pius IX *Syllabus*, Prop. 67, Denz.-Schón. 2967; Pius XII, *Allocution to the Rota* (3 Oct. 1941): "It is superfluous . . . yet it is not inappropriate to repeat that sacramental marriage which has been consummated is indissoluble by the law of God, so that it cannot be dissolved by any human power (c. 1118); whereas other marriages, though they are intrinsically indissoluble, have not absolute extrinsic indissolubility, but, granted certain necessary prerequisites (We are speaking, as you know, of cases which are relatively rare) can be dissolved, not only in virtue of the Pauline privilege, but also by the Roman Pontiff in virtue of his ministerial power."
161 c. 1143.
162 1 Cor 7:10-16.

163  Conversion to Catholicism is not required; conversion to Christianity suffices for use of the
     privilege.
164  c. 1086. Likewise it does not apply to a baptized non-Catholic who marries an unbaptized
     person.
165  c. 1144, 1.
166  *Ibid.*, 2.
167  c. 1145.
168  c. 1146.
169  c. 1147.
170  c. 1148.
171  c. 1149.
172  c. 1150.
173  c. 1151.
174  John Paul II, *Familiaris Consortio*, 83:  ''Various reasons can unfortunately lead to the
     often irreparable breakdown of valid marriages. These include mutual lack of understand-
     ing and the inability to enter into interpersonal relationships. Obviously, separation must
     be considered as a last resort, after all other reasonable attempts at reconciliation have
     proved vain.
         ''Loneliness and other difficulties are often the lot of separated spouses, especially
     when they are the innocent parties. The ecclesial community must support such people
     more than ever. It must give them much respect, solidarity, understanding and practical
     help, so that they can preserve their fidelity even in their difficult situation; and it must help
     them to cultivate the need to forgive which is inherent in Christian love, and to be ready
     perhaps to return to their former married life.
         ''The situation is similar for people who have undergone divorce, but, being well
     aware that the valid marriage bond is indissoluble, refrain from becoming involved in a
     new union and devote themselves solely to carrying out their family duties and the
     responsibilities of Christian life. In such cases their example of fidelity and Christian
     consistency takes on particular value as a witness before the world and the Church. Here it
     is even more necessary for the Church to offer continual love and assistance, without there
     being any obstacle to admission to the sacraments.''
175  c. 1152, 1.  ''If anyone says that the Church is in error when she decides that for many
     reasons husband and wife may separate from bed and board or from cohabitation for a
     definite period of time or even indefinitely, let him be anathema.'' Trent, Denz.-Schön.
     1808.
176  *Ibid.*, 1, 2, 3.
177  c. 1153, 1.
178  cc. 1154-1155.
179  c. 1153, 1.
180  *Ibid.*, 2.
181  c. 104.
182  *Familiaris Consortio*, 84:  ''Daily experience unfortunately shows that people who have
     obtained a divorce usually intend to enter into a new union, obviously not with a Catholic
     religious ceremony. Since this is an evil that, like the others, is affecting more and more
     Catholics as well, the problem must be faced with resolution and without delay. The Synod
     Fathers studied it expressly. The Church, which was set up to lead to salvation all people
     and especially the baptized, cannot abandon to their own devices those who have been
     previously bound by sacramental marriage and who have attempted a second marriage.

The Church will therefore make untiring efforts to put at their disposal her means of salvation.

"Pastors must know that, for the sake of truth, they are obliged to exercise careful discernment of situations. There is in fact a difference between those who have sincerely tried to save their first marriage and have been unjustly abandoned, and those who through their own grave fault have destroyed a canonically valid marriage. Finally, there are those who have entered into a second union for the sake of the children's upbringing, and who are sometimes subjectively certain in conscience that their previous and irreparably destroyed marriage had never been valid.

"Together with the Synod, I earnestly call upon pastors and the whole community of the faithful to help the divorced, and with solicitous care to make sure that they do not consider themselves as separated from the Church, for as baptized persons they can, and indeed must, share in her life. They should be encouraged to listen to the word of God, to attend the Sacrifice of the Mass, to persevere in prayer, to contribute to works of charity and to community efforts in favor of justice, to bring up their children in the Christian faith, to cultivate the spirit and practice of penance and thus implore, day by day, God's grace. Let the Church pray for them, encourage them and show herself a merciful mother and thus sustain them in faith and hope.

"However, the Church reaffirms her practice, which is based upon Sacred Scripture, of not admitting to Eucharistic Communion divorced persons who have remarried. They are unable to be admitted thereto from the fact that their state and condition of life objectively contradict that union of love between Christ and the Church which is signified and effected by the Eucharist. Besides this, there is another special pastoral reason: if these people were admitted to the Eucharist, the faithful would be led into error and confusion regarding the Church's teaching about the indissolubility of marriage.

"Reconciliation in the sacrament of Penance, which would open the way to the Eucharist, can only be granted to those who, repenting of having broken the sign of the Covenant and of fidelity to Christ, are sincerely ready to undertake a way of life that is no longer in contradiction to the indissolubility of marriage. This means, in practice, that when, for serious reasons such as for example the children's upbringing, a man and a woman cannot satisfy the obligation to separate, they 'take on themselves the duty to live in complete continence, that is, by abstinence from the acts proper to married couples.'

"Similarly, the respect due to the sacrament of Matrimony, to the couples themselves and their families, and also to the community of the faithful, forbids any pastor, for whatever reason or pretext even of a pastoral nature, to perform ceremonies of any kind for divorced people who remarry. Such ceremonies would give the impression of the celebration of a new sacramentally valid marriage, and would thus lead people into error concerning the indissolubility of a validly contracted marriage.

"By acting in this way, the Church professes her own fidelity to Christ and to his truth. At the same time she shows motherly concern for these children of hers, especially those who, through no fault of their own, have been abandoned by their legitimate partner.

"With firm confidence she believes that those who have rejected the Lord's command and are still living in this state will be able to obtain from God the grace of conversion and salvation, provided that they have persevered in prayer, penance and charity."

183 cc. 1156-1157.
184 c. 1158, 1.
185 *Ibid.*, 2.
186 *Ibid.*

187 c. 1159.
188 c. 1160.
189 c. 1161.
190 cc. 1162-1164.
191 c. 1164.
192 c. 1165.
193 S.C.D.F. 29 July 1972; U.S. Apost. Del., 7 Aug. 1972; NCCB, 15 Aug. 1972; S.C.D.F., 11 Apr. 1973; 21 Mar. 1975; NCCB, 26 Sept. 1975; S.C.D.F., 14 Apr. 1976. (*CLD* 8, 501-508).
194 S. Off., 25 July 1917; 31 May 1922; cf. 1917 Code, c. 139, 2; 1983 Code, c. 285, 3.

# INDEX